Warman's®
Depression Glass

FIELD GUIDE

Ellen T. Schroy

© 2002 by
Krause Publications, Inc.

Published by

**krause
publications**

700 East State Street • Iola, WI 54990-0001
715/445-2214 • FAX: 715/445-4087   www.krause.com

Please call or write for our free catalog of publications.
Our toll-free number to place an order or obtain a free catalog is 800-
258-0929 or please use our regular business telephone: 715-445-2214.

Library of Congress Catalog Number: 2001096277
ISBN: 0-87349-403-2

Printed in the United States of America

Contents

Intro

Welcome to the *Warman's Depression Glass Field Guide*. This new edition is designed to give you up-to-date pricing information on the most collectible patterns of this fascinating type of American glassware.

Each pattern includes a line drawing, helping you determine details, as well a photograph to show forms. Each pattern contains detailed information about what forms were made and in what colors. An added bonus to collectors is the reproduction notes that accompany every pattern. Special interest items have been called out to draw attention to what is important or highly sought after in some of the patterns. The compact size of this edition will make on-the-spot appraisals even easier, whether shopping at an antique shop, show, mall, or while strolling through a flea market.

Depression Glass spans the time frame from about 1900 up to the 1960s, and during those years thousands of glassware patterns were made. This edition concentrates on patterns made in complete table sets and those that are the most desired among collectors. Known for its vibrant colors, depression glass patterns have brightened the lives of generations. Today collectors eagerly seek out this interesting form of American glassware, many probably wishing they could find pieces as inexpensive as this glassware was originally. In fact, much of this glass was so inexpensive that it was used as give-away items at movies, packed in soap powder, etc. It is really this aspect of depression glass that makes it one of the fastest-growing areas in the antiques market. Prices have risen steadily over the past several years, making it a good investment.

This edition contains indexes for both pattern names and manufacturers. You'll find that many patterns are known by a variety of names, and we've tried to include them all here, further unraveling the mystery of identification.

Naturally, not everything can be included in this one small volume. For a more complete picture, see *Warman's® Depression Glass, 2nd Edition*, by Ellen T. Schroy. It contains more patterns, more listings, and full color photos of all the favorite patterns.

Happy collecting, and we hope you will enjoy this handy, pocket-sized guide.

Company Time Line

19th C   Ohio Flint Glass founded, later becomes part of National Glass Company conglomerate.
Indiana Glass Company established in 1907.
Bottle plant at Jeannette, Pennsylvania, which becomes Jeannette Glass Company.

1853   McKee and Brothers founded in Pittsburgh, Pennsylvania.

1887   Fostoria Glass Company, founded in Fostoria, Ohio, but moves to Moundsville, West Virginia, when fuel supply is depleted.

1888   McKee moves to Jeannette, Pennsylvania.

1890   Westmoreland Specialty Company established in Grapeville, Pennsylvania. Early manufacture includes bottles and food containers. During World War I, glass candy containers are made. The plant continues on to make colored and opaque glassware in both Depression patterns and later a giftware line.

1891   U.S. Glass Company organizes by combining 18 different glass houses located in Pennsylvania, Ohio, and West Virginia. The main offices are in Pittsburgh, as well as some manufacturing.

1899   Macbeth merges with Evans, creating Macbeth-Evans.
Main factory located in Charleroi, Pennsylvania, with
others located in Marion, Bethevan, and Elwood,
Indiana, as well as Toledo, Ohio.

1900   Federal Glass Company opens Columbus, Ohio, plant.
First wares are crystal with needle etching, various
decorations, and crackle finish. After switching to
automation, they soon begin production of tumblers
and many Depression-era patterns, as well as restaurant wares, all at an economical price.

1901   Imperial Glass Company organizes. Produces first glass
at Bellaire, Ohio, plant in 1904.
Morgantown Glass Works begins production in
Morgantown, West Virginia.
New Martinsville Glass Manufacturing Company is
established at New Martinsville, West Virginia.

1902   Hazel Atlas Glass Company established in Washington,
Pennsylvania, a result of the merger of the Hazel Glass
Company and its neighboring factory, Atlas Glass and
Metal Company. Corporate offices are later established
at Wheeling, West Virginia.

1903   Morgantown Glass Works reorganizes as Economy
Tumbler Company and operates using that name.
Liberty Cut Glass Works established in Egg Harbor, New
Jersey. Primarily a cutting house for years, pressed

glass is also made.

McKee Brothers reorganizes into McKee Glass Company and continues until 1951.

1905 Anchor Hocking Glass Company established in Lancaster, Ohio. Well known by the mid-1920s for their tumbler and tableware production.

1906 Fenton Art Glass Company builds new factory, Williamstown, West Virginia. While their giftware lines are well known, some Depression-era glassware is produced.

1907 Indiana Glass Company established at Dunkirk, Indiana. Early production is hand pressed. Assembly line patterns evolve during the 1920s, although some still require hand work. Later produce automobile glassware items, become a subsidiary of Lancaster Colony.

1908 Lancaster Glass Company, Lancaster, Ohio, built by first president of Fostoria.

1911 L.E. Smith begins in the glass trade. A lot of the production of this company remains utilitarian in nature as well as making lenses for automobiles.

1916 Paden City Glass Manufacturing Company established at Paden City, West Virginia. Production includes some Depression-era patterns, but is more well known for their elegant lines, vases, lamps and restaurant wares.

1923   Economy Tumbler Company changes name to Economy
Glass Company.

1924   Fostoria introduces color and starts national magazine
advertising campaign.

Jeannette touted by trade as "one of the most complete
automatic factories in the country."

Lancaster becomes subsidiary of Hocking Glass
Company. Continues to make kitchenware, cut and dec
tableware under the Lancaster name until 1937. Also
makes colored blanks for Standard Glass Company,
another Hocking subsidiary, where the glass is etched
and cut. Known as Plant #2 to Anchor Hocking.

1927   Jeannette management ceases all hand operations.

1928   Jeannette makes green and pink glass automatically in
a continuous tank, a first!

Trade journals proclaim Clarksburg, West Virginia,
Hazel-Atlas factory the "World's Largest Tumbler
Factory," which accurately describes the fully automat-
ed factory.

1929   Economy Glass Company changes name back to
Morgantown Glass Works, Inc.

1932   Liberty Cut Glass Works destroyed by fire, never to
rebuild.

1937   Corning Glass Works purchases Macbeth-Evans.

Hocking Glass Company merges with Anchor Cap and

Closure Corporation, Long Island City, New York, creating the huge Anchor-Hocking Glass Company, which has continued to have a major impact on the glassware industry.

Morgantown Glass Works, Inc., closes.

1938 U.S. Glass moves main offices to Tiffin, Ohio, and production decreases.

1939 Morgantown Glassware Guild organizes and reopens factory.

1944 New Martinsville sold and reorganizes as Viking Glass Company.

1949 Westmoreland Glass Company begins to use impressed intertwined "W" and "G" mark.

1951 The only operating company of the former U.S. Glass is Tiffin. The rest have all closed.

McKee sold to Thatcher Manufacturing Co.

1952 Fire destroys Belmont plant, Bellaire, Ohio, and with fire go records.

1955 Duncan and Miller molds acquired by Tiffin, who begins to produce colors and crystal wares with these molds.

1956 Continental Can purchases Hazel-Atlas and continues to sell tableware under name "Hazelware."

1958 Federal Glass becomes a division of Federal Paper Board Company, and continues glassware production.

1961   Jeannette buys old McKee factory in Jeannette and moves there to continue production.

1964   Brockway Glass Company buys out Continental Can's interest in Hazel-Atlas and begins operation.

1965   Fostoria Glass Company purchases Morgantown Glassware Guild.

1966   Continental Can takes over operation of Tiffin until 1969, with glass production continuing.

1971   Glass production terminated at Fostoria's Morgantown facility, ending the Morgantown Glassware Guild.

1973   Imperial Glass Company sold to Lenox, Inc.

1980   Tiffin Glass discontinues operation.

1982   Westmoreland Glass Company closes factory in May. Reorganizes in July.

1983   Lancaster Glass purchases Fostoria.
Westmoreland begins to use full name as imprinted mark.

1984   Westmoreland Glass Company again closes Grapeville plant.

1999   L.G. Wright discontinues operation. Molds, factory equipment liquidated at public auction in May.

Color
Time Line

Amber

1923: McKee
1923: New Martinsville
1924: Paden City
1924: Westmoreland's Transparent Amber
1924-1941: Fostoria
1925: Indiana
Mid-1920s: Hocking, Imperial and L.E. Smith
1926: Jeannette
Late 1920s: Liberty
1931-1942: Federal's Golden Glow
1960: Westmoreland's Golden Sunset

Amethyst

1923: McKee
1924: New Martinsville
Mid-1920s: L.E. Smith
1926: Morgantown's Old Amethyst
1933: Paden City
1939: Morgantown's Light Amethyst

Apple Green

1925: Jeannette

Black

1920s-1930s: L.E. Smith
1922: Morgantown's India Black
1923 and 1930s: Paden City
1923: New Martinsville
1924: Fostoria
1930: McKee
1931: Hazel-Atlas, Imperial, Lancaster

Blue

1920s: Lancaster
1923: McKee's Jap Blue and Transparent Blue
1923: New Martinsville
1924: Paden City
1924-1928: Fostoria
1925: McKee's Sky Blue and Westmoreland's
Mid-1920s: Hocking
1926: Imperial, Morgantown's Azure and transparent blue
1927: Imperial's Blue-Green, Morgantown's Ritz
1928: New Martinsville's Alice Blue (medium shade)
1928-1943: Fostoria's Azure Blue (lighter shade)
Late 1920s: Liberty's pale shade
1930: Hocking's Mayfair Blue (medium shade), McKee's Ritz Blue
    and Chalaine Blue
1931: Imperial's Ritz Blue, Lancaster's pale blue, Westmoreland's
    Belgian Blue
1933: Fostoria's Regal Blue
1933-1934: Federal's Madonna Blue (medium shade)

1933-1942: New Martinsville's Ritz Blue
Mid-1930s: MacBeth-Evans' Ritz Blue
1936: Hazel-Atlas's Ritz Blue, McKee's opaque Poudre Blue, Paden
    City's Ceylon Blue
1939: Morgantown's Copen Blue and Gloria Blue
1940: Anchor-Hocking's Fire King
1950s: Indiana's Blue-Green

Burgundy

1933: Fostoria
1936: Hazel-Atlas (deep shade)

Canary Yellow

1923: McKee
Mid-1920s: Hocking, L.E. Smith
1924: New Martinsville
1924-1927: Fostoria
1925: Lancaster

Cobalt Blue

1930: Liberty
1936: Paden City
1939: Morgantown

Cremax

1939: MacBeth-Evans

Crystal

1923: Paden City

1930s: Imperial

1935: New Martinsville and Westmoreland—most companies pro-
     duced crystal throughout their years of production

Delphite, Delfite

1936: Jeannette

Fired-On Colors

1920s: Federal and Lancaster

1923: Westmoreland

1926: New Martinsville

Mid-1930s: MacBeth-Evans

French Ivory (opaque)

1933: McKee

Green

1920s: Lancaster

1921: Morgantown's Venetian Green

1922: Morgantown's Meadow Green

1923: McKee

1924: Paden City

1924-1941: Fostoria

Mid-1920s: Hocking, Imperial and L.E. Smith

1925: Indiana, McKee's Grass Green and New Martinsville

1926: New Martinsville's Emerald Green

1926-1936: Federal's Springtime Green
1928: MacBeth-Evans' Emerald
Late 1920s: Liberty
1929: Hazel-Atlas, Imperial
1931: Morgantown's Stiegel Green
1931-1933: New Martinsville's Stiegel Green
1933: Fostoria's Empire Green, Hazel-Atlas's Killarney Green,
     New Martinsville's Evergreen (dark shade)
1936: Paden City's Forest Green
1939: Morgantown's Shamrock Green
1950s: Anchor-Hocking's Forest Green

Iridescent

1920s: Federal
1920s to present: Jeannette
1934-1935: Federal's Iridescent Amber

Ivory

1929: Imperial
1933: Indiana (opaque)
1940: Anchor-Hocking

Ivrene

1930s: MacBeth-Evans

Jade

1930: McKee
1931: New Martinsville

Jade Yellow

1923: McKee

Jadite

1932: Jeannette

Monax

1920s: MacBeth-Evans

Mulberry

1924: Paden City

Opalescent

1923: Morgantown's Alabaster
1931: Westmoreland's Moonstone (blue)
1942: Anchor-Hocking's Moonstone

Orchid

1927: McKee
1927-1929: Fostoria
1929: Imperial

Pink

Mid-1920s: Imperial's Rose Marie, Rose
1925: Paden City's Cheriglo
1926: McKee's Rose Pink, Morgantown's Anna

Red-Amber

1930: Liberty

Rose

1926: Indiana and Westmoreland

1926-1942: Hocking's Rose (later called Flamingo or Cerise), New
  Martinsville's Peach Melba (later known as Rose)

1927: Jeannette's Wild Rose, L.E. Smith

1928: MacBeth-Evans

1928-1941: Fostoria's Rose or Dawn

Late 1920s: Liberty

1930: Hazel-Atlas, Lancaster's deep pink

1931-1942: Federal's Rose Glow

1933: Hazel-Atlas's Sunset Pink

1939: Morgantown's Pink Champagne

1947-1949: Jeannette

Royal Blue

1932: Paden City

Ruby

1925: Morgantown

1927: McKee

1931: Imperial

1932: Paden City

1933-1942: New Martinsville

Mid-1930s: MacBeth-Evans
1935: Fostoria's Ruby
1939: Anchor-Hocking's Royal Ruby

Sea Foam

1931: Imperial, Harding Blue, Moss Green or Burnt Almond with
      opal edge

Seville Yellow

1931: McKee

Shell Pink

1958: Jeannette

Skokie Green

1931: McKee

Tan

1931: McKee's Old Rose

Topaz

1921: Morgantown's 14K Topaz
1925: Jeannette
1928: Hocking
1929: Fostoria
1930: Lancaster, Westmoreland (sometimes combined with crystal
      or black)

1930-mid-1930s: Indiana
1931: Imperial, Liberty, MacBeth-Evans, McKee, Paden City's
    Golden Glow
1933: Hazel-Atlas
1938-1940s: Fostoria's Golden Tint
1939: Morgantown's Topaz Mist

Ultramarine

1937-1938: Jeannette

Vaseline

Mid-1920s: Imperial

White

1930s: Hazel-Atlas's Platonite (opaque)
1932: Hocking (Vitrock)
1937-1942: McKee (opal) and after World War II

Wine

1923: New Martinsville

Wisteria

1931-1938: Fostoria

Shape Guide

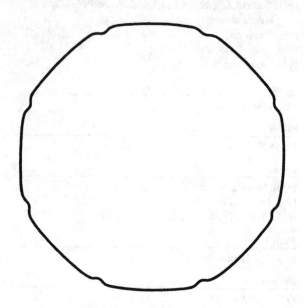

Alice (Fire-King)

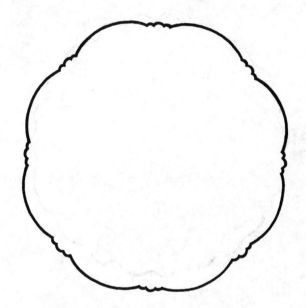

American Sweetheart

Avocado

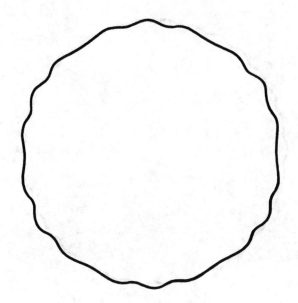

Bowknot

Bubble

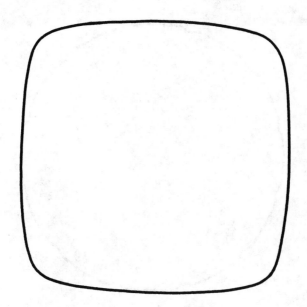

Charm (Fire-King)

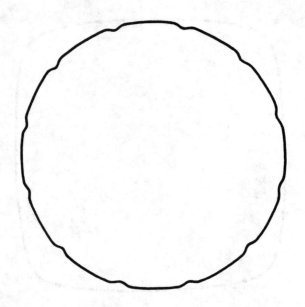

Cherry Blossom

Depression Glass

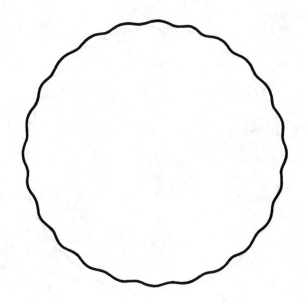

Chinex Classic

Christmas Candy

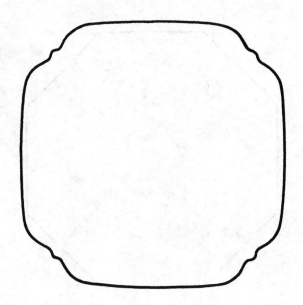

Columbia

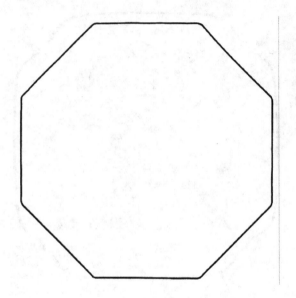

Cracked Ice

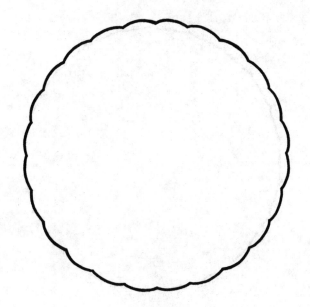

Cremax

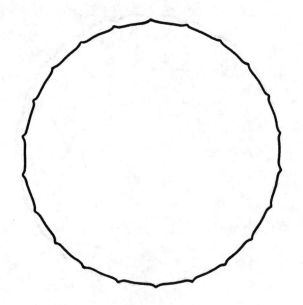

Dewdrop

English Hobnail

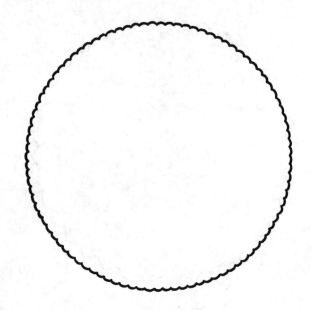

Floragold

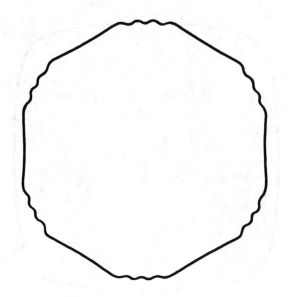

Florentine No. 1

Forest Green

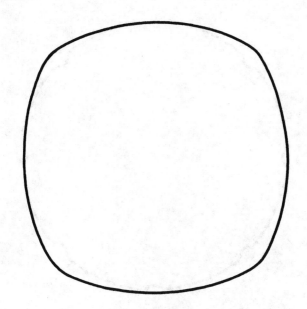

Heritage

Indiana Custard

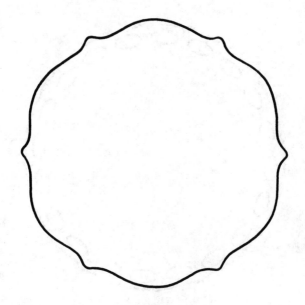

Jubilee

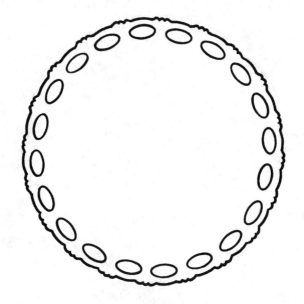

Laced Edge

Laurel

Mayfair Federal

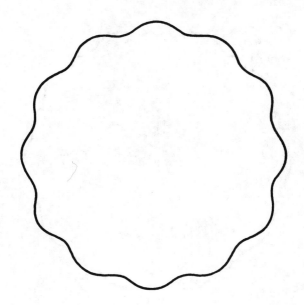

Moonstone

Mt. Pleasant

Old Café

Oyster & Pearls

Parrot

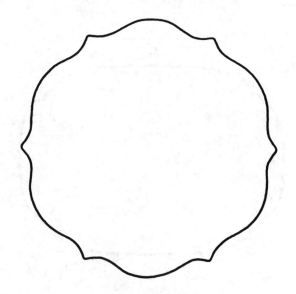

Patrick

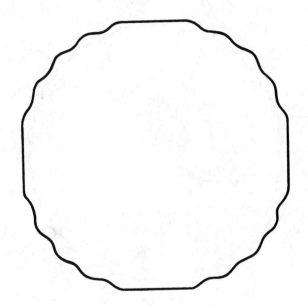

Pineapple & Floral

Pioneer

Pretzel

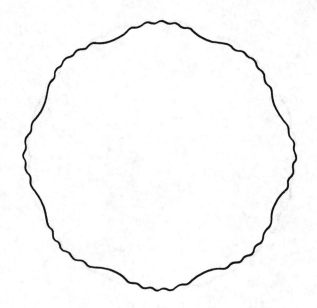

Radiance

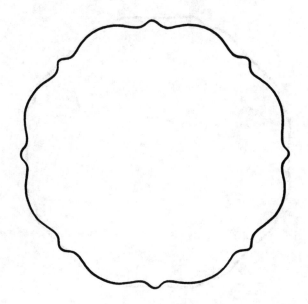

Rock Crystal

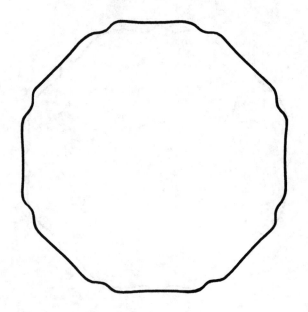

Roxana

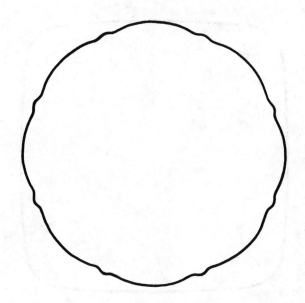

Royal Lace

Royal Ruby

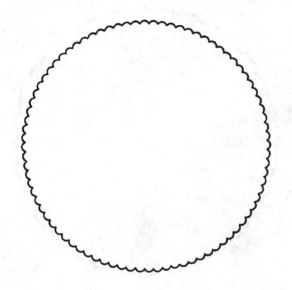

Sandwich

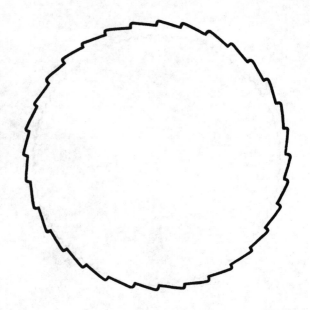

Sierra Pinwheel

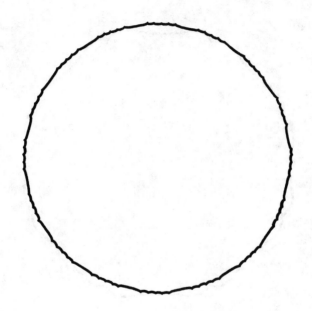

Starlight

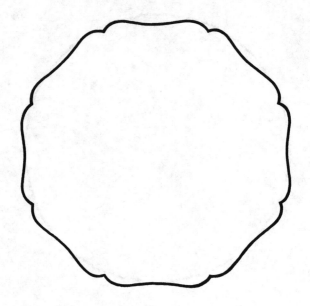

Sunburst

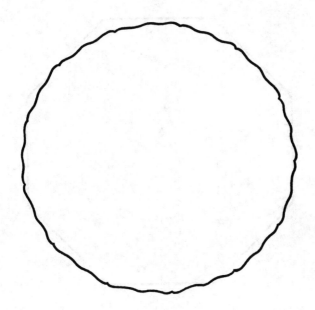

Swirl

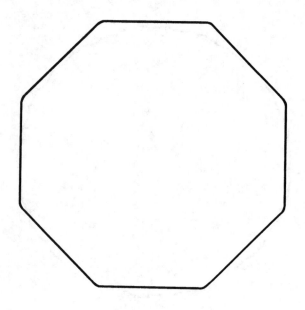

Tea Room

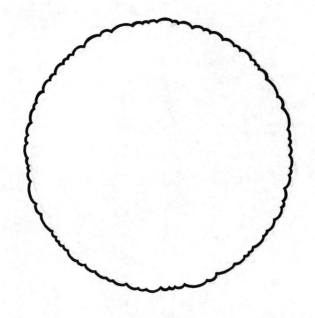

Tulip

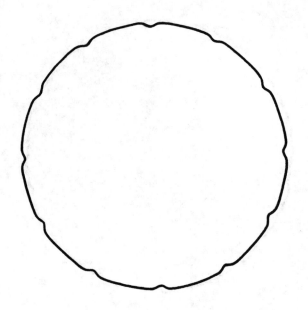

Victory

Waterford

Windsor

Thumbnail Guide

Depression-era glassware can be confusing. Many times one manufacturer came up with a neat new design and as soon as it was successful, other companies started to make patterns that were similar. To help you figure out what pattern you might be trying to research, here's a quick identification guide. The patterns are broken down into several different classifications by design elements. Try comparing your piece to these and then consult the detailed pattern listing and larger drawing for more information.

Art Deco

Ovide

Baskets

Lorain

Birds

Parrot

Georgian

Blocks

Beaded Block

Colonial Block

Bows

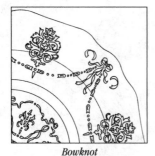

Bowknot

Cube

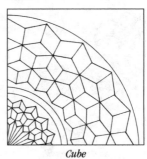

Cube

Diamonds

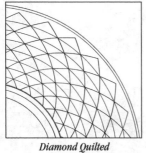

Diamond Quilted

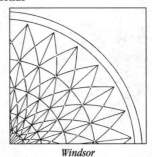

Windsor

Diamonds

English Hobnail

Miss America

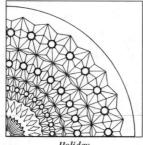

Holiday

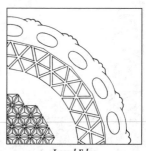

Laced Edge

Diamonds

Ellipse

Waterford

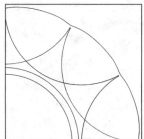

Newport

Florals

Jubilee

Indiana Custard

Florals

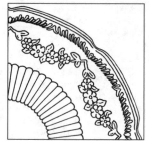

Alice (Fire-King)

Vitrock

Floral & Diamond Band

Doric

Florals

Doric & Pansy

Pineapple & Floral

Flower Garden with Butterflies

Normandie

Florals

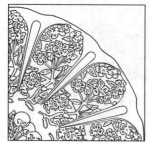

Cherry Blossom

Cloverleaf

Daisy

Dogwood

Florals

Floragold

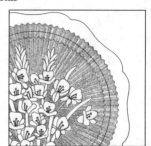

Iris

Floral

Rosemary

Florals

Mayfair (Open Rose)

Mayfair

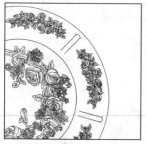

Sharon

Rose Cameo

Florals

Royal Lace

Sunflower

Thistle

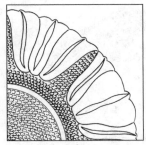

Tulip

Figure

Fruits

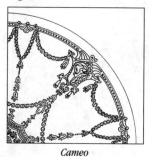

Cameo

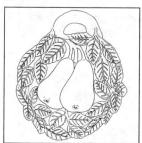

Avocado

Fruits

Cherryberry

Strawberry

Fruits

Fruits

Della Robbia

Geometric & Line Designs

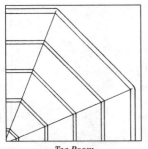

Tea Room

Cracked Ice

Geometric & Line Designs

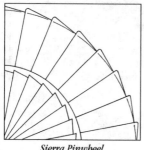

Sierra Pinwheel

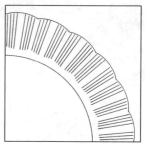

Cremax

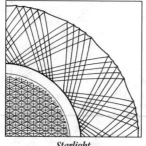

Starlight

Star

Geometric & Line Designs

Early American Prescut

Pioneer

Honeycomb

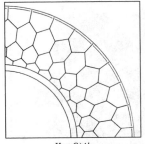

Hex Optic

Aunt Polly

Horseshoe

Lacy Designs

Horseshoe

Heritage

Lacy Designs

Harp

Sandwich (Duncan Miller)

Lacy Designs

Sandwich (Hocking)

Sandwich (Indiana)

Lacy Designs

S-Pattern

Leaves

Sunburst

Leaves

Peach Luster (Fire-King)

Laurel

Loops

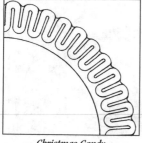

Christmas Candy

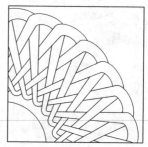

Pretzel

Petals

Victory

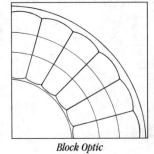

Block Optic

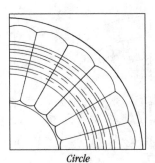

Circle

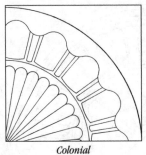

Colonial

Lacy Designs

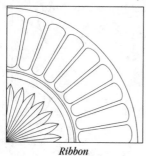

Ribbon

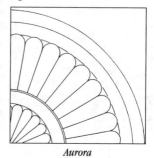

Aurora

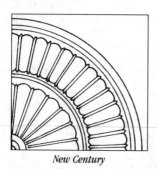

New Century

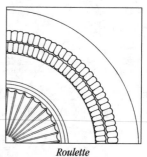

Roulette

Lacy Designs

Round Robbin

Old Café

Petals or Ridges with Diamond Accents

Coronation

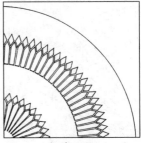

Anniversary

Petals or Ridges with Diamond Accents

Queen Mary

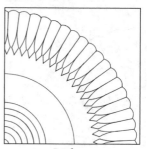

Petalware

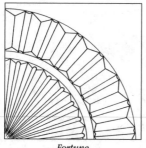

Fortune

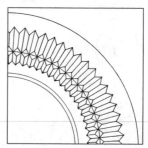

Lincoln Inn

Plain

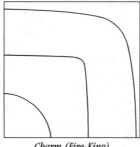

Charm (Fire-King)

Mt. Pleasant

Pyramids

Raised Bands

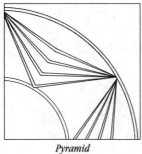

Pyramid

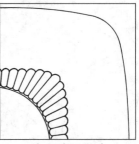

Charm (Fire-King)

Raised Bands

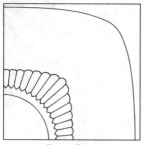

Forest Green

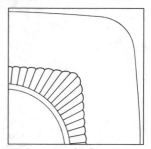

Royal Ruby

Raised Circles

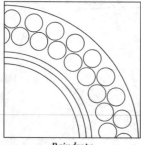

Raindrops

Oyster & Pearls

Raised Circles

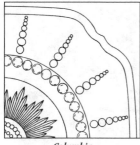

Columbia

Hobnail

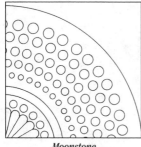

Moonstone

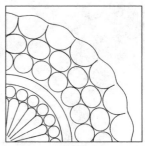

Bubble

Raised Circles

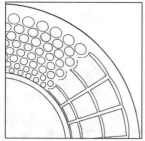

American Pioneeer

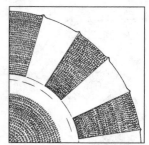

Dewdrop

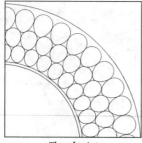

Thumbprint

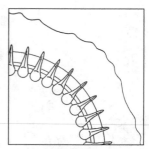

Radiance

Raised Circles

Ships

Ribs

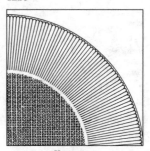

Homespun

Rings (Circles)

Moderntone

Manhattan

Rings (Circles)

Ring

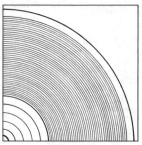

Old English

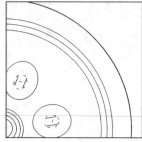

Moondrops

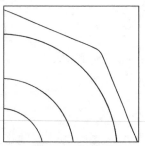

Moroccan Amethyst

Scenes

Lake Como

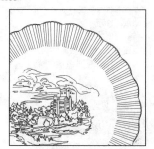

Chinex Classic

Scrolling Designs

American Sweetheart

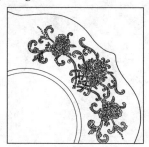

Patrick

Scrolling Designs

Princess

Roxana

Madrid

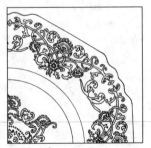

Florentine No. 1

Scrolling Designs

Florentine No. 2

Philbe (Fire King)

Adam

Vernon

Scrolling Designs

Rock Crystal

Primo

Swirls

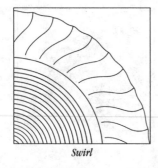

Swirl

Twisted Optic

Swirls

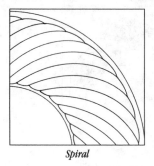

Spiral

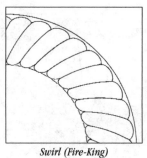

Swirl (Fire-King)

U.S. Swirl

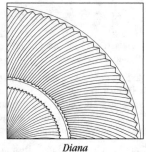

Diana

Adam

Manufactured by Jeannette Glass Company, Jeannette, Pa., from 1932 to 1934.

Made in crystal, Delphite blue, green, pink, some topaz and yellow. Delphite 4" h candlesticks are valued at $250 a pair. A yellow cup and saucer are valued at $200, and a 7-3/4" d yellow plate is valued at $115. Production in topaz and yellow was very limited. Crystal prices would be approximately 50% of the prices listed for green.

Reproductions: † Butter Dish in pink and green.

Item	Green	Pink
Ashtray, 4-1/2" d	25.00	32.00
Berry Bowl, small	20.00	18.50
Bowl, 9" d, cov	85.00	75.00
Bowl, 9" d, open	45.00	30.00
Bowl, 10" l, oval	40.00	40.00
Butter Dish, cov †	325.00	145.00
Cake Plate, 10" d, ftd	32.00	30.00
Candlesticks, pr, 4" h	125.00	100.00
Candy Jar, cov, 2-1/2" h	100.00	95.00
Casserole, cov	90.00	75.00
Cereal Bowl, 5-3/4" d	46.00	46.00
Coaster, 3-1/4" d	22.00	32.00
Creamer	22.00	20.00
Cup	24.00	26.00
Dessert Bowl, 4-3/4" d	18.50	16.50

Adam, candlestick.

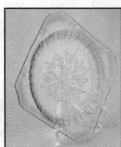

Adam, green plate.

Item	Green	Pink
Iced Tea Tumbler, 5-1/2" h	60.00	65.00
Lamp	285.00	265.00
Pitcher, 32 oz, 8" h, sq base	48.00	45.00
Plate, 6" d, sherbet	12.00	12.50
Plate, 7-3/4" d, salad, sq	18.00	19.50
Plate, 9" d, dinner, sq	32.00	38.50
Plate, 9" d, grill	20.00	20.00
Platter, 11-3/4" l, rect	38.00	35.00
Relish Dish, 8" l, divided	27.00	20.00
Salt and Pepper Shakers, pr, 4" h	130.00	95.00
Saucer, 6" sq	12.00	10.00
Sherbet, 3"	40.00	35.00
Sugar, cov	48.00	42.00
Tumbler, 4-1/2" h	30.00	35.00
Vase, 7-1/2" h	60.00	250.00
Vegetable Bowl, 7-3/4" d	30.00	30.00

Adam, pink pitcher.

Alice (Fire-King)

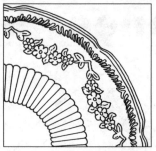

Manufactured by Anchor-Hocking, in the early 1940s.

Made in Jade-ite, white with blue trim, and white with red rim.

Item	Jade-ite	White, blue trim	White, red trim
Cup	5.00	12.00	15.00
Cup and Saucer	8.00	15.00	20.00
Plate, 9-1/2" d	25.00	28.00	30.00
Saucer	3.00	3.00	5.00

Alice (Fire-King) Jade-ite cup and saucer

American Pioneer

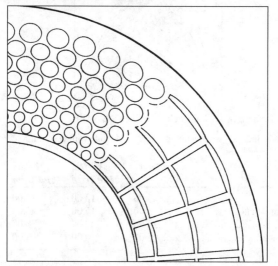

Manufactured by Liberty Works, Egg Harbor, N.J., from 1931 to 1934.

Made in amber, crystal, green and pink.

Limited production in amber.

Item	*Crystal or Pink*	*Green*
Bowl, 5" d, handle	24.00	27.50
Bowl, 8-3/4" d, cov	85.00	125.00
Bowl, 9" d, handle	24.00	30.00
Bowl, 9-1/4" d, cov	95.00	130.00
Bowl, 10" d	50.00	70.00
Candlesticks, pr, 6-1/2" h	75.00	95.00
Candy Jar, cov, 1 pound	100.00	115.00
Candy Jar, cov, 1-1/2 pound	70.00	125.00
Cheese and Cracker Set, indented plate and compote	50.00	65.00
Coaster, 3-1/2" d	20.00	32.00
Console Bowl, 10-3/4" d	50.00	75.00
Creamer, 2-3/4" h	20.00	22.00
Creamer, 3-1/2" h	30.00	32.00
Cup	10.00	12.00
Dresser Set, 2 cologne bottles, powder jar, 7-1/2" tray	300.00	345.00
Goblet, 8 oz, 6" h, water	40.00	45.00
Ice Bucket, 6" h	50.00	80.00
Juice Tumbler, 5 oz	32.00	37.50
Lamp, 1-3/4", metal pole, 9-1/2"	—	65.00
Lamp, 8-1/2" h	90.00	115.00
Mayonnaise, 4-1/4"	60.00	90.00
Pilsner, 5-3/4" h, 11 oz	100.00	110.00
Pitcher, cov, 5" h	150.00	225.00
Pitcher, cov, 7" h	175.00	250.00
Plate, 6" d	12.50	17.50

Item	*Crystal or Pink*	*Green*
Plate, 6" d, handle	12.50	17.50
Plate, 8" d	10.00	13.00
Plate, 11-1/2" d, handle	20.00	24.00
Rose Bowl, 4-1/4" d, ftd	40.00	50.00
Saucer, 6" sq	4.00	5.00
Sherbet, 3-1/2" h	18.00	22.00
Sherbet, 4-3/4" h	32.50	40.00
Sugar, 2-3/4" h	20.00	27.50
Sugar, 3-1/2" h	20.00	27.50

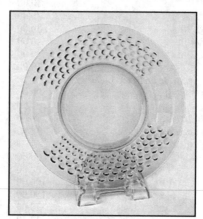

American Pioneer, green plate.

Item	Crystal or Pink	Green
Tumbler, 8 oz, 4" h	32.00	55.00
Tumbler, 12 oz, 5" h	40.00	55.00
Vase, 7" h, 4 styles	85.00	110.00
Vase, 9" h, round	—	235.00
Whiskey, 2 oz., 2-1/4" h	48.00	—

American Pioneer, cup and saucer.

American Sweetheart

Manufactured by MacBeth-Evans Glass Company, Charleroi, Pa., from 1930 to 1936.

Made in blue, Monax, pink and red. Limited production in Cremax and color-trimmed Monax.

NOTE: *A rare blue console bowl could command a $1,000 price, while a monax example would be $375, and a red cosole bowl would be $850.*

NOTE: *Pink is the only known color for the individual berry bowl, 3-1/4" dia., valued at $60.*

Item	Blue	Cremax	Monax
Berry Bowl, 9" d	—	36.00	60.00
Cereal Bowl, 6" d	—	19.50	15.00
Chop Plate, 11" d	—	—	15.00
Cream Soup, 4-1/2" d	—	—	135.00
Creamer, ftd	115.00	—	11.50
Cup	100.00	75.00	15.00
Lamp Shade	—	450.00	400.00
Pitcher, 60 oz, 7-1/2" h	—	—	—
Pitcher, 80 oz, 8" h	—	—	—
Plate, 6" d, bread and butter	—	—	5.50
Plate, 8" d, salad	75.00	25.00	10.00
Plate, 9" d, luncheon	—	—	14.00
Plate, 9-3/4" d, dinner	—	—	25.00

American Sweetheart, Monax large plate.

Item	Blue	Cremax	Monax
Plate, 10-1/4" d, dinner	—	—	30.00
Platter, 13" l, oval	—	—	85.00
Salt and Pepper Shakers, pr, ftd	—	—	325.00
Salver Plate, 12" d	180.00	—	24.00
Saucer	25.00	—	4.00
Serving Plate, 15-1/2" d	425.00	—	250.00
Sherbet, 3-3/4" h, ftd	—	—	10.50
Sherbet, 4-1/4" h, ftd	—	—	25.00
Soup Bowl, flat, 9-1/2" d	—	—	95.00
Sugar Lid	—	—	300.00
Sugar, open, ftd	115.00	—	15.00
Tidbit, 2 tier	250.00	—	95.00
Tidbit, 3 tier	650.00	—	275.00
Tumbler, 5 oz, 3-1/2" h	—	—	—
Tumbler, 9 oz, 4-1/4" h	—	—	—
Tumbler, 10 oz, 4-3/4" h	—	—	—
Vegetable Bowl, 11"	—	—	90.00

American Sweetheart, Monax sugar and creamer.

Item	Monax with color-trim	Pink	Red
Berry Bowl, 9" d	150.00	65.00	—
Cereal Bowl, 6" d	37.50	20.00	—
Cream Soup, 4-1/2" d	—	85.00	—
Creamer, ftd	85.00	12.00	110.00
Cup	70.00	18.00	75.00
Pitcher, 60 oz, 7-1/2" h	—	675.00	—
Pitcher, 80 oz, 8" h	—	575.00	—
Plate, 6" d, bread and butter	15.00	7.00	—
Plate, 8" d, salad	—	11.00	75.00
Plate, 9" d, luncheon	35.00	—	—
Plate, 9-3/4" d, dinner	70.00	38.00	—
Plate, 10-1/4" d, dinner	—	45.00	—
Platter, 13" l, oval	—	70.00	—
Salt and Pepper Shakers, pr, ftd	—	425.00	—
Salver Plate, 12" d	—	30.00	125.00
Saucer	15.00	5.75	20.00
Serving Plate, 15-1/2" d	—	—	350.00
Sherbet, 3-3/4" h, ftd	—	22.00	—
Sherbet, 4-1/4" h, ftd	70.00	17.00	—
Soup Bowl, flat, 9-1/2" d	90.00	85.00	—
Sugar, open, ftd	85.00	15.00	100.00
Tidbit, 2 tier	—	—	200.00
Tidbit, 3 tier	—	—	575.00
Tumbler, 5 oz, 3-1/2" h	—	110.00	—
Tumbler, 9 oz, 4-1/4" h	—	85.00	—
Tumbler, 10 oz, 4-3/4" h	—	185.00	—
Vegetable Bowl, 11"	—	80.00	—

Advertisement showing American Sweetheart pattern as "Rose Pink Tableware," from Crockery and Glass Journal, May 1935.

Anniversary

Manufactured by Jeannette Glass Company, Jeannette, Pa., from 1947 to 1949, late 1960s to mid 1970s.

Made in crystal, iridescent and pink.

Item	Crystal	Iridescent	Pink
Berry Bowl, 4-7/8" d	3.50	4.50	11.00
Butter Dish, cov	25.00	—	50.00
Cake Plate, 12-3/8" w, square	7.00	—	16.50
Cake Plate, 12-1/2" d, round	8.00	—	18.50
Cake Plate and metal cover	15.00	—	—
Candlesticks, pr, 4-7/8" h	20.00	25.00	—
Candy Jar, cov	24.00	—	45.00
Comport, open, 3 legs	5.00	5.00	16.00

Item	Crystal	Iridescent	Pink
Comport, ruffled, 3 legs	6.50	—	—
Creamer, ftd	6.00	6.50	14.00
Cup	5.00	4.00	9.00
Fruit Bowl, 9" d	10.00	14.00	24.00
Pickle Dish 9" d	5.50	7.50	12.00
Plate, 6-1/4" d, sherbet	2.00	3.50	4.00
Plate, 9" d, dinner	5.00	8.00	17.00
Relish Dish, 8" d	5.60	7.50	14.00
Sandwich Server, 12-1/2" d	6.50	10.00	20.00
Saucer	1.00	1.50	6.00
Sherbet, ftd	7.00	—	10.00
Soup Bowl, 7-3/8" d	8.00	7.50	18.00
Sugar, cov	12.00	10.00	20.00
Sugar, open, gold trim	4.50	—	—
Tidbit, metal handle	14.00	—	—
Vase, 6-1/2" h	16.00	—	30.00
Wall Pocket	25.00	—	30.00
Wine, 2-1/2 oz	10.00	—	20.00

Anniversary, iridescent plate.

Aunt Polly

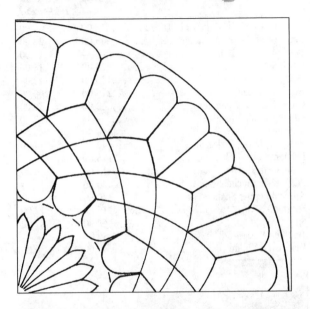

Manufactured by U.S. Glass Company, Pittsburgh, in the late 1920s.
Made in blue, green and iridescent.

Item	Blue	Green/Iridescent
Berry Bowl, 4-3/4" d, individual	18.00	9.00
Berry Bowl, 7-1/8" d, master	45.00	22.00
Bowl, 4-3/4" d, 2" h	—	15.00
Bowl, 5-1/2" d, one handle	25.00	15.00
Bowl, 8-3/8" l, oval	100.00	42.00
Butter Dish, cov	215.00	200.00
Candy Jar, cov, 2 handles	42.00	30.00
Candy Jar, ftd, 2 handles	—	27.50
Creamer	48.00	32.00
Pickle, 7-1/4" l, oval, handle	42.00	17.50
Pitcher, 48 oz, 8" h	175.00	—
Plate, 6" d, sherbet	12.00	6.00
Plate, 8" d, luncheon	20.00	—
Salt and Pepper Shakers, pr	220.00	—
Sherbet	15.00	12.00
Sugar	48.00	32.00
Tumbler, 8 oz, 3-5/8" h	30.00	—
Vase, 6-1/2" h, ftd	48.00	30.00

Aunt Polly, blue sherbet.

Aurora

Manufactured by Hazel Atlas Glass Company, Clarksburg, W.V., and Zanesville, Ohio, in the late 1930s.

Made in cobalt (Ritz) blue, crystal, green and pink.

Item	*Crystal*	*Green*	*Pink or Cobalt Blue*
Bowl, 4-1/2" d	—	—	50.00
Breakfast Set, 24 pcs, service for 4	—	—	—
Cereal Bowl, 5-3/8" d	12.00	9.50	15.00
Cup	6.00	10.00	15.00
Milk Pitcher	—	—	25.00
Plate, 6-1/2" d	—	—	12.50
Saucer	2.00	3.00	6.00
Tumbler, 10 oz, 4-3/4" h	—	—	22.00

Aurora, blue cereal bowl, berry bowl and milk pitcher.

Avocado

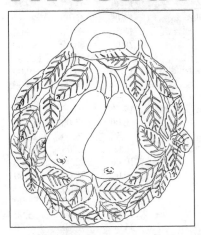

Manufactured by Indiana Glass Company, Dunkirk, Ind., from 1923 to 1933.

Made in crystal, green, pink and white.

Reproductions: † Creamer, 8" pickle, 64 oz. pitcher, plates, sherbet, sugar and tumblers. Reproductions can be found in amethyst, blue, dark green, frosted green, frosted pink, pink, red and yellow, representing several colors not made originally.

NOTE: *Pitchers in this pattern can get pricey—Crystal starts at $365, green is $1,100, pink is $800 and white is $425.*

Item	Crystal	Green	Pink
Bowl, 5-1/4" d, 2 handles 12.00		38.00	27.50
Bowl, 8" d, 2 handles, oval 17.50		30.00	25.00
Bowl, 8-1/2" d 20.00		60.00	50.00
Bowl, 9-1/2" d, 3-1/4" deep 35.00		155.00	125.00
Cake Plate, 10-1/4" d, 2 handles 17.50		60.00	40.00
Creamer, ftd † 17.50		40.00	35.00
Cup, ftd . . . . —		36.00	30.00
Pickle Bowl, 8" d, 2 handles, oval † .17.50		30.00	25.00
Plate, 6-3/8" d, sherbet † 6.00		22.00	15.00
Plate, 8-1/4" d, luncheon † 7.50		25.00	20.00
Preserve Bowl, 7" l, handle 10.00		32.00	28.00
Relish, 6" d, ftd 10.00		32.00	28.00
Salad Bowl, 7-1/2" d 9.00		55.00	37.50
Saucer 6.00		24.00	15.00
Sherbet, ftd † . . . . —		75.00	55.00
Sugar, ftd † 17.50		40.00	35.00
Tumbler † 25.00		250.00	150.00

Avocado, green sugar and creamer

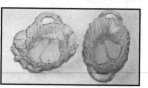

Avocado, green bowl and relish dish.

Beaded Block

Manufactured by Imperial Glass Company, Bellaire, Ohio, from 1927 to the 1930s.

Made in amber, crystal, green, ice blue, iridescent, milk white (1950s), opalescent, pink, red and vaseline. Some pieces are still being made in pink and are embossed with the "IG" trademark. The only form known in red is the 4-1/2" lily bowl, valued at $300. The secondary market for milk white is still being established.

Item	Amber	Crystal	Green
2" d, lily	8.00	6.00	10.00
Bowl, 4-1/2" d, 2 handles	10.00	8.00	10.00
Bowl, 5-1/2" sq	8.50	6.00	8.50
Bowl, 5 -/2 d, 1 handle	8.50	6.00	8.50
Bowl, 6" deep	12.00	10.00	12.00
Bowl, 6-1/4" d	9.00	7.00	9.00
Bowl, 6-1/2" d, 2 handles	9.00	7.00	9.00
Bowl, 6-3/4" d	12.00	10.00	12.00
Bowl, 7-1/4" d, flared	12.00	10.00	12.00
Bowl, 7-1/2" d, fluted	22.00	20.00	22.00
Bowl, 7-1/2" plain	20.00	18.00	20.00
Candy Dish, cov, pear shaped	—	—	275.00
Celery, 8-1/4" d	15.00	12.00	15.00
Creamer, ftd	20.00	16.00	20.00
Jelly, 4-1/2" h, stemmed	10.00	8.00	10.00
Jelly, 4-1/2" h, stemmed, flared lid	12.00	10.00	12.00
Pitcher, 1 pt, 5-1/4" h	85.00	95.00	100.00
Plate, 7-3/4" sq	7.50	5.00	7.50
Plate, 8-3/4"	20.00	16.00	20.00
Sugar, ftd	20.00	16.00	20.00
Vase, 6" h, ftd	15.00	12.00	18.00

Item	Iridescent	Opal Ice Blue or Vasoline	Pink
Bowl, 4-1/2" d, lily	15.00	18.00	15.00
Bowl, 4-1/2" d, 2 handles	16.00	18.00	10.00
Bowl, 5-1/2" sq	7.50	9.00	8.50
Bowl, 5 -/2 d, 1 handle	7.50	9.00	18.00
Bowl, 6" deep	10.00	12.50	15.00
Bowl, 6-1/4" d	9.00	9.50	8.00
Bowl, 6-1/2" d, 2 handles	9.00	9.50	8.00
Bowl, 6-3/4" d	12.00	12.00	11.00
Bowl, 7-1/4" d, flared	12.00	12.00	11.00
Bowl, 7-1/2" d, fluted	18.00	22.00	21.00
Bowl, 7-1/2" plain	18.50	20.00	18.00
Celery, 8-1/4" d	15.00	16.50	14.00
Creamer, ftd	18.50	20.00	25.00
Jelly, 4-1/2" h, stemmed	9.00	18.50	9.00
Jelly, 4-1/2" h, stemmed, flared lid . .	12.00	12.00	12.50

Beaded Block, cobalt blue bud vase and clear compote.

Item	*Iridescent*	*Opal Ice Blue or Vasoline*	*Pink*
Pitcher, 1 pt, 5-1/4" h 90.00		95.00	175.00
Plate, 7-3/4" sq 7.00		7.00	6.00
Plate, 8-3/4" 17.50		20.00	16.00
Sugar, ftd 17.50		20.00	25.00
Vase, 6" h, ftd 15.00		25.00	14.00

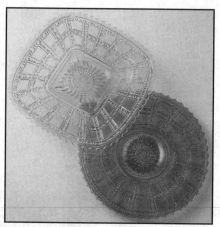

Beaded Block, vaseline square plate and iridescent round plate.

Block Optic

Block

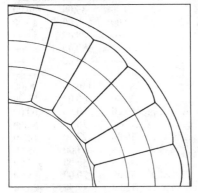

Manufactured by Hocking Glass Company, Lancaster, Ohio, from 1929 to 1933.

Made in amber, crystal, green, pink and yellow. Production in amber was very limited.

A 11-3/4" d console bowl is valued at $50, while a pair of matching 1-3/4" h candlesticks is valued at $110.

Production in yellow was also limited to basic forms. See *Warman's® Depression Glass* for a listing of values for yellow pieces.

* There are five styles of creamers and four styles of cups, each have a relative value.

Item	Crystal	Green	Pink
Berry Bowl, 8-1/2" d	20.00	35.00	40.00
Bowl, 4-1/4" d, 1-3/8" h	4.00	8.00	10.00
Bowl, 4-1/2" d, 1-1/2" h	—	28.00	—
Bowl, 8-5/8" d, low, ruffled	—	150.00	—
Butter Dish, cov	—	50.00	—
Cake Plate, 10" d, ftd	18.00	—	—
Candlesticks, pr, 1-3/4" h	—	110.00	100.00
Candy Jar, cov, 2-1/4" h	30.00	60.00	55.00
Candy Jar, cov, 6-1/4" h	40.00	80.00	60.00
Cereal Bowl, 5-1/2" d	—	20.00	30.00
Champagne, 4-3/4" h	10.00	27.50	16.50
Cocktail, 4" h	—	35.00	35.00
Comport, 4" wide	—	36.00	70.00
Console Bowl, 11-3/4" d, rolled edge	55.00	70.00	95.00
Creamer*	12.00	17.50	20.00
Cup*	7.50	9.00	7.00
Goblet, 9 oz, 5-3/4" h	12.00	27.50	40.00
Goblet, 9 oz, 7-1/2" h, thin	15.00	—	30.00
Ice Bucket	—	40.00	48.00
Ice Tub, open	—	60.00	—
Mug	—	35.00	—
Pitcher, 54 oz, 7-5/8" h, bulbous	—	75.00	75.00
Pitcher, 54 oz, 8-1/2" h	—	42.00	40.00
Pitcher, 80 oz, 8" h	—	90.00	85.00
Plate, 6" d, sherbet	1.50	3.50	3.50
Plate, 8" d, luncheon	3.50	5.50	7.00
Plate, 9" d, dinner	11.00	27.50	35.00
Plate, 9" d, dinner, snowflake center	—	16.50	—

Item	Crystal	Green	Pink
Plate, 9" d, grill	15.00	27.50	30.00
Salad Bowl, 7-1/4" d	—	155.00	—
Salad Bowl, 7-1/4" d	—	155.00	—
Salt and Pepper Shakers, pr, ftd	—	42.00	90.00
Salt and Pepper Shakers, pr, squatty ..	—	100.00	—
Sandwich Plate, 10-1/4" d	—	27.50	30.00
Sandwich Server, center handle	—	65.00	50.00
Saucer, 5-3/4" d	—	12.00	10.00
Saucer, 6-1/8" d	2.00	10.00	10.00
Sherbet, cone	—	6.50	6.00
Sherbet, 5-1/2 oz, 3-1/4" h	—	6.50	9.50
Sherbet, 6 oz, 4-3/4" h	7.00	15.50	17.50
Sugar, cone	—	17.50	15.00
Sugar, flat	—	10.00	10.00
Sugar, round, ftd	10.00	12.00	18.00
Tumbler, 3 oz, 2-5/8" h	—	27.50	25.00

*Block Optic, green large and
small berry bowl and salad bowl.*

Item	Crystal	Green	Pink
Tumbler, 3 oz, 3-1/4" h, ftd	—	27.50	25.00
Tumbler, 5 oz, 3-1/2" h, flat	—	20.00	17.50
Tumbler, 5-3/8" h, ftd	—	—	19.50
Tumbler, 9" h, ftd	—	—	17.50
Tumbler, 9-1/2 oz, 3-13/16" h, flat ...	—	17.50	14.00
Tumbler, 10 oz, 6" h, ftd	12.00	—	—
Tumbler, 10 or 11 oz, 5" h, flat	—	24.00	22.00
Tumbler, 12 oz, 4-7/8" h, flat	—	35.50	30.00
Tumbler, 15 oz, 5-1/4" h, flat	—	32.50	30.00
Tumble-Up, 3" h tumbler and bottle ..	—	90.00	75.00
Vase, 5-3/4" h, blown	—	285.00	—
Whiskey, 1 oz, 1-5/8" h	20.00	40.00	45.00
Whiskey, 2 oz, 2-1/4" h	15.00	35.00	30.00
Wine, 3-1/2" h	—	415.00	415.00
Wine, 4-1/2" h	15.00	35.00	32.00

Block Optic, green sherbet, sugar and creamer and Hasel Atlas look-alike covered candy dish.

Bowknot

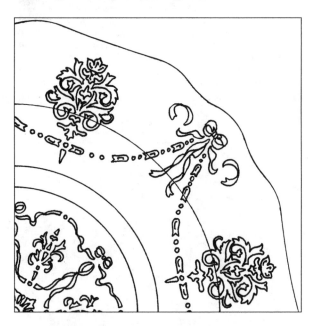

Unknown maker, late 1920s.

Made in green.

Item	*Green*
Berry Bowl, 4-1/2" d	18.00
Cereal Bowl, 5-1/2" d	20.00
Cup	15.00
Plate, 7" d, salad	12.50
Sherbet, low, ftd	24.00
Tumbler, 10 oz, 5" h, flat	15.00
Tumbler, 10 oz, 5" h, ftd	15.00

Bowknot, green tumbler and footed berry bowl.

Bubble

Bullseye, Provincial

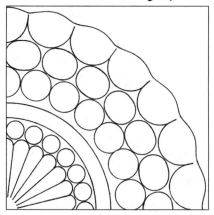

Manufactured originally by Hocking Glass Company, and followed by Anchor Hocking Glass Corporation, Lancaster, Ohio, from 1937 to 1965.

Made in crystal (1937); forest green (1937); pink, Royal Ruby (1963); and sapphire blue (1937). Production in pink was limited. The current value for a pink cup and saucer is $175.

Tumblers in Royal Ruby Bubble are the 12 oz iced tea tumbler ($19.50), juice tumbler ($10), 16 oz lemonade ($16), and 9 oz water ($16).

Item	Crystal	Forest Green or Royal Ruby	Sapphire Blue
Berry Bowl, 4" d	5.00	—	18.00
Berry Bowl, 8-3/4" d	12.00	18.00	20.00
Bowl, 9" d, fanged	8.00	—	335.00
Candlesticks, pr	24.00	40.00	—
Cereal Bowl, 5-1/4" d	8.00	17.00	17.50
Cocktail, 3-1/2 oz	4.50	10.00	—
Cocktail, 4-1/2 oz	4.50	12.50	—
Creamer	7.50	18.00	45.00
Cup	4.50	8.75	15.00
Fruit Bowl, 4-1/2" d	5.00	11.00	12.00
Goblet, 9 oz, stem, 5-1/2" h	7.50	15.00	—
Goblet, 9-1/2 oz, stem	7.50	15.00	—
Iced Tea Goblet, 14 oz	8.00	17.50	—
Iced Tea Tumbler, 12 oz, 4-1/2" h	12.50	—	—
Juice Goblet, 4 oz	3.00	8.00	—
Juice Goblet, 5-1/2 oz	5.00	12.50	—
Juice Tumbler, 6 oz, ftd	4.00	12.00	—
Lamp, 3 styles	42.00	—	—
Lemonade Tumbler, 16 oz, 5-7/8" h	16.00	—	—
Old Fashioned Tumbler, 8 oz, 3-1/4" h	6.50	16.00	—
Pitcher, 64 oz, ice lip	60.00	—	—
Plate, 6-3/4" d, bread and butter	3.50	4.50	3.75
Plate, 9-3/8" d, dinner	7.50	28.00	8.00
Plate, 9-3/8" d, grill	—	20.00	22.00

Item	Crystal	Forest Green or Royal Ruby	Sapphire Blue
Platter, 12" l, oval	10.00	—	18.00
Sandwich Plate, 9-1/2" d	7.50	25.00	8.00
Saucer	1.50	5.00	1.50
Sherbet, 6 oz	4.50	9.50	—
Soup Bowl, flat, 7-3/4" d	10.00	—	16.00
Sugar	6.00	13.00	28.00
Tumbler, 9 oz, water	6.00	—	—

Bubble, blue grill plate, platter and bowls.

Cameo
Ballerina, Dancing Girl

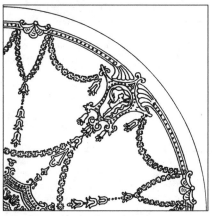

Manufactured by Hocking Glass Company, Lancaster, Ohio, from 1930 to 1934.

Made in crystal, green, pink and yellow. Only the crystal has a platinum rim.

Reproductions: † Salt shakers made in blue, green and pink. Children's dishes have been made in green and pink, but were never part of the original pattern. Recently, a squatty candy dish in cobalt blue has also been made. Again, this was not an original color.

Item	Crystal	Green	Pink
Berry Bowl, 4-1/4" d	15.00	—	—
Berry Bowl, 8-1/4" d	—	45.00	175.00
Butter Dish, cov	—	245.00	—
Cake Plate, 10" d, 3 legs	—	22.00	—
Cake Plate, 10-1/2" d, flat	—	115.00	165.00
Candlesticks, pr, 4" h	—	85.00	—
Candy Jar, cov, 4" h	—	90.00	495.00
Candy Jar, cov, 6-1/2" h	—	195.00	—
Cereal Bowl, 5-1/2" d	8.50	35.00	160.00
Cocktail Shaker	600.00	—	—
Comport, 5" w	—	42.00	200.00
Console Bowl, 3 legs, 11" d	—	75.00	45.00
Cookie Jar, cov	—	60.00	—
Cream Soup, 4-3/4" d	—	175.00	—

Cameo, 8" luncheon plate.

Cameo, clear tumbler.

Item	Crystal	Green	Pink
Creamer, 3-1/4" h	—	30.00	110.00
Creamer, 4-1/4" h	—	30.00	115.00
Cup	10.00	19.00	85.00
Decanter, 10" h	225.00	195.00	
Domino Tray, 7" l	150.00	165.00	250.00
Goblet, 6" h, water	—	65.00	175.00
Ice Bowl, 3" h, 5-1/2" d	265.00	190.00	700.00
Jam Jar, cov, 2" h	175.00	185.00	—
Juice Pitcher, 6" h, 36 oz	—	65.00	—
Juice Tumbler, 3 oz, ftd	—	55.00	90.00
Juice Tumbler, 5 oz, 3-3/4" h	—	25.00	—
Pitcher, 8-1/2" h, 56 oz	550.00	65.00	1,450.00
Plate, 6" d, sherbet	6.00	9.00	90.00
Plate, 7" d, salad	12.00	—	—
Plate, 8" d, luncheon	8.00	14.00	36.00
Plate, 9-1/2" d, dinner	—	24.00	85.00

Cameo, green vegetable bowl.

Item	Crystal	Green	Pink
Plate, 10-1/2" d, dinner, rimmed	—	115.00	175.00
Plate, 10-1/2" d, grill	—	12.00	55.00
Platter, 12" l	—	30.00	—
Relish, 7-1/2" l, ftd, 3 part	175.00	35.00	—
Salad Bowl, 7-1/4" d	—	60.00	—
Salt and Pepper Shakers, pr, ftd †	—	70.00	90.00
Sandwich Plate, 10" d	—	18.00	45.00
Sandwich Server, center handle	—	6,500.00	—
Saucer	4.00	4.00	90.00
Sherbet, 3-1/8" h, blown	—	17.50	75.00
Sherbet, 3-1/8" h, molded	—	16.00	75.00
Sherbet, 4-7/8" h	—	40.00	100.00
Soup Bowl, rimmed, 9" d	—	75.00	135.00
Sugar, 3-1/4" h	—	21.00	—
Sugar, 4-1/4" h	—	30.00	125.00

Cameo, green sugar.

Item	Crystal	Green	Pink
Syrup Pitcher, 20 oz, 5-3/4" h	—	250.00	—
Tumbler, 9 oz, 4" h	16.00	30.00	80.00
Tumbler, 9 oz, 5" h, ftd	—	29.00	115.00
Tumbler, 10 oz, 4-3/4" h, flat	—	35.00	95.00
Tumbler, 11" oz, 5" h, flat	—	30.00	90.00
Tumbler, 11 oz, 5-3/4" h, ftd	—	70.00	135.00
Tumbler, 15 oz, 5-1/4" h	—	80.00	145.00
Tumbler, 15 oz, 6-3/8" h, ftd	—	495.00	—
Vase, 5-3/4" h	—	245.00	—
Vase, 8" h	—	65.00	—
Vegetable, oval, 10" l	—	50.00	—
Wine, 3-1/2" h	—	1,200.00	950.00
Wine, 4" h	—	95.00	250.00

Note: *Yellow Cameo is limited to a butter dish ($1,500), candy jar ($120), cereal bowl ($35), console bowl ($95), creamer ($25), 8" cup and saucer ($13), luncheon plate ($12.50), 9-1/2" dinner plate ($12), 10-1/2" grill plate ($10), 12" platter ($42), 10" sandwich plate ($37), 4-7/8" sherbet with plate ($50), sugar ($20), 9 oz tumbler ($14), 11 oz tumbler ($48) and a 10" oval vegetable bowl, ($45). The ultimate piece of yellow Cameo is the 20 oz syrup, valued at $1,950.*

Charm (Fire-King)

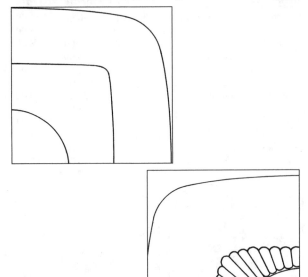

Manufactured by Anchor-Hocking, from 1950 to 1954.

Made in Azur-ite and Jade-ite.

Item	Azur-ite	Jade-ite
Creamer	6.50	17.00
Cup	4.50	15.00
Cup and Saucer	6.00	15.00
Dessert Bowl, 4-3/4" d	5.00	15.00
Plate, 6-5/8" d, salad	4.00	5.00
Plate, 8-3/4" d, luncheon	7.00	9.00
Plate, 9-1/2" d, dinner	20.00	25.00
Platter, 11" x 8"	15.00	30.00
Salad Bowl, 7-3/8" d	15.00	30.00
Saucer, 5-3/8" d	2.50	3.50
Soup Bowl, 6" d	20.00	24.00
Sugar	6.00	18.00

Charm, (Fire-King) blue plate, cup and saucer.

Charm, (Fire-King) cup and saucer.

Cherryberry

Manufactured by U.S. Glass Company, Pittsburgh, early 1930s.

Made in crystal, green, iridescent and pink.

Item	Crystal	Green or Pink	Iridesc.
Berry Bowl, 4" d	7.00	8.75	7.00
Berry Bowl, 7-1/2" d, deep	17.50	20.00	17.50
Bowl, 6-1/4" d, 2" deep	40.00	55.00	40.00
Butter Dish, cov	150.00	175.00	150.00
Comport, 5-3/4"	17.50	25.00	17.50
Creamer, large, 4-5/8"	40.00	45.00	40.00
Creamer, small	15.00	20.00	15.00
Olive Dish, 5" l, one handle	10.00	15.00	10.00
Pickle Dish, 8-1/4" l, oval	10.00	15.00	10.00
Pitcher, 7-3/4" h	165.00	175.00	165.00
Plate, 6" d, sherbet	6.50	11.00	6.50
Plate, 7-1/2" d, salad	8.50	15.00	9.00
Salad Bowl, 6-1/2" d, deep	17.50	22.00	17.50
Sherbet	9.00	10.00	9.50
Sugar, large, cov	45.00	75.00	45.00
Sugar, small, open	15.00	20.00	15.00
Tumbler, 9 oz, 3-5/8" h	20.00	35.00	20.00

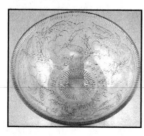

Cherryberry, clear bowl.

Cherry Blossom

Manufactured by Jeannette Glass Company, Jeannette, Pa., from 1930 to 1939.

Made in Crystal, Delphite, green, Jade-ite, pink and red (production was very limited in crystal, Jade-ite and red).

Reproductions: † Reproductions include: small berry bowl, 8-1/2" d bowl, cov butter dish, cake plate, cereal bowl, cup, pitcher, 6" and 9" plates, divided 13" platter, salt shaker, sandwich tray, saucer, 3-3/4" and 4-1/2" h ftd tumblers. Reproductions have been made in cobalt blue, Delphite, green, pink and red. A children's butter dish has also been made, which was never included in the original production.

Note: *Cherry Blossom collectors are always looking for salt and pepper shakers with the original tops, and no wonder: a pair in green is valued at $995 while a pink pair is valued at $1,250.*

Item	Delphite	Green	Pink
Berry Bowl, 4-3/4" d †	17.50	20.00	22.50
Berry Bowl, 8-1/2" d †	55.00	22.00	65.00
Bowl, 9" d, 2 handles	27.50	75.00	48.00
Butter Dish, cov †	—	85.00	75.00
Cake Plate, 10-1/4" d, 3 legs †	—	28.00	25.00
Cereal Bowl, 5-3/4" d †	—	35.00	32.00
Coaster	—	15.00	15.00
Creamer	30.00	35.00	35.00
Cup †	28.00	25.00	24.00
Fruit Bowl, 10-1/2" d	32.00	89.00	89.00
Juice Tumbler, 1 oz, 3-1/2"	—	35.00	24.00
Mug, 7 oz	—	195.00	265.00
Pitcher, 36 oz, 6-3/4" h, 36 oz †	89.00	60.00	72.00
Pitcher, 36 oz, 8", PAT, ftd	—	65.00	60.00
Pitcher, 42 oz, 8", PAT, flat	—	65.00	60.00
Plate, 6" d, sherbet †	12.50	9.50	10.00
Plate, 7" d, salad	—	27.50	24.00
Plate, 9" d, dinner †	18.00	28.00	25.00
Plate, 9" d, grill	—	32.50	32.50
Plate, 10" d, grill	—	30.00	—

Cherry Blossom, delphite small bowls.

Cherry Blossom, cup & saucer & dinner plate in pink.

Item	Delphite	Green	Pink
Platter, 11" l, oval	40.00	48.00	35.00
Platter, 13" d	—	72.00	43.00
Platter, 13" divided †	—	72.00	43.00
Salt and Pepper Shakers, pr, scalloped base †	—	995.00	1,250.00
Sandwich Tray, 10-1/2" d †	20.00	24.00	30.00
Saucer †	6.00	7.50	6.00
Sherbet	18.00	20.00	19.50
Soup, flat, 7-3/4" d	—	85.00	80.00
Sugar, cov	24.00	37.50	35.00
Tumbler, 3-3/4" h, AOP, ftd †	—	22.00	24.00
Tumbler, 5" h	20.00	70.00	72.00
Tumbler, 8 oz, 4-1/2" h, scalloped ftd base, AOP	—	40.00	35.00
Tumbler, 9 oz, 4-1/4" h	—	24.00	22.00
Tumbler, 9 oz, 4-1/2" h †	20.00	30.00	32.00
Vegetable Bowl, 9" l, oval	45.00	42.00	40.00

Children's

Item	Delphite	Green	Pink
Creamer		50.00	50.00
Cup †		42.00	42.00
Plate, 6" d		15.00	15.00
Saucer		7.50	7.50
Sugar		50.00	50.00

Chinex Classic

Manufactured by MacBeth-Evans Division of Corning Glass Works, from the late 1930s to early 1940s.

Made in Chinex (ivory) and Chinex with Classic Bouquet or Classic Castle decal.

Item	Chinex	Chinex, Classic Bouquet decal	Chinex, Classic Castle decal
Bowl, 11" d	20.00	36.00	48.00
Butter Dish, cov	55.00	80.00	135.00
Cake Plate, 11-1/2" d	10.00	15.00	25.00
Cereal Bowl, 5- 3/4" d	6.00	8.50	15.00
Creamer	8.50	12.00	20.00
Cup	6.00	9.50	17.50
Plate, 6-1/4" d, sherbet	3.50	4.50	8.00
Plate, 9-3/4" d, dinner	4.00	8.00	16.00
Sandwich Plate, 11-1/2" d	8.00	15.00	25.00
Saucer	2.00	4.00	7.00
Sherbet, low, ftd	9.50	12.00	29.00
Soup Bowl, 7-3/4" d	14.00	25.00	40.00
Sugar, open	7.50	12.50	20.00
Vegetable Bowl, 7" d	15.00	25.00	35.00
Vegetable Bowl, 9" d	15.00	25.00	35.00

Chinese Classic, plate with castle decal.

Christmas Candy

No. 624

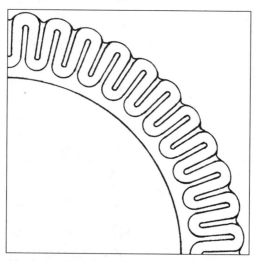

Manufactured by Indiana Glass Company, Dunkirk, Ind., 1950s.
Made in crystal and Terrace Green (teal).

Item	Crystal	Terrace Green
Bowl, 5-3/4" d	6.50	—
Creamer	15.00	27.50
Cup	8.00	35.00
Mayonnaise, ladle, liner	24.00	—
Plate, 6" d, bread and butter	6.00	16.00
Plate, 8-1/4" d, luncheon	8.00	28.00
Plate, 9-5/8"d, dinner	12.00	36.00
Sandwich Plate, 11-1/4" d	24.00	65.00
Saucer	5.00	15.00
Soup Bowl, 7-3/8" d	12.00	75.00
Sugar	15.00	35.00
Tidbit, 2 tier	20.00	—
Vegetable Bowl, 9-1/2" d	—	235.00

Christmas Candy, crystal sugar and creamer.

Circle

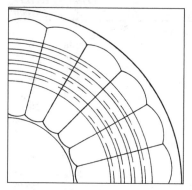

Manufactured by Hocking Glass Company, Lancaster, Ohio, in the 1930s.

Made in crystal, green and pink. Crystal is listed in the original catalogs, but few pieces have surfaced to date. A 3-1/8" d sherbet is known and valued at $4.

Item	Green	Pink
Bowl, 4-1/2" d	15.00	15.00
Bowl, 5-1/2" d, flared	17.50	17.50
Bowl, 8" d	16.00	16.00
Bowl, 9-3/8" d	18.50	18.50
Creamer, ftd	9.00	16.00
Cup	6.00	7.50

Item	Green	Pink
Goblet, 8 oz, 5-3/4" h	16.50	15.00
Iced Tea Tumbler, 10 oz	17.50	17.50
Juice Tumbler, 4 oz	9.50	9.00
Pitcher, 60 oz	35.00	35.00
Pitcher, 80 oz	30.00	32.00
Plate, 6" d, sherbet	3.00	3.00
Plate, 8-1/4"d, luncheon	11.00	11.00
Plate, 9-1/2" d, dinner	12.00	12.00
Sandwich Plate, 10" d	15.00	17.50
Saucer, 6" d	2.50	2.50
Sherbet, 3-1/8"	5.00	5.00
Sherbet, 4-3/4"	12.00	12.00
Sugar, ftd	12.00	16.00
Tumbler, 8 oz	10.00	10.00
Tumbler, 15 oz, flat	17.50	17.50
Wine, 4-1/2" h	15.00	15.00

Circle, green cup.

Cloverleaf

Manufactured by Hazel Atlas Glass Company, Clarksburg, W.V., and Zanesville, Ohio, from 1930 to 1936.

Made in black, crystal, green, pink and yellow. Collector interest in crystal is minimal; prices would be about 50% of those listed for green.

Pink cloverleaf production is limited to cup and saucer ($16.50), dessert bowl ($15), luncheon plate ($10), sherbet ($8.50), 9 oz flat tumbler ($26.50) and 10 oz flat tumbler ($22.50).

Item	*Black*	*Green*	*Yellow*
Ashtray, match holder in center, 4" d	.65.00	—	—
Ashtray, match holder in center, 5-3/4" d	.75.00	20.00	—
Bowl, 8" d	—	50.00	—

Item	Black	Green	Yellow
Candy Dish, cov	—	45.00	95.00
Cereal Bowl, 5" d	—	25.00	34.00
Creamer, 3-5/8" h, ftd	25.00	12.00	20.00
Cup	16.00	9.00	10.00
Dessert Bowl, 4" d	—	18.00	25.00
Plate, 6" d, sherbet	38.00	4.50	7.00
Plate, 8" d, luncheon	16.00	8.00	14.00
Plate, 10-1/4" d, grill	—	20.00	34.00
Salad Bowl, 7" d	—	40.00	48.00
Salt and Pepper Shakers, pr	95.00	24.00	120.00
Saucer	7.00	6.00	5.00
Sherbet, 3" h, ftd	22.00	15.00	12.00
Sugar, 3-5/8" h, ftd	25.00	12.00	20.00
Tumbler, 9 oz, 4" h, flat	—	50.00	35.00
Tumbler, 10 oz, 3-3/4" h, flat	—	35.00	—
Tumbler, 10 oz, 5-3/4" h, ftd	—	22.00	32.00

*Cloverleaf, green saucer
and pink plate and cup.*

Colonial

Knife and Fork

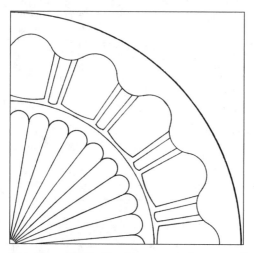

Manufactured by Hocking Glass Company, Lancaster, Ohio, from 1934 to 1938.

Made in crystal, green and pink.

Note: *A rare form of depression glass, a 12 oz 5-1/2" mug is found in colonial pattern. Green is valued at $825, while pink is $500.*

Item	Crystal	Green	Pink
Berry Bowl, 3-3/4" d	—	—	45.00
Berry Bowl, 4-1/2"	12.00	22.00	18.00
Berry Bowl, 9" d	24.00	55.00	35.00
Butter Dish, cov	40.00	60.00	625.00
Cereal Bowl, 5-1/2" d	32.00	85.00	60.00
Claret, 4 oz, 5-1/4" h	20.00	25.00	—
Cocktail, 3 oz, 4" h	15.00	25.00	—
Cordial, 1 oz, 3-3/4" h	20.00	30.00	—
Cream Soup Bowl, 4-1/2" d	70.00	85.00	72.00
Creamer, 8 oz, 5" h	17.00	25.00	60.00
Cup	8.00	15.00	12.00
Goblet, 8-1/2 oz, 5-3/4" h	25.00	35.00	40.00
Ice Tea Tumbler, 12 oz	28.00	55.00	45.00

Colonial, crystal wine and cocktail.

Item	*Crystal*	*Green*	*Pink*
Juice Tumbler, 5 oz, 3" h	.17.50	27.50	22.00
Lemonade Tumbler, 15 oz	.47.50	75.00	65.00
Milk Pitcher, 8 oz, 5" h	.17.00	25.00	60.00
Pitcher, 54 oz, 7" h, ice lip	.40.00	45.00	48.00
Pitcher, 54 oz, 7" h, no lip	.40.00	45.00	48.00
Pitcher, 68 oz, 7-3/4" h, ice lip	.35.00	72.00	65.00
Pitcher, 68 oz, 7-3/4" h, no lip	.35.00	72.00	65.00
Plate, 6" d, sherbet	.4.50	7.50	7.00
Plate, 8-1/2" d, luncheon	.6.00	8.00	10.00
Plate, 10" d, dinner	.32.00	45.00	46.00
Plate, 10"d, grill	.17.50	27.00	27.50
Plate, 12" d, oval	.17.50	25.00	30.00
Platter, 12" l, oval	.17.50	25.00	35.00
Salt and Pepper Shakers, pr	.65.00	140.00	148.00
Saucer	.4.50	7.50	6.50
Sherbet, 3" h	—	—	24.00
Sherbet, 3-3/8" h	.10.00	15.00	12.50

Colonial, green saucer.

Colonial, crystal butter dish, covered

Item	Crystal	Green	Pink
Soup Bowl, 7" d	.30.00	85.00	82.00
Spoon Holder or Celery Vase	.80.00	125.00	135.00
Sugar, cov	.35.00	45.00	42.00
Sugar, 5", open	.10.00	12.00	15.00
Tumbler, 3 oz, 3-1/4" h, ftd	.11.00	15.00	14.00
Tumbler, 5 oz, 4" h, ftd	.15.00	35.00	30.00
Tumbler, 9 oz, 4" h	.15.00	20.00	25.00
Tumbler, 10 oz, 5-1/4" h, ftd	.30.00	46.50	50.00
Tumbler, 11 oz, 5-1/8" h	.25.00	37.00	40.00
Vegetable Bowl, 10" l, oval	.18.00	25.00	30.00
Whiskey, 2-1/2" h, 1-1/2 oz	.9.00	20.00	15.00
Wine, 4-1/2" h, 2-1/2 oz	.16.00	28.00	11.00
Tumbler, 3 oz, 3-1/4" h, ftd	.11.00	15.00	16.50
Tumbler, 5 oz, 4" h, ftd	.15.00	35.00	27.50
Tumbler, 9 oz, 4" h	.15.00	20.00	25.00
Tumbler, 10 oz, 5-1/4" h, ftd	.30.00	46.50	50.00
Tumbler, 11 oz, 5-1/8" h	.25.00	37.00	40.00
Vegetable Bowl, 10" l, oval	.18.00	25.00	45.00
Whiskey, 2-1/2" h, 1-1/2 oz	.10.00	20.00	15.00
Wine, 4-1/2" h, 2-1/2 oz	.17.00	30.00	14.00

*Colonial, salt &
pepper shakers.*

Colonial Block

Manufactured by Hazel Atlas Glass Company, Clarksburg, W.V., and Zanesville, Ohio, early 1930s.

Made in black, cobalt blue (rare), crystal, green, pink and white (1950s).

Note: *Production in black is limited to a covered powder jar ($30). Production in white includes a creamer ($7.50), open sugar ($9.50), and covered sugar ($18).*

Item	Crystal	Green	Pink
Bowl, 4" d .6.00		7.50	7.50
Bowl, 7" d 16.00		20.00	20.00
Butter Dish, cov 35.00		45.00	45.00
Butter Tub, cov 35.00		40.00	40.00
Candy Jar, cov 30.00		40.00	40.00
Compote, 4" h, 4-3/4" w 12.00		—	—
Creamer 15.00		16.00	15.00
Goblet, 5-3/4" h 9.00		12.00	15.00
Pitcher, 20 oz, 5-3/4" h 40.00		50.00	50.00
Powder Jar, cov 20.00		24.00	24.00
Sherbet 6.00		9.50	9.50
Sugar, cov 20.00		25.00	25.00
Sugar, open 6.00		8.00	8.00

Colonial Block, green covered butter dish.

Colonial Fluted

Rope

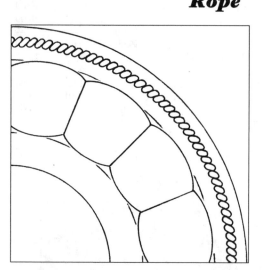

Manufactured by Federal Glass Company, Columbus, Ohio, from 1928 to 1933.

Made in crystal and green.

Item	Crystal	Green
Berry Bowl, 4" d 11.00		12.00
Berry Bowl, 7-1/2" d 16.00		18.00
Cereal Bowl, 6" d 15.00		18.00
Creamer, ftd 12.00		14.00
Cup 5.00		7.50
Plate, 6" d, sherbet 2.50		4.00
Plate, 8" d, luncheon 5.00		10.00
Salad Bowl, 6-1/2" d, 2-1/2" deep 22.00		35.00
Saucer 2.50		4.00
Sherbet 6.00		8.50
Sugar, cov 21.00		25.00
Sugar, open 8.00		10.00

Colonial Fluted, green sugar and creamer.

Columbia

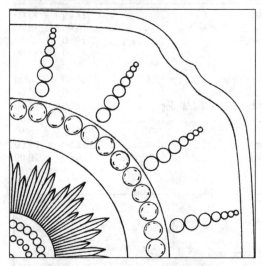

Manufactured by Federal Glass Company, Columbus, Ohio, from 1938 to 1942.

Made in crystal and pink. Several flashed (stained) colors are found, and some decaled pieces are known.

Reproductions: † The 2-7/8" h juice tumbler has been reproduced. Look for the "France" on the base to clearly identify the reproductions.

Item	Crystal	Flashed	Pink
Bowl, 10-1/2" d, ruffled edge	.24.00	20.00	—
Butter Dish, cov	.20.00	25.00	—
Cereal Bowl, 5" d	.18.00	—	—
Chop Plate, 11" d	.17.00	12.00	—
Crescent Shaped Salad	.27.00	—	—
Cup	.9.50	10.00	25.00
Juice Tumbler, 4 oz, 2-3/4" h † . . .	.30.00	—	—
Plate, 6" d, bread & butter	.5.00	—	14.00
Plate, 9-1/2" d, luncheon	.15.00	—	32.00
Salad Bowl, 8-1/2" d	.20.00	—	—
Saucer	.4.00	3.50	10.00
Soup Bowl, 8" d, low	.25.00	—	—
Tumbler, 9 oz	.42.50	—	—

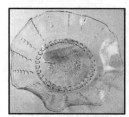

Columbia, crystal ruffled bowl.

Columbia, crystal plate, cup and saucer.

Coronation
Banded Fine Rib, Saxon

Manufactured by Hocking Glass Company, Lancaster, Ohio, from 1936 to 1940.

Made in crystal, green, pink and Royal Ruby.

Crystal forms are limited to cup and saucer ($7), 6-1/2" nappy bowl ($15), 6" plate ($2), and 8-1/2" plate ($5).

Item	Green	Pink	Royal Ruby
Berry Bowl, 4-1/4" d	34.00	8.50	6.50
Berry Bowl, 8" d, handle	—	18.00	20.00
Berry Bowl, 8" d	150.00	—	—
Cup	—	6.00	7.50
Nappy Bowl, 6-1/2" d	—	7.50	15.00
Pitcher, 68 oz, 7-3/4" h	—	500.00	—
Plate, 6" d, sherbet	—	4.50	—
Plate, 8-1/2" d, luncheon	42.00	12.00	8.50
Saucer	—	4.00	—
Sherbet	70.00	7.00	—
Tumbler, 10 oz, 5" h, ftd	165.00	35.00	—

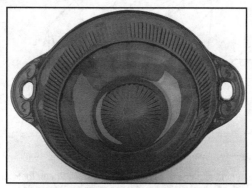

Coronation, ruby handled bowl.

Cracked Ice

Manufactured by Indiana Glass, Dunkirk, Ind., in the 1930s.

Made in pink and green. Often mistaken for Tea Room, look for the additional diagonal line, giving it a more Art Deco style.

Item	Green	Pink
Creamer	30.00	35.00
Plate, 6-1/2" d	15.00	18.00
Sherbet	12.00	15.00
Sugar, cov	30.00	35.00
Tumbler	15.00	18.00

Cracked Ice, pink creamer and covered sugar.

Cremax

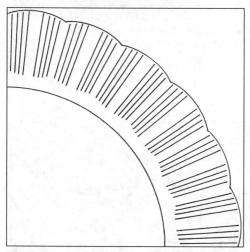

Manufactured by MacBeth-Evans Division of Corning Glass Works, late 1930s to early 1940s.

Made in Cremax, Cremax with fired-on colors, Delphite and Robin's Egg Blue. One set is known as Bordette.

Note: *A rare form of depression glass was made in this pretty pattern, but only in Bordette—value the 2-3/4" h egg cup at $10. Value for the other Bordette pieces would be approximately $1 less than those listed for Cremax.*

Item	Cremax	Cremax Fired-On	Delphite or Robin's Egg Blue
Cereal Bowl, 5-3/4" d	4.00	7.00	8.00
Creamer	4.50	4.00	9.00
Cup	4.00	6.00	5.00
Demitasse Cup	14.00	16.00	24.00
Demitasse Saucer	5.00	6.00	18.00
Plate, 6-1/4" d, bread and butter	2.50	3.50	5.00
Plate, 9-3/4" d, dinner	5.00	9.00	10.00
Sandwich Plate, 11-1/2" d	8.00	13.00	15.00
Saucer	2.00	2.00	4.00
Sugar, open	4.50	4.00	9.00
Vegetable Bowl, 9" d	9.00	8.00	18.00

Cremax, plate with blue edge.

Cube

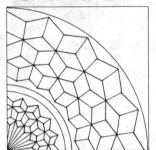

Cubist

Manufactured by Jeannette Glass Company, Jeannette, Pa., from 1929 to 1933.

Made in amber, crystal, green, pink, ultramarine and white. Production in amber and white is limited to the 2-3/8" h sugar bowl, $3.

Production in ultramarine is limited to the 2-3/8" h sugar bowl ($70) and a 4-1/2" dia deep bowl, ($35).

Item	Crystal	Green	Pink
Bowl, 4-1/2" d, deep	—	7.00	9.50
Butter Dish, cov	—	60.00	65.00
Candy Jar, cov, 6-1/2" h	—	30.00	30.00
Coaster, 3-1/4" d	—	10.00	10.00
Creamer, 2-5/8" h	5.00	10.00	9.00
Creamer, 3-9/16" h	—	8.50	9.00

Item	Crystal	Green	Pink
Cup	—	7.00	8.00
Dessert Bowl, 4-1/2" d, pointed rim	4.00	8.50	9.50
Pitcher, 8-3/4" h, 45 oz	—	235.00	215.00
Plate, 6" d, sherbet	—	11.00	3.50
Plate, 8" d, luncheon	—	8.50	7.50
Powder Jar, cov, 3 legs	—	30.00	35.00
Salad Bowl, 6-1/2" d	6.00	15.00	15.00
Salt and Pepper Shakers, pr	—	35.00	36.00
Saucer	1.50	3.00	3.50
Sherbet, ftd	—	8.50	12.00
Sugar, cov, 2-3/8" h	4.00	22.00	6.00
Sugar, cov, 3" h	—	25.00	25.00
Sugar, open, 3"	5.00	8.00	7.00
Tray, 7-1/2" l	9.00	—	5.00
Tumbler, 9 oz, 4" h	—	70.00	65.00

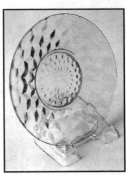

Cube, pink plate.

Daisy

No. 620

Manufactured by Indiana Glass Company, Dunkirk, Ind., from late 1930s to 1980s.

Made in amber (1940s), crystal (1933-40), dark green (1960s-80s), fired-on red (late 1930s) and milk glass (1960s-80s).

Item	Amber or Fired-On Red	Crystal	Dk Grn or Milk Wht
Berry Bowl, 4-1/2" d	9.50	6.00	6.00
Berry Bowl, 7-3/8" d deep	17.50	8.50	9.50
Berry Bowl, 9-3/8" d, deep	35.00	14.00	14.00
Cake Plate, 11-1/2" d	16.50	14.00	14.00
Cereal Bowl, 6" d	25.00	10.00	10.00
Cream Soup Bowl, 4-1/2" d	13.50	7.50	7.50
Creamer, ftd	10.00	8.00	8.00
Cup	6.50	5.00	6.00
Plate, 6" d, sherbet	3.00	2.50	2.50
Plate, 7-3/8" d, salad	7.50	4.00	4.50
Plate, 8-3/8" d, luncheon	8.50	6.00	6.00
Plate, 9-3/8" d, dinner	10.00	8.00	8.00

Daisy, green luncheon plate.

Daisy, crystal sandwich plate.

Item	Amber or Fired-On Red	Crystal	Dk Grn or Milk Wht
Plate, 10-3/8" d, grill	15.00	8.00	8.00
Plate, 10-3/8" d, grill, indent for soup	15.00	8.00	8.00
Platter, 10-3/4" d	15.00	11.00	11.00
Relish Dish, 8-3/8" d, 3 part	22.00	12.00	12.00
Sandwich Plate, 11-1/2" d	17.50	14.00	14.00
Saucer	2.00	1.50	2.00
Sherbet, ftd	9.00	5.00	5.00
Sugar, ftd	10.00	8.00	8.00
Tumbler, 9 oz, ftd	16.00	10.00	10.00
Tumbler, 12 oz, ftd	40.00	15.00	15.00
Vegetable Bowl, 10" l, oval	18.00	12.00	12.00

Daisy, amber luncheon plate.

Daisy, amber Footed sugar.

Della Robbia

#1058

Manufactured by Westmoreland Glass Company, Grapeville, Pa., from late 1920s to 1940s.

Made in crystal, with applied luster colors and milk glass. Examples of milk white prices are: hand-painted dec candy jar, $45; creamer, $18; goblet, $20; tumbler, $15; wine, $18.

Item	*Crystal*
Basket, 9"	195.00
Basket, 12"	275.00
Bowl, 8" d, bell, handle	48.00
Bowl, 8"d, heart shape, handle.	95.00
Bowl, 12" d, ftd	12.00
Bowl, 13" d, rolled edge	115.00
Bowl, 14" d, oval, flange	155.00
Bowl, 15" d, bell	175.00
Cake Salver, 14" d, ftd	120.00
Candlesticks, pr, 4" h	65.00
Candlesticks, pr, 4" h, 2 light	160.00
Candy Jar, cov, scalloped edge	85.00

Della Robbia, clear plate.

Item	*Crystal*
Champagne, 6 oz.	.25.00
Chocolate Candy, round, flat	.75.00
Cocktail, 3-1/4 oz.	.15.00
Comport, 12" d, ftd, bell	.115.00
Comport, 13" d, flanged	.125.00
Creamer, ftd	.18.00
Cup and saucer	.28.00
Finger Bowl, 5" d	.30.00
Ginger Ale Tumbler, 5 oz	.25.00
Goblet, 8 oz., 6" h	.28.00
Iced Tea Tumbler 11 oz., ftd	.35.00
Iced Tea Tumbler 12 oz., 5-3/16" h, straight	.40.00
Iced Tea Tumbler 12 oz., bell	.32.00
Iced Tea Tumbler, 12 oz., bell, ftd	.32.00
Mint Comport, 6-1/2" d, 3-5/8" h, ftd	.45.00
Nappy, 7-1/2"d	.42.00
Nappy, 8" d, bell	.45.00
Nappy, 4-1/2" d	.30.00
Nappy, 6" d, bell	.35.00
Nappy, 6-1/2"d , one handle	.32.00
Nappy, 9" d	.60.00
Pitcher, 32 oz.	.200.00
Plate, 6" d, finger bowl liner	.12.00
Plate, 6-1/8" d, bread & butter	.14.00
Plate, 7-1/4" d, salad	.22.00
Plate, 9" d, luncheon	.35.00
Plate, 10-1/2" d, dinner	.95.00
Plate, 18" d	.175.00

Item	Crystal
Platter, 14" l, oval	175.00
Punch Bowl, 14"d	225.00
Punch Bowl Liner, 18" d plate, upturned edge	165.00
Punch Cup	15.00
Salt and Pepper Shakers, pr	55.00
Sherbet, 5 oz, low foot	22.00
Sherbet, 5 oz, 4-3/4" h, ftd	24.00
Sugar, ftd	27.50
Sweetmeat Comport, 8" d	100.00
Torte Plate, 14"d	115.00
Tumbler 8 oz., ftd	30.00
Tumbler, 8 oz, water	32.00
Wine, 3 oz	25.00

Della Robbia, stained decorated compote.

Dewdrop

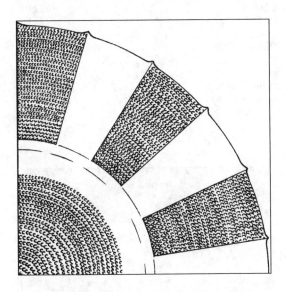

Manufactured by Jeannette Glass Company, Jeannette, Pa., from 1953 to 1956.

Made in crystal.

Item	Crystal
Bowl, 4-3/4" d	9.00
Bowl, 8-1/2" d	22.00
Bowl, 10-3/8" d	24.00
Butter, cov	32.00
Candy Dish, cov, 7" d	30.00
Casserole, cov	27.50
Creamer	8.50
Iced Tea Tumbler, 15 oz	17.50
Lazy Susan, 13" d tray	32.00
Pitcher, 1/2 gallon, ftd	48.00

Dewdrop, crystal sugar and creamer

Item	Crystal
Plate, 11-1/2" d	.20.00
Punch Cup	.4.00
Punch Bowl Set, bowl, 12 cups	.65.00
Snack Cup	.4.00
Snack Plate, indent for cup	.5.00
Relish, leaf-shape, handle	.9.00
Sugar, cov	.14.00
Tumbler, 9 oz	.15.00

Dewdrop, clear tumbler and iridescent pitcher.

Diamond
Quilted

Flat Diamond

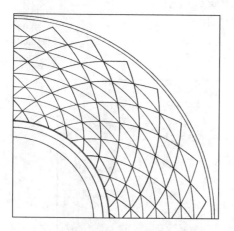

Manufactured by Imperial Glass Company, Bellaire, Ohio, from late 1920 to early 1930s.

Made in amber, black, blue, crystal, green, pink and red. Amber and red prices would be valued slightly higher than black, while blue and crystal would be slightly less.

Item	Black	Green	Pink
Bowl, 5-1/2" d, one handle	20.00	15.00	18.00
Bowl, 7" d, crimped edge	22.00	18.00	20.00
Cake Salver, 10" d, tall	—	60.00	65.00
Candlesticks, pr	60.00	32.00	28.00
Candy Jar, cov, ftd	—	65.00	65.00
Cereal Bowl, 5" d	15.00	9.00	8.50
Champagne, 9 oz, 6" h	—	12.00	—
Compote, 6" h, 7-1/4" w	—	45.00	48.00
Compote, cov, 11-1/2" d	—	80.00	75.00
Console Bowl, 10-1/2" d, rolled edge	65.00	20.00	24.00
Cordial, 1 oz	—	12.00	15.00
Cream Soup Bowl, 4-3/4" d	22.00	12.00	14.00
Creamer	18.50	12.00	12.00
Cup	18.00	10.00	12.00
Ice Bucket	90.00	50.00	50.00
Iced Tea Tumbler, 12 oz	—	10.00	10.00
Mayonnaise Set, comport, plate, ladle	60.00	37.50	40.00
Pitcher, 64 oz	—	50.00	55.00

Diamond Quilted, pink sugar.

Item	Black	Green	Pink
Plate, 6" d, sherbet	10.00	7.00	7.50
Plate, 7" d, salad	10.00	8.50	8.50
Plate, 8" d, luncheon	12.00	6.50	8.50
Punch Bowl and Stand	—	450.00	450.00
Sandwich Plate, 14" d	—	15.00	15.00
Sandwich Server, center handle	50.00	25.00	25.00
Saucer	5.00	4.00	4.00
Sherbet	16.00	6.00	5.00
Sugar	20.00	15.00	13.50
Tumbler, 6 oz, ftd	—	9.00	10.00
Tumbler, 9 oz	—	14.00	16.00
Tumbler, 9 oz, ftd	—	14.00	16.00
Tumbler, 12 oz, ftd	—	15.00	15.00
Vase, fan	80.00	50.00	50.00
Whiskey, 1-1/2" oz	—	10.00	12.00
Wine, 2 oz	—	12.50	12.50
Wine, 3 oz	—	15.00	15.00

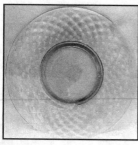

Diamond Quilted, 8" luncheon plate.

Diana

Manufactured by Federal Glass Company, Columbus, Ohio, from 1937 to 1941.

Made in amber, crystal and pink.

Reproductions: † A 13-1/8" d scalloped pink bowl has been made, which was not original to the pattern.

Item	Amber	Crystal	Pink
Ashtray, 3-1/2" d	—	4.00	5.00
Bowl, 12" d, scalloped edge	20.00	10.00	32.00
Candy Jar, cov, round	40.00	18.50	48.00
Cereal Bowl, 5" d	15.00	6.50	13.00
Coaster, 3-1/2" d	12.00	4.00	7.00
Console/Fruit Bowl, 11" d	10.00	20.00	44.00
Cream Soup Bowl, 5-1/2" d	18.00	14.00	24.00
Creamer, oval	9.00	4.00	12.50
Cup and saucer	10.00	6.00	25.00
Demitasse Cup and Saucer, 2 oz, 4-1/2" d saucer	—	15.00	50.00
Junior Set, 6 cups and saucers, rack ..	—	125.00	300.00
Plate, 6" d, bread & butter	3.50	3.00	5.50
Plate, 9-1/2" d, dinner	9.00	7.00	18.50
Platter, 12" l, oval	15.00	12.00	28.00
Salad Bowl, 9"d	18.00	15.00	20.00
Salt and Pepper Shakers, pr	100.00	30.00	75.00
Sandwich Plate, 11-3/4" d	10.00	8.00	28.00
Sandwich Plate, 11-3/4" d, advertising in center	—	15.00	—
Sherbet	10.00	7.00	12.00
Sugar, open, oval	10.00	10.00	16.00
Tumbler, 9 oz, 4-1/8" h	27.50	18.00	45.00

Diana, clear tumbler.

Diana, pink sherbet.

Diana, salad bowl 9".

Dinnerware
(Fire-King)
Jade-ite Restaurant Ware

Manufactured by Anchor-Hocking, from 1950 to 1956.

Made in Jade-ite.

Item	Jade-ite
Batter Bowl	.45.00
Bowl, 4-7/8" d	.12.00
Bowl, 10 oz deep	.15.00
Bowl, 15 oz deep	.20.00
Butter Dish, cov	.150.00
Cereal Bowl, 8 oz, flanged rim	.24.00
Chili Bowl, 15 oz, 5-5/8" d, rolled rim	.20.00
Coffee Mug, 7 oz	.12.00
Cup, 6 oz, straight	.10.00
Cup, 7 oz, extra heavy	.8.50
Cup, 7 oz, narrow rim	.7.20
Demitasse Cup and Saucer	.75.00
Egg Cup, double	.24.00

Item	*Jade-ite*
Fruit Bowl, 4-3/4" d 8.50	
Plate, 5-1/2" d, bread and butter 8.00	
Plate, 6-3/4" d, pie or salad 12.00	
Plate, 8" d, luncheon 17.50	
Plate, 8-7/8" d, oval, partitioned .24.00	
Plate, 9" d, dinner 18.00	
Plate, 9-3/4" l, oval, sandwich 20.00	
Plate, 9-5/8" d, 3 sections 18.00	
Plate, 9-5/8" d, 5 sections 24.00	
Platter, 9-1/2" d, oval 24.00	
Platter, 11-1/2" l, oval 20.00	
Saucer, 6" d 4.00	

*Dinnerware, (Fire-King) Jade-ite cup &
saucer.*

Dogwood

Apple Blossom, Wild Rose

Dogwood, pink sugar, creamer and plate.

Manufactured by MacBeth-Evans Company, Charleroi, Pa., from 1929 to 1932.

Made in Cremax, crystal, green, Monax, pink and yellow. Yellow is rare; a cereal bowl is known and valued at $95. Crystal items are valued at 50% less than green.

Item	Cremax or Monax	Green	Pink
Berry Bowl, 8-1/2" d	40.00	100.00	65.00
Cake Plate, 11" d, heavy solid foot . . .	—	—	650.00

Item	Cremax or Monax	Green	Pink
Cake Plate, 13" d, heavy solid foot	185.00	130.00	165.00
Cereal Bowl, 5-1/2" d	6.00	32.00	35.00
Coaster, 3-1/4" d	—	—	500.00
Creamer, 2-1/2" h, thin	—	48.00	22.50
Creamer, 3-1/4" h, thick	—	—	25.00
Cup, thin	—	32.00	18.00
Cup, thick	36.00	40.00	25.00
Fruit Bowl, 10-1/4" d	100.00	250.00	435.00
Pitcher, 8" h, 80 oz, (American Sweetheart style)	—	—	420.00
Pitcher, 8" h, 80 oz, decorated	—	500.00	265.00
Plate, 6" d, bread & butter	22.00	10.00	9.50
Plate, 8" d, luncheon	—	9.00	9.00
Plate, 9-1/4" d, dinner	—	—	42.00
Plates, 10-1/2" d, grill, AOP or border design only	—	22.00	25.00
Platter, 12" d, oval	—	—	500.00
Salver, 12" d	20.00	—	35.00
Saucer	20.00	10.00	8.50
Sherbet, low, ftd	—	95.00	40.00
Sugar, 2-1/2" h, thin	—	50.00	22.50
Sugar, 3-1/4" h, thick, ftd	—	—	24.50
Tidbit, 2 tier	—	—	90.00
Tumbler, 10 oz, 4" h, decorated	—	85.00	53.00
Tumbler, 11 oz, 4-3/4" h, decorated	—	95.00	75.00
Tumbler, 12 oz, 5" h, decorated	—	100.00	65.00
Tumbler, moulded band	—	—	25.00

Doric

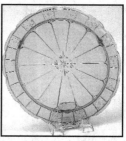

Doric, green cake plate.

Manufactured by Jeannette Glass Company, Jeannette, Pa., from 1935 to 1938.

Made in Delphite, green, pink and yellow. Yellow is rare.

Note: *Doric is another pattern in which the pitcher prices are high. A 36 oz flat pitcher in delphite is valued at $1,200, but the same size in green is $50 and $45 in pink. The 48 oz footed pitcher in green is valued at $1,000 and at $750 in pink.*

Note: *The forms found in delphite include a 4-1/2" berry bowl ($45), an 8-1/2" d berry b owl ($135), a 3-part candy dish ($10) and footed sherbet, ($10).*

Item	Green	Pink
Berry Bowl, 4-1/2" d	12.00	12.00
Berry Bowl, 8-1/4" d	25.00	17.00
Bowl, 9" d, two handles	45.00	45.00
Butter Dish, cov	90.00	75.00
Cake Plate, 10" d, 3 legs	30.00	30.00
Candy Dish, cov, 8" d	40.00	45.00
Candy Dish, 3 part	9.50	12.50
Cereal Bowl, 5-1/2" d	65.00	90.00
Coaster, 3" d	28.00	20.00
Cream Soup, 5" d, 2 handles	385.00	—
Creamer, 4" h	17.00	14.00
Cup	10.00	10.00
Plate 9" d, grill	20.00	25.00
Plate, 6" d, sherbet	7.50	7.50
Plate, 7" d, salad	20.00	18.00
Plate, 9" d, dinner	24.00	12.00
Platter, 12" l, oval	32.00	35.00
Relish Tray, 4" x 4"	12.00	14.00
Relish Tray, 4" x 8"	10.00	11.00
Salt and Pepper Shakers, pr	40.00	45.00
Saucer	7.00	7.00
Sherbet, footed	17.50	15.00
Sugar, cov	35.00	32.00
Tray, 8" x 8", serving	30.00	42.50
Tray, 10" l, handle	25.00	16.00
Tumbler, 9 oz, 4-1/2" h, flat	100.00	75.00
Tumbler, 10 oz, 4" h, ftd.	90.00	65.00
Tumbler, 12 oz, 5" h, ftd.	125.00	85.00
Vegetable Bowl, 9" l, oval	35.00	30.00

Doric & Pansy

Manufactured by Jeannette Glass Company, Jeannette, Pa., from 1937 to 1938.

Made in ultramarine, with limited production in pink and crystal.

Note: *Collectors only pay $600 for ultramarine salt and pepper shakers if the tops are original and in very good condition.*

Item	Crystal	Pink	Ultra-marine
Berry Bowl, 4-1/2" d	10.00	12.00	22.00
Berry Bowl, 8" d	—	24.00	75.00
Bowl, 9" d, handle	15.00	20.00	35.00
Butter Dish, cov	—	—	600.00
Cup	12.00	14.00	20.00
Creamer	72.00	90.00	145.00
Plate, 6" d, sherbet	8.00	12.00	14.50
Plate, 7" d, salad	—	—	35.00
Plate, 9" d, dinner	7.50	8.00	30.00
Salt and Pepper Shakers, pr,	—	—	600.00
Saucer	4.50	4.50	5.50
Sugar, open	80.00	85.00	115.00
Tray, 10" l, handles	45.00	—	25.00
Tumbler, 9 oz, 4-1/2" h	—	—	124.00

Doric and Pansy, pink plate.

Children's

Item	*Pink*	*Ultra-marine*
Creamer	.35.00	50.00
Cup	.35.00	48.00
Plate	.10.00	12.00
Saucer	.7.00	8.50
Sugar	.35.00	50.00
14-pc set	.400.00	425.00

Doric & Pansy, teal child's creamer & sugar.

Early American Prescut

Manufactured by Anchor Hocking, Lancaster, Ohio, from 1960 & 1999. Made in crystal with some limited production in colors.

Item	*Crystal*
Ashtray, 4" d	.4.00
Ashtray, 5" d	.8.00
Ashtray, 7-3/4" d	.12.00
Basket, 6" x 4-1/2"	.20.00
Bowl, 4-1/4" d, plain rim	.20.00
Bowl, 4-1/4" d, scalloped	.7.50
Bowl, 6-3/4" d, 3 legs	.5.00
Bowl, 7-1/4" d, scalloped	.18.50
Bowl, 8-3/4" d	.9.00
Bowl, 9" d, oval	.8.00
Bowl, 11-3/4" d, paneled	.200.00
Bud Vase, 5" h, ftd	.295.00
Butter, cov, 1/4 lb	.7.50
Butter, cov, metal handle, knife	.15.00
Cake Plate	.25.00
Candlesticks, pr, 2-lite	.28.50
Candy, cov, 5-1/4"	.12.00
Candy, cov, 7-1/4"	.14.50
Chip and Dip, 10-1/4" bowl, metal holder	.25.00
Coaster	.4.00
Cocktail Shaker, 30 oz	.300.00
Console Bowl, 9" d	.15.00
Creamer	.3.50
Creamer and Sugar Tray	.3.00
Cruet, os	.9.50
Dessert Bowl, 5-3/8" d	.3.00
Deviled Egg Plate, 11-3/4" d	.42.00

Item	*Crystal*
Gondola Dish, 9-1/2" l	.4.50
Hostess Tray, 6-1/2" x 12"	.14.00
Iced Tea Tumbler, 15 oz, 6" h	.20.00
Juice Tumbler, 5 oz, 4" h	.5.00
Lamp, oil	.250.00

Early American Prescut, 11" d crystal plate.

Item	*Crystal*
Lazy Susan, 9 pcs	60.00
Pitcher, 18 oz	12.00
Pitcher, 40 oz, sq	60.00
Pitcher, 60 oz	20.00
Plate, 6-3/4" d, salad	55.00
Plate, 6-3/4" d, snack, ring for cup	40.00
Plate, 10" d, snack	15.00
Plate, 11" d	15.00
Punch Cup	3.00
Punch Set, 15 pcs	35.00
Relish, 2-part, 10" l, tab handle	7.50
Relish, 3-part, 8-1/2" l, oval	6.50
Relish, 5-part, 13-1/2" d	30.00
Salad Bowl, 10-3/4" d	15.00
Salt and Pepper Shakers, pr, individual size	72.00
Salt and Pepper Shakers, pr, metal tops	10.00
Salt and Pepper Shakers, pr, plastic tops	12.00
Serving Plate, 11" d, 4 part	90.00
Serving Plate, 13-1/2" d	15.00
Sherbet, 6 oz	90.00
Snack Cup	3.00
Sugar, cov	4.50
Syrup Pitcher, 12 oz	24.00
Tumbler, 10 oz, 4-1/2" h	6.50
Vase, 8-1/2" h	8.00
Vase, 10" h	15.00

English Hobnail

Line #555

Manufactured by Westmoreland Glass Company, Grapeville, Pa., from the 1920s to 1983.

Made in amber, cobalt blue, crystal, crystal with various color treatments, green, ice blue, pink, red and turquoise blue. Values for cobalt blue, red or turquoise blue pieces would be about 25% higher than ice blue values. Currently, a turquoise basket is valued at $150; a red basket at $100. Crystal pieces with a color accent would be slightly higher than crystal values.

Reproductions: † A creamer and sugar with a hexagonal foot have been reproduced as well as nut bowl and pickle dish.

Note: *The values for green and pink English Hobnail are usually the same. A few exceptions where pink forms are more expensive are: 12" oval bowl ($95), ftd. candy dish ($125), oval celery ($90), cigarette jar ($55), claret ($65), hex. ftd. creamer ($48), ice tub ($85), 5-1/2" h ice tub ($100), marmalade ($70), 23 oz rounded pitcher ($165), 10" plate ($65), cov. puff box ($80), hex ft. sugar ($48), toilet bottle ($80), 8-1/2" vase ($235), wine ($65).*

Item	Amber or Crystal	Green or Pink	Ice Blue
Ashtray, 3" d	20.00	22.00	—
Ashtray, 4-1/2" d	9.00	15.00	24.00
Ashtray, 4-1/2" sq	9.50	15.00	
Basket, 5" d, handle	20.00	—	
Basket, 6" d, handle, tall	40.00	—	
Bonbon, 6-1/2" h, handle	15.00	30.00	40.00
Bowl, 7" d, 6 part	17.50	—	—
Bowl, 7" d, oblong spoon	17.50	—	—
Bowl, 8" d, ftd	30.00	48.00	—
Bowl, 8" d, hexagonal foot, 2 handles	38.00	75.00	115.00
Bowl, 8", 6 pt	24.00	—	—
Bowl, 9-1/2" d, round, crimped	30.00	—	—
Bowl, 10" d, flared	35.00	40.00	—
Bowl, 10" l, oval, crimped	40.00	—	—

Item	Amber or Crystal	Green or Pink	Ice Blue
Bowl, 11" d, bell	35.00	—	—
Bowl, 11" d, rolled edge	35.00	40.00	85.00
Bowl, 12" d, flared	32.00	40.00	—
Bowl,12" l, oval crimped	32.00	—	—
Candelabra, 2 light	20.00	—	—
Candlesticks, pr, 3-1/2" h, round base	24.00	36.00	—
Candlesticks, pr, 5-1/2" h, sq base .	30.00	—	—
Candlesticks, pr, 9" h, round base .	50.00	72.00	—
Candy Dish, 3 foot	35.00	50.00	—
Candy Dish, cov, 1/2 lb, cone shape .	35.00	55.00	—
Celery, 12" l, oval	24.00	36.00	—
Celery, 9" d	18.00	32.00	—
Champagne, two ball, round foot . . .	8.00	20.00	—
Chandelier, 17" shade, 200 prisms .	425.00	—	—
Cheese, cov, 6" d	40.00	—	—
Cheese, cov, 8-3/4" d	50.00	—	—
Cigarette Box, cov, 4-1/2" x 2-1/2" . .	24.50	30.00	—
Cigarette Jar, cov, round	16.00	25.00	—
Claret, 5 oz, round	15.00	—	—
Coaster, 3"	5.00	—	—
Cocktail, 3 oz, round	8.50	—	—
Cocktail, 3-1/2 oz, round, ball	15.00	—	—
Compote, 5" d, round, round foot . .	22.00	25.00	—
Compote, 5" d, round, sq foot	24.00	—	—
Compote, 5-1/2" d, bell	12.00	—	—
Compote, 5-1/2" d, bell, sq foot . . .	20.00	—	—

Item	Amber or Crystal	Green or Pink	Ice Blue
Console Bowl, 12" d, flange	30.00	40.00	—
Cordial, 1 oz, round, ball	16.50	—	—
Cordial, 1 oz, round, foot	16.50	—	—
Cream Soup Bowl, 4-5/8" d	15.00	—	—
Cream Soup Liner, round, 6-1/2" d	5.00	—	—
Creamer, hexagonal foot †	20.00	25.00	—
Creamer, low, flat	10.00	—	—
Creamer, sq foot	24.00	45.00	—
Cruet, 12 oz	—	—	—
Cup	6.50	18.00	—
Decanter, 20 oz	55.00	—	—

English Hobnail, clear tumbler.

Item	Amber or Crystal	Green or Pink	Ice Blue
Demitasse Cup 17.50		55.00	—
Dish, 6" d, crimped 15.00		—	—
Egg Cup 15.00		—	—
Finger Bowl, 4-1/2" d 7.50		15.00	35.00
Finger Bowl, 4-1/2" sq, foot 9.50		18.00	40.00
Finger Bowl Liner, 6" sq 6.50		20.00	—
Finger Bowl Liner, 6-1/2" d, round . .12.00		10.00	—
Ginger Ale Tumbler, 5 oz, flat 10.00		18.00	—
Ginger Ale Tumbler, 5 oz, round foot 10.00		—	—
Ginger Ale Tumbler, 5 oz, sq foot 8.00		32.00	—
Goblet, 8 oz, 6-1/4" h, round, water .11.00		—	50.00
Goblet, 8 oz, sq foot, water 9.00		—	—
Grapefruit Bowl, 6-1/2" d 12.00		22.00	—
Hat, high 18.00		—	—
Hat, low .15.00		—	—
Honey Compote, 6" d, round foot . . .18.00		35.00	—
Honey Compote, 6" d, sq foot 18.00		—	—
Ice Tub, 4" h 18.00		50.00	—
Ice Tub, 5-1/2" h 36.00		65.00	—
Iced Tea Tumbler, 10 oz 14.00		30.00	—
Iced Tea Tumbler, 11 oz, round, ball .12.00		—	—
Iced Tea Tumbler, 11 oz, sq foot 13.50		—	—
Iced Tea Tumbler, 12-1/2 oz, round foot 14.00		—	—
Iced Tea Tumbler, 12 oz, flat 14.00		32.00	—
Icer, sq base, patterned insert 45.00		—	—
Ivy Bowl, 6-1/2" d, sq foot, crimp top 35.00		—	—

Item	Amber or Crystal	Green or Pink	Ice Blue
Juice Tumbler, 7 oz, round foot	27.50	—	—
Juice Tumbler, 7 oz, sq foot	6.50	—	—
Lamp Shade, 17" d	175.00	—	—
Lamp, 6-1/2" h, electric	45.00	50.00	—
Lamp, 9-1/2" d, electric	45.00	115.00	—
Lamp, candlestick	32.00	—	—
Marmalade, cov	40.00	45.00	—
Mayonnaise, 6"	12.00	22.00	—
Mustard, cov, sq, foot	18.00	—	—
Nappy, 4-1/2" d, round	8.00	15.00	30.00
Nappy, 4-1/2" w, sq	8.50	—	—
Nappy, 5" d, round	10.00	15.00	35.00
Nappy, 5-1/2" d, bell	12.00	—	—
Nappy, 6" d, round	10.00	17.50	—
Nappy, 6" d, sq	10.00	17.50	—
Nappy, 6-1/2" d, round	12.50	20.00	—
Nappy, 6-1/2" d, sq	14.00	—	—
Nappy, 7" d, round	14.00	24.00	—
Nappy, 7-1/2" d, bell	15.00	—	—
Nappy, 8" d, cupped	22.00	30.00	—
Nappy, 8" d, round	22.00	35.00	—
Nappy, 9" d, bell	25.00	—	—
Nut, individual, ftd †	6.00	14.50	—
Oil Bottle, 2 oz, handle	25.00	—	—
Oil Bottle, 6 oz, handle	27.50	—	—
Old Fashioned Tumbler, 5 oz	15.00	—	—

Item	Amber or Crystal	Green or Pink	Ice Blue
Oyster Cocktail, 5 oz, sq foot	12.00	17.50	—
Parfait, round foot	17.50	—	—
Pickle, 8" d †	15.00	—	—
Pitcher, 23 oz, rounded	48.00	150.00	—
Pitcher, 32 oz, straight side	50.00	175.00	—
Pitcher, 38 oz, rounded	65.00	215.00	—
Pitcher, 60 oz, rounded	70.00	295.00	—
Pitcher, 64 oz, straight side	75.00	310.00	—
Plate, 5-1/2" d, round	7.00	10.00	—
Plate, 6" w, sq	5.00	—	—
Plate, 6-1/2" d, round	6.25	10.00	—
Plate, 6-1/2" d, round, depressed center	6.00	—	—
Plate, 8" d, round	9.00	14.00	—
Plate, 8" d, round, ftd	13.00	—	—
Plate, 8-1/2" d, plain edge	9.00	—	—
Plate, 8-1/2" d, round	7.00	17.50	—
Plate, 8-3/4" w, sq	9.25	—	—
Plate, 10" d, round	15.00	45.00	—
Plate, 10" w, sq	15.00	—	—
Plate, 10-1/2" d, round, grill	18.00	—	—
Plate, 12" w, sq	20.00	—	—
Plate, 15" w, sq	28.00	—	—
Preserve, 8" d	15.00	—	—
Puff Box, cov, 6" d, round	20.00	47.50	—
Punch Bowl and Stand	215.00	—	—
Punch Cup	7.00	—	—

Item	Amber or Crystal	Green or Pink	Ice Blue
Relish, 8" d, 3 part	18.00	—	—
Rose Bowl, 4" d	17.50	48.00	—
Rose Bowl, 6" d	20.00	—	—
Salt and Pepper Shakers, pr, round foot	27.50	150.00	—
Salt and Pepper Shakers, pr, sq, foot	15.00	—	—
Saucer, demitasse, round	10.00	15.00	—
Saucer, demitasse, sq	10.00	—	—
Saucer, round	2.00	6.00	—
Saucer, sq	2.00	—	—
Sherbet, high, round foot	7.00	18.00	—
Sherbet, high, sq foot	8.00	18.00	—
Sherbet, high, two ball, round foot	10.00	—	—
Sherbet, low, one ball, round foot	12.00	—	—
Sherbet, low, round foot	12.50	—	—
Sherbet, low, sq foot	6.50	15.00	—

English Hobnail, crystal nappy with handle.

Item	Amber or Crystal	Green or Pink	Ice Blue
Straw Jar, 10" h	65.00	—	—
Sundae	9.00	—	—
Sugar, hexagonal, ftd †	9.00	25.00	—
Sugar, low, flat	8.00	—	—
Sugar, sq foot	9.00	48.00	—
Sweetmeat, 5-1/2" d, ball stem	30.00	—	—
Sweetmeat, 8" d, ball stem	40.00	60.00	—
Tidbit, 2 tier	27.50	65.00	85.00
Toilet Bottle, 5 oz	25.00	40.00	65.00
Torte Plate, 14" d, round	35.00	48.00	—
Torte Plate, 20-1/2" round	55.00	—	—
Tumbler, 8 oz, water	10.00	24.00	—
Tumbler, 9 oz, round, ball, water	10.00	—	—
Tumbler, 9 oz, round, ftd water	10.00	—	—
Tumbler, 9 oz, sq foot, water	10.00	—	—
Urn, cov, 11" h	35.00	350.00	—
Vase, 6-1/2" h, sq foot	24.00	—	—
Vase, 7-1/2" h, flip	27.50	70.00	—
Vase, 7-1/2" h, flip jar with cov	55.00	85.00	—
Vase, 8" h, sq foot	35.00	—	—
Vase, 8-1/2" h, flared top	40.00	120.00	—
Whiskey, 1-1/2 oz	10.00	—	—
Whiskey, 3 oz	12.00	—	—
Wine, 2 oz, round foot	13.00	—	—
Wine, 2 oz, sq ft	15.00	35.00	—
Wine, 2-1/2 oz, ball, foot	10.00	—	—

Floragold

Louisa

Manufactured by Jeannette Glass Company, Jeannette, Pa., 1950s.

Made in iridescent. Some large comports were later made in ice blue, crystal, red-yellow and shell pink.

Note: *Carefully measure the square base of the covered butter dish. The smaller 5-1/2" square base is valued at $800, while the more common 6-1/4" square base is valued at $45.*

Item	Iridescent
Ashtray, 4" d	10.00
Bowl, 4-1/2" sq	6.50
Bowl, 5-1/4" d, ruffled	16.00
Bowl, 8-1/2" d, sq	8.00
Bowl, 8-1/2" d, ruffled	14.00
Butter Dish, cov, 1/4 pound, oblong	30.00
Butter Dish, cov, round, 5-1/2" sq base	800.00
Butter Dish, cov, round, 6-1/4" w sq base	45.00
Candlesticks, pr, double branch	60.00
Candy Dish, 1 handle	16.50
Candy or Cheese Dish, cov, 6-3/4" d	95.00
Candy, 5-3/4" l, 4 feet	9.50
Celery Vase	395.00
Cereal Bowl, 5-1/2" d, round	40.00
Coaster, 4" d	10.00
Comport, 5-1/4", plain top	795.00
Comport, 5-1/4", ruffled top	895.00
Creamer	12.00
Cup	8.00
Fruit Bowl, 5-1/2" d, ruffled	8.50
Fruit Bowl, 12" d, ruffled, large	15.00
Nappy, 5" d, one handle	12.00
Pitcher, 64 oz	45.00
Plate, 5-1/4" d, sherbet	15.00
Plate, 8-1/2" d, dinner	40.00
Platter, 11-1/4" d	22.00
Salad Bowl, 9-1/2" d, deep	42.50

Item	Iridescent
Salt and Pepper Shakers, pr, plastic tops	60.00
Saucer, 5-1/4" d	12.00
Sherbet, low, ftd	16.00
Sugar	18.00
Sugar Lid	15.00
Tidbit, wooden post	35.00
Tray, 13-1/2" d	22.50
Tray, 13-1/2" d, with indent	65.00
Tumbler, 11 oz, ftd	20.00
Tumbler, 10 oz, ftd	20.00
Tumbler, 15 oz, ftd	110.00
Vase	395.00

Floragold, iridescent plate and ruffled berry bowl.

Floral

Poinsettia

Manufactured by Jeannette Glass Company, Jeannette, Pa., from 1931 to 1935.

Made in amber, crystal, Delphite, green, Jad-ite, pink, red and yellow. Production in amber, crystal, jade-ite, red and yellow was very limited. A crystal 6-7/8" h vase would be valued at $295.

Reproductions: † Reproduction salt and pepper shakers have been made in cobalt blue, dark green, green, pink and red.

Note: *Jade-ite was made in limited forms. A canister set valued at $60 and a refrigerator set would be $15.*

Item	Delphite	Green	Pink
Berry Bowl, 4" d	40.00	25.00	25.00
Butter Dish, cov	—	95.00	90.00
Candlesticks, pr, 4" h	—	90.00	95.00
Candy Jar, cov	80.00	45.00	45.00
Canister Set	—	—	—
Casserole, cov	—	45.00	28.00
Coaster, 3-1/4" d	—	15.00	—
Comport, 9"	—	875.00	795.00
Cream Soup, 5-1/2" d	—	735.00	735.00
Creamer, flat	—	24.00	24.00

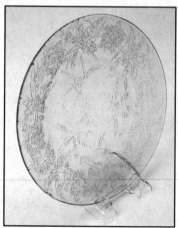

Floral, pink plate.

Item	Delphite	Green	Pink
Cup	—	15.00	15.00
Dresser Set	—	1,350.00	—
Dresser Tray, 9-1/4" l, oval	—	200.00	—
Flower Frog	—	695.00	—
Ice Tub, 3-1/2" h, oval	—	850.00	825.00
Juice Tumbler, ftd	—	24.00	27.50
Juice Tumbler, 5 oz, 4" h, flat	—	35.00	35.00
Lamp	—	275.00	260.00
Lemonade Pitcher, 48 oz, 10-1/4" h	—	265.00	350.00
Lemonade Tumbler, 9 oz, 5-1/4" h, ftd	—	60.00	55.00
Pitcher, 23 or 24 oz, 5-1/2" h	—	50.00	—
Pitcher, 32 oz, ftd, cone, 8" h	—	36.00	42.00
Plate, 6" d, sherbet	—	8.50	8.50
Plate, 8" d, salad	—	15.00	17.00
Plate, 9" d, dinner	145.00	30.00	27.50
Plate, 9" d, grill	—	185.00	—
Plate, 10-3/4" l, oval	—	20.00	17.50
Platter, 11" l	150.00	25.00	25.00
Refrigerator Dish, cov, 5" sq	—	—	—
Relish, 2 part oval	165.00	24.00	18.50
Rose Bowl, 3 legs	—	500.00	—
Salad Bowl, 7-1/2" d	—	40.00	40.00
Salad Bowl, 7-1/2" d, ruffled	65.00	125.00	120.00
Salt and Pepper Shakers, pr, 4" h, ftd †	—	45.00	45.00
Salt and Pepper Shakers, pr, 6" flat	—	—	60.00
Saucer	—	12.50	12.50
Sherbet	90.00	20.00	20.00

Item	Delphite	Green	Pink
Sugar, cov	—	26.00	30.00
Sugar, open	75.00	—	—
Tray, 6" sq, closed handles	—	195.00	
Tumbler, 3 oz, 3-1/2" h, ftd	—	18.00	25.00
Tumbler, 7 oz, 4-1/2", ftd	175.00	25.00	25.00
Tumbler, 5-1/4" h, ftd	—	60.00	55.00
Vase, flared, 3 legs	—	485.00	—
Vase, 6-7/8" h	—	475.00	—
Vegetable Bowl, 8" d, cov	—	50.00	40.00
Vegetable Bowl, 8" d, open	80.00	—	30.00
Vegetable Bowl, 9" l, oval	—	35.00	35.00

Floral, green tumblers and footed pitcher.

Floral and Diamond Band

Manufactured by U.S. Glass Company, Pittsburgh, late 1920s.

Made in pink and green with limited production in black, crystal and iridescent.

Item	*Green*	*Pink*
Berry Bowl, 4-1/2" d	10.00	12.00
Berry Bowl, 8" d	15.00	18.00
Butter Dish, cov	140.00	175.00
Compote, 5-1/2" h	18.00	17.50
Creamer, 4-3/4"	20.00	17.50
Iced Tea Tumbler, 5" h	38.00	32.50
Nappy, 5-3/4" d, handle	12.00	11.00
Pitcher, 42 oz, 8" h	95.00	90.00
Plate, 8" d, luncheon	40.00	40.00
Sherbet	8.00	9.50
Sugar, 5-1/4"	15.00	15.00
Water tumbler, 4" h, ...	25.00	25.00

*Floral and Diamond Band,
green plate.*

Florentine No. 1

Old Florentine, Poppy No. 1

Manufactured by Hazel Atlas Glass Company, Clarksburg, W.V., and Zanesville, Ohio, from 1932 to 1935.

Made in crystal, green, pink, yellow and limited production in cobalt blue.

Reproductions: † Salt and pepper shakers have been reproduced in cobalt blue, pink and red.

Production in cobalt blue was limited to 5" berry bowl ($20), ruffled comport ($60), cream soup ($50), ruffled creamer and sugar ($120), cup and saucer ($100), and 36 oz pitcher ($850).

item	Crystal or Green	Pink	Yellow
Ashtray, 5-1/2" d	24.00	28.00	28.00
Berry Bowl, 5" d	12.00	15.00	15.00
Berry Bowl, 8-1/2" d	25.00	28.00	28.00
Butter Dish, cov	115.00	165.00	160.00
Cereal Bowl, 6" d	32.00	35.00	35.00
Coaster/Ashtray, 3-3/4" d	20.00	25.00	25.00
Comport, 3-1/2" h, ruffled	25.00	15.00	—
Cream Soup, 5" d, ruffled	14.00	18.00	—
Creamer	12.00	25.00	20.00
Creamer, ruffled	35.00	37.00	—
Cup	8.00	9.00	10.00
Iced Tea Tumbler, 12 oz, 5-1/4" h, ftd	28.00	30.00	24.00
Juice Tumbler, 5 oz, 3-3/4" h, ftd	16.00	20.00	22.00
Lemonade Tumbler, 9 oz, 5-1/4" h	—	100.00	—
Pitcher, 36 oz, 6-1/2", ftd	45.00	65.00	50.00

Florentine No. 1, green creamer and covered sugar.

item	Crystal or Green	Pink	Yellow
Pitcher, 48 oz, 7-1/2", flat, with or without ice lip	75.00	135.00	195.00
Plate, 6" d, sherbet	9.00	7.50	9.00
Plate, 8-1/2" d, salad	10.00	12.00	12.00
Plate, 10" d, dinner	16.00	22.00	24.00
Plate, 10" d, grill	12.50	20.00	22.00
Platter, 11-1/2" l, oval	10.00	22.00	28.00
Salt and Pepper Shakers, pr, ftd † . . .	32.00	55.00	58.00
Saucer	3.50	4.00	3.00
Sherbet, 3 oz, ftd	7.50	10.00	16.00
Sugar, cov	12.50	25.00	12.00
Sugar, ruffled	30.00	42.50	—
Tumbler, 4 oz, 3-1/4" h, ftd	16.00	—	—
Tumbler, 9 oz, 4" h, ribbed	14.00	22.00	—
Tumbler, 10 oz, 4-3/4" h, ftd	20.00	22.00	24.00
Vegetable Bowl, cov, 9-1/2" l, oval .	42.00	60.00	60.00

*Florentine No. 1,
green covered
butter dish.*

Florentine No. 2

Poppy No. 2

Manufactured by Hazel Atlas Glass Company, Clarksburg, W.V., and Zanesville, Ohio, from 1932 to 1935.

Made in amber, cobalt blue, crystal, green, ice blue, pink and yellow. Ice blue production is limited to 7-1/2" h pitcher, valued at $525. Amber production is limited to 9 oz and 12 oz tumblers, both currently valued at $80; cup and saucer, valued at $75; and sherbet, valued at $45. Cobalt blue production is limited to 3-1/2" comport, valued at $60 and 9 oz tumbler, valued at $80.

Reproductions: † 7-1/2" h cone-shaped pitcher and 4" h ftd tumbler. Reproductions found in amber, cobalt blue, crystal, deep green and pink.

Item	Crystal or Green	Pink	Yellow
Ashtray, 3-1/2" d	18.50	—	25.00
Ashtray, 5-1/2" d	25.00	—	35.00
Berry Bowl, 4-1/2" d	16.50	17.50	22.50
Berry Bowl, 8" d	26.00	30.00	35.00
Bowl, 5-1/2" d	35.00	—	42.00
Bowl, 7-1/2" d, shallow	—	—	85.00
Bowl, 9" d, flat	27.50	—	—
Butter Dish, cov	125.00	—	165.00
Candlesticks, pr, 2-3/4" h	48.00	—	70.00
Candy Dish, cov	110.00	150.00	165.00
Cereal Bowl, 6" d	28.00	—	40.00
Coaster, 3-1/4" d	—	—	25.00
Coaster, 3-3/4" d	18.50	—	25.00
Coaster, 5-1/2" d	25.00	—	35.00

Florentine No. 2, yellow cup.

Item	Crystal or Green	Pink	Yellow
Cocktail, 3-1/4" h, ftd	—	—	14.50
Comport, 3-1/2" d, ruffled	25.00	25.00	—
Condiment Tray, round	—	—	65.00
Cream Soup, 4-3/4" d, 2 handles . . .	16.00	18.50	20.00
Creamer	11.00	—	14.50
Cup	7.50	—	12.00
Custard Cup	60.00	—	85.00
Gravy Boat	—	—	55.00
Gravy Boat Underplate, 11-1/2" l	—	—	115.00
Iced Tea Tumbler, 12 oz, 5" h	35.00	—	45.00
Juice Tumbler, 5 oz, 3-1/8" h, flat . . .	14.50	14.50	22.00
Juice Tumbler, 5 oz, 3-1/8" h, ftd . . .	15.00	—	21.00
Parfait, 6" h	32.00	—	65.00
Pitcher, 24 oz, cone, ftd, 6-1/4" h	—	—	35.00
Pitcher, 28 oz, cone ftd, 7-1/2" h † . .	40.00	—	50.00
Pitcher, 48 oz, 7-1/2" h	70.00	120.00	32.00
Pitcher, 76 oz, 8-1/4" h	95.00	225.00	400.00
Plate, 6" d, sherbet	4.00	—	7.50
Plate, 6-1/2" d, indent	17.50	—	30.00
Plate, 8-1/2" d, salad	9.50	9.00	10.00
Plate, 10" d, dinner	16.00	—	19.00
Plate, 10-1/4" d, grill	15.00	—	14.50
Plate, 10-1/4" d, grill, cream soup ring	35.00	—	—
Platter, 11" oval	16.00	18.50	24.00
Relish, 10" d, divided, 3 part	24.00	26.00	32.00
Relish, 10" d, plain	24.00	26.00	32.00

Item	Crystal or Green	Pink	Yellow
Salt and Pepper Shakers, pr	48.00	—	65.00
Saucer	4.00	—	3.50
Sherbet, ftd	12.50	—	14.50
Sugar, cov	9.00	—	38.00
Tumbler, 5 oz, 3-1/4" h, ftd	15.00	15.00	—
Tumbler, 5 oz, 4" h, ftd †	15.00	18.00	20.00
Tumbler, 5 oz, 3-5/16" h, blown	18.50	—	—
Tumbler, 6 oz, 3-9/16" h, blown	18.50	—	—
Tumbler, 9 oz, 4" h	18.50	16.00	22.50
Tumbler, 9 oz, 4-1/2" h, ftd	25.00	—	38.00
Tumbler, 10 oz, 4-11/16 h, blown	19.00	—	—
Tumbler, 12 oz, 5" h, blown	20.00	—	20.00
Vase, 6" h	32.00	—	65.00
Vegetable Bowl, cov, 9" l, oval	60.00	—	85.00

REPRODUCTION! Florentine No. 2, green pitcher and tumbler.

Flower Garden with Butterflies

Butterflies and Roses

Manufactured by U.S. Glass Company, Pittsburgh, late 1920s.

Made in amber, black, blue, blue-green, canary yellow, crystal, green and pink.

Amber or crystal prices would be 10% less than those shown for blue-green.

Note: *The rare heart-shaped covered candy dish can command $1,550 for blue-green, green, or pink, and $2,500 for blue or canary yellow.*

Item	Black	Blue-Green, Green or Pink	Blue or Canary Yellow
Ashtray	—	185.00	195.00
Bonbon, cov, 6-5/8" d	265.00	—	—
Bowl, 9" d, rolled edge	225.00	—	—
Candlesticks, pr, 4" h	—	60.00	100.00
Candlesticks, pr, 8" h	325.00	145.00	145.00
Candy, cov, 6" d, flat	—	165.00	—
Candy, cov, 7-1/2" cone shape	100.00	165.00	175.00
Cologne Bottle, 7-1/2" h	—	225.00	365.00
Comport, 2-7/8" h	250.00	40.00	45.00
Comport, 3" h	—	30.00	35.00
Comport, 4-1/4" h, 4-3/4" w	—	—	65.00
Comport, 4-3/4" h, 10-1/4" w	250.00	70.00	90.00
Comport, 5-7/8" h, 11" w	—	—	95.00
Comport, 7-1/4" h, 8-1/4" w	175.00	85.00	—
Creamer	—	75.00	—
Cup	—	70.00	—
Mayonnaise, ftd, 4-3/4" h, 6-1/4" w, 7" d plate, ladle	—	95.00	145.00
Orange Bowl, 11" d, ftd	250.00	—	—
Plate, 7" d	—	25.00	30.00
Plate, 8" d	—	20.00	27.50
Plate, 10" d	—	45.00	50.00
Plate, 10" d, indent	150.00	45.00	50.00
Powder Jar, 3-1/2", flat	—	75.00	—

Item	Black	Blue-Green, Green or Pink	Blue or Canary Yellow
Powder Jar, 6-1/4" h, ftd	—	130.00	175.00
Powder Jar, 7-1/2" h, ftd	—	135.00	195.00
Sandwich Server, center handle	135.00	75.00	100.00
Saucer	—	30.00	—
Tray, 5-1/2" x 10", oval	—	75.00	9.00
Tray, 11-3/4" x 7-3/4", rect	—	75.00	90.00
Tumbler, 7-1/2 oz	—	—	—
Vase, 6-1/4" h	145.00	135.00	145.00
Vase, 8" h, Dahlia, cupped	275.00	—	—
Vase, 10" h, 2 handles	250.00	—	—
Vase, 10-1/2" h	—	150.00	225.00
Wall Pocket, 9" l	365.00	—	—

Flower Garden with Butterflies, blue compote.

Forest Green

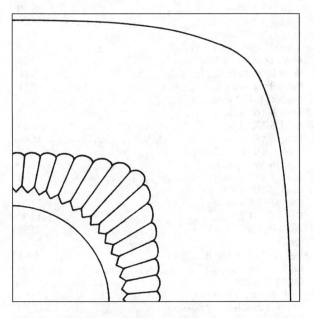

Manufactured by Anchor Hocking Glass Company, Lancaster, Ohio, and Long Island City, N.Y., from 1950 to 1967.

Made only in forest green.

Item	Forest Green
Ashtray, 3-1/2" sq	3.50
Ashtray, 4-5/8" sq	5.50
Ashtray, 5-3/4" hexagon	8.00
Ashtray, 5-3/4" sq	7.50
Batter Bowl, spout	25.00
Berry Bowl, large	15.00
Berry Bowl, small	5.50
Bonbon, 6-1/4" w, tricorn	12.00
Bowl, 4-1/2" w, sq	5.50
Bowl, 5-1/4" deep	8.50
Bowl, 6" w, sq	18.00
Bowl, 6-1/2" d, scalloped	9.00
Bowl, 6-3/8" d, 3 toes	15.00
Bowl, 7-3/8" w, sq	30.00
Bowl, 7-1/2" d, crimped	10.00
Cocktail, 3-1/2 oz	12.00
Cocktail, 4-1/2 oz	14.00
Creamer, flat	7.50
Cup, sq	7.00
Dessert Bowl, 4-3/4" d	7.00
Goblet, 9 oz	10.00
Goblet, 9-1/2 oz	14.00
Iced Tea Tumbler, 13 oz	8.00
Iced Tea Tumbler, 14 oz, Boopie	8.00
Iced Tea Tumbler, 15 oz, tall	10.00
Iced Tea Tumbler, 32 oz, giant	18.00
Ivy Ball, 4" h	5.00

Item	Forest Green
Juice Tumbler, 4 oz	10.00
Juice Tumbler, 5-1/2 oz	12.50
Juice Roly Poly Tumbler, 3-3/8" h	6.00
Ladle, all green glass	80.00
Mixing Bowl, 6" d	9.50
Pitcher, 22 oz	22.50
Pitcher, 36 oz	25.00
Pitcher, 86 oz, round	45.00
Plate, 6-3/4" d, salad	7.50
Plate, 7" w, sq	6.75
Plate, 8-3/8" d, luncheon	9.00
Plate, 9-1/4" d, dinner	33.50
Platter, 11" l, rect	22.00
Popcorn Bowl, 5-1/4" d	10.00
Punch Bowl	25.00
Punch Bowl and Stand	60.00
Punch Cup	4.25
Relish Tray, 4-3/4" x 6-3/4" l, 2 handles	25.00
Roly Poly Tumbler, 5 1/8" h	7.50
Salad Bowl, 7-3/8" d	15.00
Sandwich Plate, 13-3/4" d	45.00
Saucer, 5-3/8" w	3.00
Sherbet, 6 oz	9.00
Sherbet, 6 oz, Boopie	7.00
Sherbet, flat	7.50
Soup Bowl, 6" d	17.00
Sugar, flat	7.00
Tray, 6" x 10", 2 handles	30.00

Item	*Forest Green*
Tumbler, 5 oz, 3-1/2" h	.4.00
Tumbler, 7 oz	.4.50
Tumbler, 5-1/4" h	.4.00
Tumbler, 9-1/2 oz, tall	.8.00
Tumbler, 9 oz, fancy	.7.00
Tumbler, 9 oz, table	.5.00
Tumbler, 10 oz, 4-1/2" h, ftd	.7.50
Tumbler, 11 oz	.7.00
Tumbler, 14 oz, 5" h	.8.00
Tumbler, 15 oz, long boy	.10.00
Vase, 6-3/8" h, Harding	.10.00
Vase, 7" h, crimped	.15.00
Vase, 9" h	.8.00
Vegetable Bowl, 8-1/2" l, oval	.24.00

Forest Green, cup and suacer.

Forest Green, tumbler.

Fortune

Manufactured by Hocking Glass Company, Lancaster, Ohio, from 1937 to 1938.

Made in crystal and pink.

Item	Crystal	Pink
Berry Bowl, 4" d	5.00	6.00
Berry Bowl, 7-3/4" d	15.00	15.00
Bowl, 4-1/2" d, handle	4.50	4.50
Bowl, 5-1/4" d, rolled edge	6.00	6.50
Candy Dish, cov, flat	22.50	25.00
Cup	7.50	10.00
Dessert Bowl, 4-1/2" d	5.00	5.00
Juice Tumbler, 5 oz, 3-1/2" h	8.00	10.00
Plate, 6" d, salad	5.00	12.50
Plate, 8" d, luncheon	17.50	17.50
Salad Bowl, 7-3/4" d	15.00	15.00
Saucer	4.00	6.50
Tumbler, 9 oz, 4" h	12.00	12.50

Fortune, pink fruit bowl.

Fruits

Manufactured by Hazel Atlas Company, and several other small glass companies, from 1931 to 1935.

Made in crystal, green, iridized and pink. Iridized production includes only a 4" tumbler, valued at $10.

Item	*Crystal*	*Green*	*Pink*
Berry Bowl, 5" d	.14.00	28.00	22.00
Berry Bowl, 8" d	.30.00	60.00	40.00
Cup	.5.00	10.00	7.00
Juice Tumbler, 5 oz, 3-1/2" h	.15.00	24.00	22.00
Pitcher, 7" h	.45.00	85.00	—
Plate, 8" d, luncheon	.5.00	9.00	7.50
Saucer	.2.50	5.00	4.50
Sherbet	.4.50	9.00	7.50
Tumbler, 4" h, multiple fruits	.15.00	24.00	22.00
Tumbler, 4" h, single fruit	.20.00	30.00	25.00
Tumbler, 12 oz, 5" h	.70.00	200.00	95.00

Fruits, green cup and saucer.

Fruits, green plate.

Georgian

Lovebirds

Manufactured by Federal Glass Company, Columbus, Ohio, from 1931 to 1936.

Made in green. A crystal hot plate is valued at $25.

Note: *The high price of $875 for the cold cuts server represents a piece in very good condition, with all of the components present.*

Item	Green
Berry Bowl, 4-1/2" d	10.00
Berry Bowl, 7-1/2" d, large	65.00
Bowl, 6-1/2" d, deep	65.00
Butter Dish, cov	80.00
Cereal Bowl, 5-3/4" d	30.00
Cold Cuts Server, 18-1/2" d, wood, seven openings for 5" d coasters	875.00
Creamer, 3" d, ftd	16.00
Creamer, 4" d, ftd	16.50
Cup	8.50
Hot Plate, 5" d, center design	48.00
Plate, 6" d, sherbet	6.50
Plate, 8" d, luncheon	10.00
Plate, 9-1/4" d, center design only	25.00
Plate, 9-1/4" d, dinner	36.00

Georgian, green sherbet.

Item	Green
Platter, 11-1/2" l, closed handle	70.00
Saucer	3.50
Sherbet, ftd	16.00
Sugar Cover, 3" d	12.00
Sugar Cover, 4" d	12.00
Sugar, 3" d, ftd	15.00
Sugar, 4" d, ftd	15.00
Tumbler, 9 oz, 4" h, flat	65.00
Tumbler 12 oz, 5-1/4" h, flat	135.00
Vegetable Bowl, 9" l, oval	65.00

Georgian, green cup & saucer.

Harp

Manufactured by Jeannette Glass Company, Jeannette, Pa., from 1954 to 1957.

Made in crystal, crystal with gold trim, limited pieces made in ice blue, iridescent white, pink and shell pink.

Item	Crystal	Ice Blue	Shell Pink
Ashtray	6.00	—	—
Cake Stand, 9" d	35.00	45.00	45.00
Coaster	6.00	—	—
Cup	28.00	—	—
Parfait	20.00	—	—
Plate, 7" d	20.00	25.00	—
Saucer	12.00	—	—
Snack Set, cup, saucer, 7" plate	48.00	—	—
Tray, 2 handles, rectangular	35.00	35.00	65.00
Vase, 7-1/2" h	35.00	—	—

Harp, crystal, gold-edge plate and cake stand.

Heritage

Manufactured by Federal Glass Company, Columbus, Ohio, from 1940 to 1955.

Made in blue, crystal, green and pink.

Reproductions: † Bowls have been reproduced in amber, crystal and green. Some are marked with N or MC.

Item	Blue or Green	Crystal	Pink
Berry Bowl, 5" d †	60.00	12.00	50.00
Berry Bowl, 8-1/2" d †	190.00	48.00	115.00
Creamer, ftd	—	30.00	—
Cup	—	8.00	—
Fruit Bowl, 10-1/2" d	—	18.00	—
Plate, 8" d, luncheon	—	10.00	—
Plate, 9-1/4" d, dinner	—	12.00	—
Sandwich Plate, 12" d	—	15.00	—
Saucer	—	4.00	—
Sugar, open, ftd	—	22.00	—

Heritage, crystal plate.

Heritage, crystal cup and saucer.

Hex Optic

Honeycomb

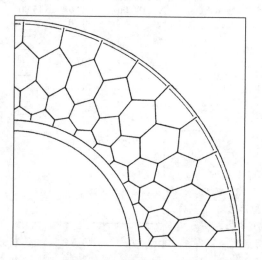

Manufactured by Jeannette Glass Company, Jeannette, Pa., from 1928 to 1932.

Made in green and pink. Ultramarine tumblers have been found. Iridescent tumblers and pitchers were made about 1960 and it is assumed that they were made by Jeannette.

Item	Green	Pink
Berry Bowl, 4-1/4" d, ruffled	7.50	6.50
Berry Bowl, 7-1/2" d	12.00	10.00
Bucket Reamer	60.00	50.00
Butter Dish, cov, rect, 1 lb size	75.00	72.00
Creamer, two style handles	8.00	7.00
Cup, two style handles	5.00	5.00
Ice Bucket, metal handle	20.00	20.00
Mixing Bowl, 7-1/4" d	14.00	14.00
Mixing Bowl, 8-1/4" d	16.00	16.00
Mixing Bowl, 9" d	18.00	18.00
Mixing Bowl, 10" d	20.00	20.00
Pitcher, 32 oz, 5" h	24.00	24.00
Pitcher, 48 oz, 9" h, ftd	48.00	50.00
Pitcher, 96 oz, 8" h	235.00	245.00

Hex Optic, green plate.

Item	Green	Pink
Plate, 6" d, sherbet	3.00	3.00
Plate, 8" d, luncheon	6.00	6.00
Platter, 11" d, round	14.00	16.00
Refrigerator Dish, 4" x 4"	10.00	10.00
Refrigerator Stack Set, 4 pc	60.00	60.00
Salt and Pepper Shakers, pr	30.00	30.00
Saucer	4.00	4.00
Sherbet, 5 oz, ftd	5.00	5.00
Sugar, two styles of handles	6.00	6.00
Sugar Shaker	175.00	175.00
Tumbler, 12 oz, 5" h	8.00	8.00
Tumbler, 5-3/4" h, ftd	10.00	10.00
Tumbler, 7" h, ftd	12.00	12.00
Tumbler, 7 oz, 4-3/4" h, ftd	8.00	8.00
Tumbler, 9 oz, 3-3/4" h	5.00	5.00
Whiskey, 1 oz, 2" h	8.50	8.50

Hex Optic, green ice tub.

Hobnail

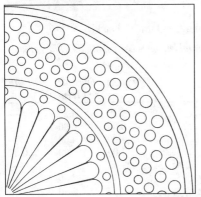

Hobnail, pink sherbet.

Manufactured by Hocking Glass Company, Lancaster, Ohio, from 1934 to 1936.

Made in crystal, crystal with red trim and pink.

Note: *Reproduction tumblers have been spotted in blue, green, pink & yellow.*

Item	*Crystal*	*Crystal, red trim*	*Pink*
Cereal Bowl, 5-1/2" d	4.25	4.25	—
Cordial, 5 oz, ftd	6.00	6.00	—
Creamer, ftd	4.00	4.00	—
Cup	5.00	5.00	6.00
Decanter and Stopper, 32 oz	27.50	27.50	—
Goblet, 10 oz	7.50	7.50	—
Iced Tea Goblet, 13 oz	8.50	8.50	—
Iced Tea Tumbler, 15 oz	8.50	8.50	—
Juice Tumbler, 5 oz	4.00	4.00	—
Milk Pitcher, 18 oz	22.00	22.00	—
Pitcher, 67 oz	25.00	25.00	—
Plate, 6" d, sherbet	2.50	2.50	3.50
Plate, 8-1/2" d, luncheon	5.50	5.50	7.50
Salad Bowl, 7" d	5.00	5.00	—
Saucer	2.00	2.00	3.00
Sherbet	4.00	4.00	5.00
Sugar, ftd	4.00	4.00	—
Tumbler, 9 oz, 4-3/4" h, flat	5.00	5.00	—
Whiskey, 1-1/2 oz	5.00	5.00	—
Wine, 3 oz, ftd	6.50	6.50	—

Holiday

Button and Bows

Manufactured by Jeannette Glass Company, Jeannette, Pa., from 1947 to the 1950s.

Made in crystal, iridescent, pink and shell pink. Shell pink production was limited to the console bowl, valued at $48.

Few forms were made in crystal. The 16 oz, 4-3/4" h pitcher is valued at $17.50, and the 5 oz, 4" h footed tumbler is $8.

Item	*Iridescent*	*Pink*
Berry Bowl, 5-1/8" d	—	14.00
Berry Bowl, 8-1/2" d	—	25.00
Butter Dish, cov	—	45.00
Cake Plate, 10-1/2" d, 3 legs	—	100.00
Candlesticks, pr, 3" h	—	110.00
Chop Plate, 13-3/4" d	—	100.00
Console Bowl, 10-1/4" d	—	120.00
Creamer, ftd	—	10.00
Cup, plain	—	8.00
Cup, rayed bottom, 2" d base	—	8.50
Cup, rayed bottom, 2-3/8" d base	—	10.00
Juice Tumbler, 5 oz, 4" h, ftd	—	55.00
Pitcher, 16 oz, 4-3/4" h	35.00	60.00
Pitcher, 52 oz, 6-3/4" h	—	42.00

Holiday, pink water pitcher.

Item	*Iridescent*	*Pink*
Plate, 6" d, sherbet	—	6.50
Plate, 9" d, dinner	—	22.50
Platter, 11-3/8" l, oval 15.00		24.00
Sandwich Tray, 10-1/ 2" l 17.50		18.00
Saucer, plain center	—	4.00
Saucer, rayed center, 2-1/8" d ring	—	6.00
Saucer, rayed center, 2-1/2" d ring	—	6.00
Sherbet	—	8.50
Soup Bowl, 7-3/4" d	—	50.00
Sugar, cov	—	25.00
Sugar Lid	—	16.00
Tumbler, 5 oz, 4" h, ftd 10.00		35.00
Tumbler, 5-1/4 oz, 4-1/4" h, ftd	—	45.00
Tumbler, 6" h, ftd	—	195.00
Tumbler, 9 oz, 4" h, ftd	—	25.00
Tumbler, 10 oz, 4" h, flat	—	24.00
Vegetable Bowl, 9-1/2" l, oval	—	19.00

*Holiday, pink 5-1/8"
berry bowl.*

Homespun

Fine Rib

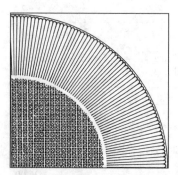

Homespun, pink sugar and look-alike tumbler.

Manufactured by Jeannette Glass Company, Jeannette, Pa., from 1939 to 1949.

Made in crystal and pink.

Item	Crystal	Pink
Ashtray	6.00	6.00
Berry Bowl, 4-1/2" d, closed handles	12.00	13.00
Berry Bowl, 8-1/4" d	20.00	20.00
Butter Dish, cov	50.00	55.00
Cereal Bowl, 5" d, closed handles	25.00	25.00
Coaster	6.00	6.00
Creamer, ftd	12.50	12.50
Cup	12.00	12.00
Iced Tea Tumbler, 13 oz, 5-1/4" h	32.00	32.00
Plate, 6" d, sherbet	7.50	7.50
Plate, 9-1/4" d, dinner	18.00	18.00
Platter, 13" d, closed handles	20.00	20.00
Saucer	5.50	5.50
Sherbet, low, flat	17.50	19.00
Sugar, ftd	12.50	12.50
Tumbler, 5 oz, 4" h, ftd	8.00	8.00
Tumbler, 6 oz, 3-7/8" h, straight	7.00	7.00
Tumbler, 9 oz, 4" h, flared top	17.50	17.50
Tumbler, 9 oz, 4-1/4" h, band at top	17.50	17.50
Tumbler, 15 oz, 6-1/4" h, ftd	38.00	38.00
Tumbler, 15 oz, 6-3/8" h, ftd	36.00	36.00

Children's

	Crystal	Pink
Cup	25.00	35.00
Plate	10.00	15.00
Saucer	9.00	12.00
Teapot	—	125.00

Horseshoe

No. 612

Manufactured by Indiana Glass Company, Dunkirk, Ind., from 1930 to 1933.

Made in crystal, green, pink and yellow. Limited collector interest in crystal and pink at the current time.

Item	Green	Yellow
Berry Bowl, 4-1/2" d	30.00	25.00
Berry Bowl, 9-1/2" d	40.00	35.00
Butter Dish, cov	750.00	—
Candy Dish, metal holder	175.00	
Cereal Bowl, 6-1/2" d	25.00	35.00
Creamer, ftd	18.00	20.00
Cup and Saucer	18.50	17.50
Pitcher, 64 oz, 8-1/2" h	250.00	295.00
Plate, 6" d, sherbet	9.00	9.00
Plate, 8-3/8" d, salad	10.00	10.00
Plate, 9-3/8" d, luncheon	13.00	17.50
Plate, 10-3/8" d, grill	85.00	85.00
Platter, 10-3/4" l, oval	25.00	25.00
Relish, 3 part ftd	20.00	24.00
Salad Bowl, 7-1/2" d	24.00	24.00
Sandwich Plate, 11-1/2" d	24.00	27.50

*Horseshoe, No. 612
yellow cup.*

Item	Green	Yellow
Saucer	6.00	6.50
Sherbet	16.00	18.50
Sugar, open	16.50	17.00
Tumbler, 9 oz, ftd	25.00	28.00
Tumbler, 9 oz, 4-1/4" h	150.00	—
Tumbler, 12 oz, ftd	140.00	150.00
Tumbler, 12 oz, 4-3/4" h	150.00	—
Vegetable Bowl, 8-1/2" d	30.00	30.00
Vegetable Bowl, 10-1/2" d, oval	25.00	28.50

Horseshoe, No. 612 yellow plate.

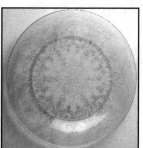

Horseshoe, No. 612 pitcher.

Indiana Custard

Flower and Leaf Band

Manufactured by Indiana Glass Company, Dunkirk, Ind., in the 1930s and in the 1950s.

Made in custard color, known as French Ivory. White was made in the 1950s.

Item	French Ivory	White
Berry Bowl, 5-1/2" d	16.50	8.00
Berry Bowl, 9" d, 1-3/4" deep	36.00	—
Butter Dish, cov	68.00	—
Cereal Bowl, 6-1/2" d	8.00	—
Creamer	17.50	—
Cup	38.00	18.00
Plate, 5-3/4" d, bread and butter	7.00	—
Plate, 7-1/2" d, salad	16.00	—
Plate, 8-7/8" d, luncheon	18.00	—
Plate, 9-3/4" d, dinner	28.00	—
Platter, 11-1/2" l, oval	30.00	—
Saucer	12.00	6.00
Sherbet	90.00	—
Soup Bowl, 7-1/2" d, flat	32.00	—
Sugar, cov	30.00	—

Indiana Custard,
covered sugar.

Iris

Iris and Herringbone

Manufactured by Jeannette Glass Company, Jeannette, Pa., from 1928 to 1932 and in the 1950s and 1970s.

Made in crystal, iridescent, some green and pink. Recent color combinations of yellow and red and blue and green and white have been made. A record price of $495 is noted for a rare amethyst demitasse cup and saucer. Green is limited to footed creamer ($150), covered sugar ($150), and ruffled salad bowl. Pink is limited to footed creamer ($150), footed sugar ($150), ruffled salad bowl ($135), and 9" vase ($225).

Reproductions: † Some collectors and dealers feel strongly that the newer re-issues of this pattern are actually reproductions. Forms that have the potential to fool buyers are the 4-1/2" berry bowl, covered candy jar, 10" d dinner plate, 6-1/2" h ftd tumbler, and vase. Careful examination of the object, plus careful consideration of the color should help determine age.

Item	Crystal	Iridescent
Berry Bowl, 4-1/2" d, beaded edge †	50.00	20.00
Berry Bowl, 8" d, beaded edge	110.00	30.00
Bowl, 5-1/2" d, scalloped	10.00	23.00
Bowl, 9-1/2" d, scalloped	17.50	14.00
Bread Plate, 11-3/4" d	20.00	38.00
Butter Dish, cov	50.00	55.00
Candlesticks, pr	48.50	48.00
Candy Jar, cov †	150.00	—
Cereal Bowl, 5" d	150.00	—
Coaster	105.00	—
Cocktail, 4 oz, 4-1/4" h	29.50	—
Creamer, ftd	15.00	17.50
Cup	20.00	30.00
Demitasse Cup and Saucer	210.00	350.00
Fruit Bowl, 11" d, or 11-1/2"	15.00	18.00
Fruit Set	110.00	—
Goblet, 4 oz, 5-3/4" h	30.00	135.00
Goblet, 8 oz, 5-3/4" h	27.50	175.00
Iced Tea Tumbler, 6-1/2" h, ftd	42.00	—
Lamp Shade, 11-1/2"	90.00	—
Nut Set	90.00	—
Pitcher, 9-1/2" h, ftd	50.00	50.00
Plate, 5-1/2" d, sherbet	16.00	15.00
Plate, 7" d	95.00	—
Plate, 8" d, luncheon	125.00	115.00
Plate, 9" d, dinner †	65.00	48.00

Item	*Crystal*	*Iridescent*
Salad Bowl, 9-1/2" d, ruffled	20.00	20.00
Sandwich Plate, 11-3/4" d	20.00	38.00
Sauce, 5" d, ruffled	12.50	24.00
Sherbet, 2-1/2" h, ftd	30.00	15.50
Sherbet, 4" h, ftd	22.00	15.50
Soup Bowl, 7-1/2" d	165.00	80.00
Sugar, cov	32.00	23.00
Tumbler, 4" h, flat	125.00	18.00
Tumbler, 6" h, ftd	30.00	25.00
Tumbler, 6-1/2" h, ftd †	40.00	—
Tumbler, flat, water	135.00	—
Vase, 9" h †	38.00	35.00
Wine, 4" h	20.00	33.50
Wine, 4-1/4" h, 3 oz	24.00	—
Wine, 5-1/2" h	27.50	—

*Iris, crystal
candlesticks and
iridescent plate.*

Jane Ray
(Fire-King)

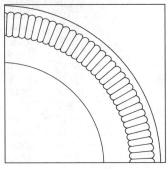

Jane Ray (Fire-King) Jade-ite plate.

Manufactured by Anchor-Hocking, from 1945 to 1963.

Made in ivory, Jade-ite, Peach Lustre, white and white with gold trim.

Item	Ivory	Jade-ite	Peach Lustre	White
Berry Bowl, 4-7/8" d	—	12.00	—	—
Cereal Bowl	8.00	11.00	—	8.00
Chili Bowl	8.00	6.00	—	8.00
Creamer	9.00	10.00	15.00	9.00
Cup	5.00	7.00	6.00	5.00
Cup, St. Denis	—	7.50	—	—
Demitasse Cup	18.00	45.00	30.00	18.00
Demitasse Saucer	20.00	45.00	25.00	20.00
Dessert Bowl, 4-7/8" d ...	4.00	7.50	6.00	4.00
Egg Cup, double	—	18.50	—	—
Mug	—	8.00	—	—
Oatmeal Bowl, 5-7/8" d ..	8.00	22.00	—	8.00
Plate, 7-3/4" d, salad ...	9.00	10.00	6.00	9.00
Plate, 9-1/8" d, dinner ..	12.00	15.00	8.00	12.00
Platter, 9" x 12"	15.00	30.00	—	15.00
Saucer	2.00	5.00	4.00	2.00
Soup Bowl	8.00	35.00	—	8.00
Soup Plate, 7-5/8" d ...	12.00	140.00	8.00	12.00
Sugar, cov	15.00	12.00	15.00	15.00
Sugar Cover only	5.00	6.00	—	5.00
Sugar, no lid	5.00	5.00	—	5.00
Vegetable Bowl, 8-1/4" d	14.00	35.00	—	14.00

Jubilee

Manufactured by Lancaster Glass Company, Lancaster, Ohio, early 1930s.

Made in pink and yellow.

Item	Pink	Yellow
Bowl, 8" d, 5-1/8" h, 3 legs	275.00	225.00
Bowl, 11-1/2" d, 3 legs	265.00	250.00
Bowl, 11-1/2" d, 3 legs, curved in	—	250.00
Bowl, 13" d, 3 legs	250.00	245.00
Cake Tray, 11" d, 2 handles	75.00	85.00
Candlesticks, pr	190.00	195.00
Candy Jar, cov, 3 legs	325.00	325.00
Cheese and Cracker Set	265.00	255.00
Cordial, 1 oz, 4" h	—	245.00
Creamer	45.00	30.00
Cup	40.00	17.50
Fruit Bowl, 9" d, handle	—	125.00
Fruit Bowl, 11-1/2" h, flat	200.00	165.00
Goblet, 3 oz, 4-7/8" h	—	150.00
Goblet, 11 oz, 7-1/2" h	—	75.00
Iced Tea Tumbler, 12-1/2 oz, 6-1/8" h	—	135.00

Jubilee, yellow cup and saucer.

Item	Pink	Yellow
Juice Tumbler, 6 oz, 5" h, ftd	—	100.00
Mayonnaise, plate, orig ladle	315.00	285.00
Mayonnaise Underplate	125.00	110.00
Plate, 7" d, salad	25.00	14.00
Plate, 8-3/4" d, luncheon	30.00	16.50
Plate, 14" d, 3 legs	—	210.00
Sandwich Plate, 13-1/2" d	95.00	85.00
Sandwich Tray, 11" d, center handle	215.00	250.00
Saucer	15.00	8.00
Sherbet, 8 oz, 3" h	—	75.00
Sherbet/Champagne, 7 oz, 5-1/2" h	—	75.00
Sugar	40.00	24.00
Tumbler, 10 oz, 6" h, ftd	75.00	50.00
Vase, 12" h	—	385.00

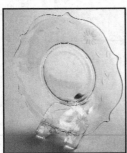

Jubilee, yellow serving plate with handles.

Jubilee, yellow goblet.

Laced Edge
Katy Blue

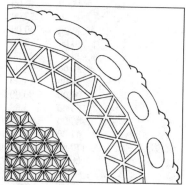

Manufactured by Imperial Glass Company, Bellaire, Ohio, early 1930s.

Made in blue and green with opalescent edges.

Item	Blue	Green
Basket, 9" d	265.00	—
Bowl, 5" d	40.00	40.00
Bowl, 5-1/2" d	42.00	42.00
Bowl, 5-7/8" d	42.00	42.00
Bowl, 11" l, oval	295.00	285.00
Bowl, 11" l, oval, divided	165.00	165.00

Item	Blue	Green
Candlesticks, pr, double light	175.00	180.00
Creamer	45.00	40.00
Cup and saucer	55.00	55.00
Fruit Bowl, 4-1/2" d	32.00	30.00
Mayonnaise, 3 piece	100.00	125.00
Plate, 6-1/2" d, bread and butter	24.00	24.00
Plate, 8" d, salad	35.00	35.00
Plate, 10" d, dinner	95.00	95.00
Plate, 12" d, luncheon	90.00	90.00
Platter, 13" l	175.00	165.00
Soup Bowl, 7" d	85.00	80.00
Sugar	45.00	40.00
Tidbit, 2 tiers, 8" and 10" plates	110.00	100.00
Tumbler, 9 oz	60.00	60.00
Vegetable Bowl, 9" d	95.00	95.00

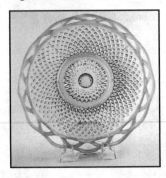

Laced Edge, blue-opalescent bowl.

Lake Como

Manufactured by Hocking Glass Company, Lancaster, Ohio, from 1934 to 1937.

Made in opaque white with a blue scene.

Item	White
Cereal Bowl, 6" d	30.00
Creamer, ftd	35.00
Cup, regular	32.00
Cup, St Denis	35.00
Plate, 7-1/4" d, salad	30.00
Plate, 9-1/4" d, dinner	35.00
Platter, 11" d	70.00
Salt and Pepper Shakers, pr	48.00
Saucer	12.00
Saucer, St Denis	12.00
Soup Bowl, flat	95.00
Sugar, ftd	35.00
Vegetable Bowl, 9-3/4" l	65.00

Lake Como, blue and white plate.

Laurel

Manufactured by McKee Glass Company, Pittsburgh, Pa., 1930s.

Made in French Ivory, Jade Green, Poudre Blue and White Opal.

Prices for White Opal are 50% more than French Ivory Prices.

Prices for children's items with no decoration are 50% less than decorated items.

Item	French Ivory	Jade Green	Poudre Blue
Berry Bowl, 4-3/4" d	9.00	12.50	16.00
Berry Bowl, 9" d	28.50	32.00	55.00
Bowl, 6" d, 3 legs	15.00	18.00	—
Bowl, 10-1/2" d, 3 legs	37.50	50.00	68.00
Bowls, 11" d	40.00	50.00	85.00
Candlesticks, pr, 4" h	50.00	60.00	—
Cereal Bowl, 6" d	12.00	20.00	28.00
Cheese Dish, cov	60.00	80.00	—
Creamer, short	12.00	20.00	—
Creamer, tall	15.00	24.00	40.00
Cup	9.50	12.50	20.00
Plate, 6" d, sherbet	6.00	12.00	10.00
Plate, 7-1/2" d, salad	10.00	15.00	17.50
Plate, 9-1/8" d, dinner	15.00	20.00	30.00
Plate, 9-1/8" d, grill, round	15.00	20.00	—
Plate, 9-1/8" d, grill, scalloped	15.00	20.00	—
Platter, 10-3/4" l, oval	32.00	35.00	45.00
Salt and Pepper Shakers, pr	48.00	75.00	—
Saucer	3.25	3.75	7.50
Sherbet	12.50	18.00	—
Sherbet/Champagne, 5"	50.00	62.00	—
Soup Bowl, 7-7/8" d	35.00	40.00	—
Sugar, short	12.00	20.00	—
Sugar, tall	15.00	24.00	40.00
Tumbler, 9 oz, 4-1/2" h, flat	40.00	60.00	—
Tumbler, 12 oz, 5" h, flat	60.00	—	—
Vegetable Bowl, 9-3/4" l, oval	18.50	20.00	45.00

Children's

Item	Green or Decorated	Scotty Dog Green	Scotty Dog Ivory
Creamer	.50.00	155.00	100.00
Cup	.36.00	85.00	50.00
Plate	.17.50	55.00	35.00
Saucer	.10.00	55.00	25.00
Sugar	.50.00	155.00	100.00

Laurel, green plate.

Laurel Leaf
(Fire-King)
Gray Laurel, Peach Lustre

Manufactured by Anchor-Hocking, from 1952 to 1963.

Made in gray, ivory, peach lustre, and white.

Reproductions: † Reproductions of the cup and saucer have been found.

Item	Gray Laurel	Ivory or White	Peach Lustre
Creamer	8.00	10.00	6.00
Cup †	4.50	7.50	5.00
Dessert Bowl, 4-7/8" d	7.00	9.00	5.00
Plate, 7-3/8" d, salad	7.00	9.00	6.50
Plate, 9-1/8" d, dinner	10.00	12.00	8.00
Saucer, 5-3/4" d †	2.00	5.50	1.50
Serving Plate, 11" d	25.00	28.00	18.00
Soup Plate, 7-5/8" d	15.00	18.00	10.00
Sugar, ftd	8.00	10.00	6.50
Vegetable Bowl, 8-1/4" d	25.00	28.00	18.00

Peach Lustre (Fire-King), iridescent sugar and creamer.

Peach Lustre (Fire-King) iridescent plate.

Lincoln Inn

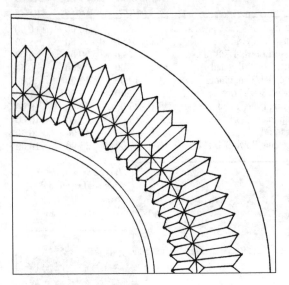

Manufactured by Fenton Art Glass Company, Williamstown, W.V., late 1920s.

Made in amber, amethyst, black, cobalt blue, crystal, green, green opalescent, light blue, opaque jade, pink and red. Production in black was limited to salt and pepper shakers, valued at $325. Some rare pieces have been identified in several other colors.

Item	Cobalt Blue or Red	Crystal	Other Colors
Ashtray	17.50	12.00	12.00
Bonbon, oval, handle	17.50	12.00	14.00
Bonbon, sq, handle	15.00	12.00	14.00
Bowl, 6" d, crimped	14.50	7.50	10.00
Bowl, 9" d, shallow	—	9.00	—
Bowl, 9-1/4" d, ftd	45.00	18.00	20.00
Bowl, 10-1/2" d, ftd	50.00	28.00	30.00
Candy Dish, ftd, oval	24.00	14.00	14.50
Cereal Bowl, 6" d	12.50	7.50	9.50
Comport	25.00	14.00	15.00
Creamer	24.00	12.00	15.00
Cup	17.50	8.50	9.50
Finger Bowl	20.00	14.00	14.50
Fruit Bowl, 5" d	14.00	7.00	9.00
Goblet, 6" h	30.00	18.50	16.00
Iced Tea Tumbler, 12 oz ftd	40.00	22.00	24.00
Juice Tumbler, 4 oz, flat	27.50	9.00	14.00
Nut Dish, ftd	20.00	14.50	16.00
Olive Bowl, handle	15.00	8.50	12.00
Pitcher, 46 oz, 7-1/4" h	820.00	700.00	715.00
Plate, 6" d	19.50	12.00	12.50
Plate, 8" d	27.50	15.00	14.00
Plate, 9-1/4" d	30.00	15.00	16.50
Plate, 12" d	35.00	16.00	18.00
Salt and Pepper Shakers, pr	215.00	175.00	175.00
Sandwich Server, center handle	115.00	95.00	100.00
Saucer	5.00	4.00	4.50

Item	Cobalt Blue or Red	Crystal	Other Colors
Sherbet, 4-1/2" h, cone shape	18.00	12.00	14.00
Sherbet, 4-3/4" h	20.00	14.00	14.50
Sugar	24.00	12.00	15.00
Tumbler, 5 oz, ftd	24.00	14.00	14.50
Tumbler, 9 oz, flat	15.00	14.00	15.00
Tumbler, 9 oz, ftd	28.00	32.00	35.00
Vase, 9-3/4" h	150.00	85.00	95.00
Vase, 12" h, ftd	185.00	115.00	125.00
Wine	35.00	20.00	24.00

Lincoln Inn, pink plate.

Lincoln Inn, cobalt blue goblet.

Lorain

Basket, No. 615

Manufactured by Indiana Glass Company, Dunkirk, Ind., from 1929 to 1939.

Made in crystal, green and yellow.

Reproduction: † A fantasy sherbert has been reported in both milk white and avocado green.

Item	Crystal	Green	Yellow
Berry Bowl, 8" d	85.00	90.00	165.00
Cereal Bowl, 6" d	40.00	40.00	60.00
Creamer, ftd	20.00	20.00	27.00
Cup and Saucer	32.00	32.00	25.00
Plate, 5-1/2" d, sherbet	10.00	12.00	15.00
Plate, 7-3/4" d, salad	15.00	18.00	24.00
Plate, 8-3/4" d, luncheon	20.00	24.00	32.50
Plate, 10-1/4" d, dinner	30.00	40.00	60.00
Platter, 11-1/2" l	32.50	32.50	48.00
Relish, 8" d, 4 part	32.00	32.00	40.00
Salad Bowl, 7-3/4" d	40.00	40.00	75.00
Saucer	6.00	6.00	8.00
Sherbet, ftd †	32.00	20.00	40.00
Snack Tray, crystal trim	32.00	37.50	—
Sugar, ftd	20.00	24.00	28.00
Tumbler, 9 oz, 4-3/4" h, ftd	32.00	35.00	40.00
Vegetable Bowl, 9-3/4" l, oval	40.00	40.00	60.00

*Lorain, yellow
plate and tumbler.*

Madrid

Manufactured by Federal Glass Company, Lancaster, Ohio, from 1932 to 1939.

Made in amber, blue, crystal, green, iridescent and pink. Iridized pieces are limited to a console set, consisting of a low bowl and pair of candlesticks, valued at $40.

Note: *Production in blue Madrid was limited. Expect to pay 50% more than amber prices.*

Reproductions: † Reproductions include candlesticks, cups, saucers and vegetable bowl. Reproductions are found in amber, blue, crystal and pink. Federal Glass Company reissued this pattern under the name "Recollection." Some of these pieces were dated 1976. When Federal went bankrupt, the molds were sold to Indiana Glass, which removed the date and began production of crystal, then pink. Several pieces were made recently that were not part of the original production and include a footed cake stand, goblet, two-section grill plate, preserves stand, squatty salt and pepper shakers, 11 oz tumbler and vase.

Item	Amber or Crystal	Green	Pink
Ashtray, 6" sq	250.00	200.00	—
Berry Bowl, small	7.50	—	—
Berry Bowl, 9-3/8" d	25.00	—	20.00
Bowl, 7" d	17.50	17.50	—
Butter Dish, cov	70.00	90.00	—
Cake Plate, 11-1/4" d	24.00	—	28.00
Candlesticks, 2-1/4" h, pr †	18.50	—	28.00
Coaster, 5" d	40.00	35.00	—
Console Bowl, 11" d	20.00	—	36.00
Cookie Jar	50.00	—	40.00
Creamer	12.00	10.00	—
Cream Soup, 4-3/4" d	16.00	—	—
Cup †	8.00	12.00	8.50
Gelatin Mold, 2-1/2" h	25.00	—	—
Gravy Boat	900.00	—	—

Madrid, amber creamer.

Item	*Amber or Crystal*	*Green*	*Pink*
Gravy Boat Platter	.900.00	—	—
Hot Dish Coaster, 3-1/2" d	.95.00	45.00	—
Iced Tea Tumbler, round	.24.00	22.00	—
Jam Dish, 7" d	.24.00	25.00	—
Juice Pitcher	.50.00	—	—
Juice Tumbler, 5 oz, 3-7/8 h, ftd . .	.16.50	30.00	—
Pitcher, jug-type	.60.00	190.00	—
Pitcher, 60 oz, 8" h, sq	.50.00	145.00	50.00
Pitcher, 80 oz, 8-1/2" h, ice lip	.75.00	225.00	—
Plate, 6" d, sherbet	.5.50	4.50	4.00

Madrid, amber bowl.

Item	*Amber or Crystal*	*Green*	*Pink*
Plate, 7-1/2" d, salad	12.00	9.00	9.00
Plate, 8-7/8" d, luncheon	10.00	12.00	10.00
Plate, 10-1/2" d, dinner	45.00	45.00	—
Plate, 10-1/2" d, grill	12.00	18.50	—
Platter, 11-1/2" oval	20.00	18.00	18.00
Relish Dish, 10-1/2" d	14.50	16.00	20.00
Salad Bowl, 8" d	17.00	15.50	—
Salad Bowl, 9-1/2" d	32.00	—	—
Salt and Pepper Shakers, 3-1/2" h	125.00	68.00	—

Madrid, amber 60 oz. 8" b. pitcher.

Item	Amber or Crystal	Green	Pink
Sauce Bowl, 5" d	9.00	8.50	11.00
Saucer †	5.00	5.00	5.00
Sherbet, cone	7.00	9.50	—
Sherbet, ftd	7.50	11.00	—
Soup Bowl, 7" d †	15.00	15.50	—
Sugar, cov †	46.00	48.00	—
Sugar, open †	10.00	10.00	—
Tumbler, 9 oz, 4-1/2" h	20.00	25.00	25.00
Tumbler, 12 oz, 5-1/4" h, ftd or flat	35.00	40.00	—
Vegetable Bowl, 10" l, oval †	28.00	24.00	30.00

Madrid, amber 5-1/4 oz.
12" tumbler.

Manhattan
Horizontal Ribbed

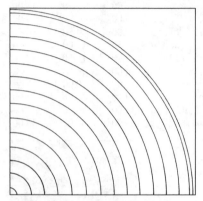

Manufactured by Anchor Hocking Glass Company, from 1938 to 1943.

Made in crystal, green, iridized, pink and ruby. Ruby pieces are limited to relish tray inserts, currently valued at $8 each. Green and iridized production was limited to ftd tumblers, currently valued at $17.50.

Anchor Hocking introduced a similar pattern, Park Avenue, in 1987. Anchor Hocking was very careful to preserve the Manhattan pattern. Collectors should pay careful attention to measurements if they are uncertain of the pattern.

Item	Crystal	Pink
Ashtray, 4" d, round	12.00	10.00
Ashtray, 4-1/2" w, sq	25.00	—
Berry Bowl, 5-3/8" d, handles	20.00	24.00
Berry Bowl, 7-1/2" d	24.00	—
Bowl, 4-1/2" d	9.00	—
Bowl, 8" d, closed handles	28.00	25.00
Bowl, 8" d, metal handle	25.00	—
Bowl, 9-1/2" d, handle	—	45.00
Candlesticks, pr, 4-1/2" h	25.00	—
Candy Dish, 3 legs	—	16.00
Candy Dish, cov	40.00	—
Cereal Bowl, 5-1/4" d, no handles	45.00	—
Coaster, 3-1/2"	19.50	—
Cocktail	15.00	—
Comport, 5-3/4" h	32.00	40.00
Creamer, oval	9.00	17.50
Cup and saucer	28.00	190.00
Fruit Bowl, 9-1/2" d, 2 open handles	40.00	35.00
Juice Pitcher, 24 oz	35.00	—

Manhattan, relish tray with ruby inserts and
crystal base; and crystal compote, vase and bowl.

Item	Crystal	Pink
Pitcher, 80 oz, tilted	55.00	85.00
Plate, 8-1/2" d, salad	24.00	—
Plate, 10-1/4" d, dinner	30.00	120.00
Relish Tray Insert	2.50	6.00
Relish Tray, 14" d, inserts	40.00	50.00
Relish Tray, 14" d, 4 part	65.00	—
Salad Bowl, 9" d	20.00	—
Salt and Pepper Shakers, pr, 2" h, sq	50.00	48.00
Sandwich Plate, 14" d	22.00	—
Sauce Bowl, 4-1/2" d, handles	12.00	—
Sherbet and 6" plate	20.00	65.00
Sugar, oval	12.00	17.50
Tumbler, 10 oz, 5-1/4" h, ftd	16.00	25.00
Vase, 8" h	20.00	—
Wine, 3-1/2" h	15.00	—

Manhattan, small crystal bowl (on pedestal); pink sugar and creamer; crystal salt and pepper shakers; crystal iced tea tumbler, pitcher, relish with metal stand; and pink footed bowl.

Mayfair

Federal

Manufactured by Federal Glass Company, Columbus, Ohio, 1934.

Made in amber, crystal and green.

Item	Amber	Crystal	Green
Cereal Bowl, 6" d	18.50	15.00	22.00
Cream Soup, 5" d	22.00	12.00	20.00
Creamer, ftd	17.50	14.00	16.00
Cup	8.50	5.00	8.50
Plate, 6-3/4" d, salad	7.00	4.50	8.50
Plate, 9-1/2" d, dinner	14.00	12.00	14.50
Plate, 9-1/2" d, grill	17.50	15.00	17.50
Platter, 12" l, oval	27.50	22.00	30.00
Sauce Bowl, 5" d	8.50	7.00	12.00
Saucer	4.50	2.50	4.50
Sugar, ftd	14.00	12.00	14.00
Tumbler, 9 oz, 4-1/2" h	27.50	16.50	32.00
Vegetable, 10" l, oval	32.00	32.00	32.00

*Mayfair Federal,
amber plate.*

Mayfair

Open Rose

Manufactured by Hocking Glass Company, Lancaster, Ohio, from 1931 to 1937.

Made in crystal, green, ice blue, pink and yellow.

Reproductions: † This pattern has been plagued with reproductions since 1977. Items reproduced include cookie jars, salt and pepper shakers, juice pitchers and whiskey glasses. Reproductions are found in amethyst, blue, cobalt blue, green, pink and red.

Note: *The 9" console bowl is rare and known only in green and pink. It is currently valued at $5,000 for each of those colors. The 1 oz cordial is also rare and now is valued at $1,000 for green or pink.*

Item	Crystal	Green	Ice Blue
Bowl, 11-3/4" l, flat	—	35.00	75.00
Butter Dish, cov	—	1,295.00	325.00
Cake Plate, 10" d, ftd	—	115.00	75.00
Cake Plate, 12" d, handles	—	40.00	70.00
Candy Dish, cov	—	575.00	325.00
Celery Dish, 9" l, divided	—	155.00	60.00
Celery Dish, 10" l, divided	.20.00	65.00	200.00
Celery Dish, 10" l, not divided	—	115.00	80.00
Cereal Bowl, 5-1/2" d	—	24.00	48.00
Claret, 4-1/2 oz, 5-1/4" h	—	950.00	—
Cocktail, 3 oz, 4" h	—	975.00	—
Cookie Jar, cov †	—	575.00	295.00
Cream Soup, 5" d	—	—	—
Creamer, ftd	—	—	—

Mayfair Open Rose, divided crystal celery dish.

Item	*Crystal*	*Green*	*Ice Blue*
Cup	—	150.00	55.00
Decanter, stopper, 32 oz	—	—	225.00
Fruit Bowl, 12" d, scalloped	—	50.00	100.00
Goblet, 2-1/2 oz, 4-1/8"	—	950.00	—
Goblet, 9 oz, 5-3/4" h	—	465.00	—
Goblet, 9 oz, 7-1/4" h, thin	—	—	225.00
Iced Tea Tumbler, 13-1/2 oz, 5-1/4" h .	—	—	225.00
Iced Tea Tumbler, 15 oz, 6-1/2" h, ftd .	—	250.00	285.00
Juice Pitcher, 37oz, 6" h † 24.50		525.00	150.00
Juice Tumbler, 3 oz, 3-1/4" h, ftd	—	—	—
Juice Tumbler, 5 oz, 3-1/2"	—	—	120.00

REPRODUCTION! Mayfair Open Rose, green and blue cookie jras.

Item	Crystal	Green	Ice Blue
Pitcher, 60 oz, 8" h	—	475.00	175.00
Pitcher, 80 oz, 8-1/2" h	—	725.00	295.00
Plate, 5-3/4" d	—	90.00	25.00
Plate, 6-1/2" d, off-center indent	—	115.00	35.00
Plate, 6-1/2" d, sherbet	—	—	24.00
Plate, 8-1/2" d, luncheon	—	85.00	55.00
Plate, 9-1/2" d, dinner	—	150.00	90.00
Plate, 9-1/2" d, grill	—	75.00	70.00
Plate, 11-1/2" d, grill, handles	—	—	—

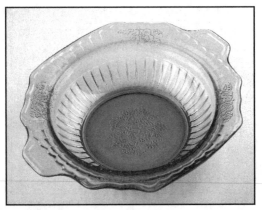

Mayfair Open Rose, blue vegetable bowl.

Item	Crystal	Green	Ice Blue
Platter, 12" l, oval, open handles 17.50		175.00	60.00
Platter, 12-1/2" oval, 8" wide, closed handles . . . . —		245.00	—
Relish, 8-3/8" d, 4 part . . . . —		160.00	65.00
Relish, 8-3/8" d, non-partitioned . . . . —		275.00	—
Salt and Pepper Shakers, pr, flat † . .20.00		999.00	295.00
Sandwich Server, center handle . . . . . . —		48.00	85.00
Saucer . . . . —		90.00	30.00
Sherbet, 2-1/4" flat . . . . —		—	135.00
Sherbet, 3" ftd . . . . —		—	—
Sherbet, 4-3/4" ftd . . . . —		150.00	75.00
Sugar, ftd . . . . —		195.00	85.00
Sweet Pea Vase . . . . —		285.00	125.00
Tumbler, 9 oz, 4-1/4" h . . . . —		—	100.00
Tumbler, 10 oz, 5-1/4" h . . . . —		—	145.00
Tumblers, 11 oz, 4-3/4" h . . . . —		200.00	165.00
Vegetable Bowl, 7" d, 2 handles . . . . . —		33.00	75.00
Vegetable Bowl, 9-1/2" l, oval . . . . —		110.00	70.00
Vegetable Bowl, 10" d cov . . . . —		—	120.00
Vegetable Bowl, 10" d open . . . . —		—	75.00
Whiskey, 1-1/2 oz, 2-1/4" h † . . . . —		—	—
Wine, 3 oz, 4-1/2" h . . . . —		450.00	—

Item	Pink	Pink Satin	Yellow
Bowl, 11-3/4" l, flat	.65.00	70.00	195.00
Butter Dish, cov	.80.00	95.00	1,295.00
Cake Plate, 10" d, ftd	.40.00	45.00	—
Cake Plate, 12" d, handles	.48.00	50.00	—
Candy Dish, cov	.70.00	85.00	475.00
Celery Dish, 9" l, divided	—	—	150.00
Celery Dish, 10" l, divided	—	—	
Celery Dish, 10" l, not divided	.45.00	50.00	115.00
Cereal Bowl, 5-1/2" d	.30.00	35.00	75.00
Claret, 4-1/2 oz, 5-1/4" h	.1,150.00	—	—
Cocktail, 3 oz, 4" h	.75.00	—	—
Cookie Jar, cov †	.47.00	37.00	860.00
Cream Soup, 5" d	.65.00	68.00	—
Creamer, ftd	.35.00	30.00	—
Cup	.24.00	27.50	150.00
Decanter, stopper, 32 oz	—	—	
Fruit Bowl, 12" d, scalloped	.65.00	75.00	215.00
Goblet, 2-1/2 oz, 4-1/8"	.950.00	—	—
Goblet, 9 oz, 5-3/4" h	.80.00	—	—
Goblet, 9 oz, 7-1/4" h, thin	.250.00	—	—
Iced Tea Tumbler, 13-1/2 oz, 5-1/4" h	.70.00	—	—
Iced Tea Tumbler, 15 oz, 6-1/2" h, ftd	.65.00	65.00	—
Juice Pitcher, 37oz, 6" h †	.70.00	65.00	525.00
Juice Tumbler, 3 oz, 3-1/4" h, ftd	.80.00	—	—
Juice Tumbler, 5 oz, 3-1/2"	.45.00	—	—

Item	Pink	Pink Satin	Yellow
Pitcher, 60 oz, 8" h	95.00	100.00	425.00
Pitcher, 80 oz, 8-1/2" h	130.00	135.00	725.00
Plate, 5-3/4" d	15.00	15.00	90.00
Plate, 6-1/2" d, off-center indent	30.00	35.00	—
Plate, 6-1/2" d, sherbet	14.50	—	—
Plate, 8-1/2" d, luncheon	40.00	35.00	80.00
Plate, 9-1/2" d, dinner	65.00	62.00	150.00
Plate, 9-1/2" d, grill	50.00	35.00	80.00
Plate, 11-1/2" d, grill, handles	—	—	100.00
Platter, 12" l, oval, open handles	40.00	35.00	115.00
Platter, 12-1/2" oval, 8" wide, closed handles	—	—	245.00
Relish, 8-3/8" d, 4 part	37.50	37.50	160.00
Relish, 8-3/8" d, non-partitioned	200.00	—	275.00
Salt and Pepper Shakers, pr, flat †	65.00	70.00	800.00
Sandwich Server, center handle	65.00	50.00	130.00
Saucer	45.00	35.00	140.00
Sherbet, 2-1/4" flat	185.00	—	—
Sherbet, 3" ftd	20.00	—	—
Sherbet, 4-3/4" ftd	75.00	75.00	150.00
Sugar, ftd	35.00	40.00	185.00
Sweet Pea Vase	140.00	145.00	—
Tumbler, 9 oz, 4-1/4" h	30.00	—	—
Tumbler, 10 oz, 5-1/4" h	65.00	—	185.00
Tumblers, 11 oz, 4-3/4" h	225.00	225.00	215.00
Vegetable Bowl, 7" d, 2 handles	65.00	70.00	195.00
Vegetable Bowl, 9-1/2" l, oval	40.00	30.00	125.00

Item	*Pink*	*Pink Satin*	*Yellow*
Vegetable Bowl, 10" d cov 120.00		120.00	900.00
Vegetable Bowl, 10" d open 20.00		19.00	200.00
Whiskey, 1-1/2 oz, 2-1/4" h † 58.00		—	—
Wine, 3 oz, 4-1/2" h 120.00		—	—

Mayfair Open Rose, pink tumbler and pink satin-finish covered cookie jar.

Miss America

Diamond Pattern

Manufactured by Hocking Glass Company, Lancaster, Ohio, from 1935 to 1938.

Made in crystal, green, ice blue, Jade-ite, pink, and royal ruby.

Forms made in green in this pretty pattern include: berry bowl ($15), cereal bowl ($18), cup and saucer ($20), 6-3/4" plate ($12), 8-1/2" salad plate ($14), salt and pepper shakers ($300), sherbet and underplate ($20), and 10 oz, 4-1/2" h tumbler ($20).

Note: *All pieces of Miss America pattern found in cobalt blue are reproductions.*

Reproductions: † Reproductions include the butter dish, (including a new importer,) creamer, 8" pitcher, salt and pepper shakers, sugar, and tumbler. Reproductions are found in amberina, blue, cobalt blue, crystal, green, pink, red.

Item	Crystal	Pink	Royal Ruby
Berry Bowl, 4-1/2" d	—	—	—
Bowl, 8" d, curved at top	.48.00	95.00	—
Bowl, 8" d, straight sides	—	85.00	—
Bowl, 11" d, shallow	—	—	800.00
Butter Dish, cov †	.200.00	550.00	—
Cake Plate, 12" d, ftd	.27.50	45.00	—
Candy Jar, cov, 11-1/2"	.65.00	175.00	—
Celery Dish, 10-1/2" l, oval	.19.50	38.50	—
Cereal Bowl, 6-1/4" d...........	.12.00	25.00	—
Coaster, 5-3/4" d	.19.50	35.00	—
Comport, 5" d	.20.00	35.00	—
Creamer, ftd †	.12.50	24.00	215.00

Miss America,
crystal 5" compote.

Item	*Crystal*	*Pink*	*Royal Ruby*
Cup	.12.50	28.00	235.00
Fruit Bowl, 8-3/4" d	.39.50	60.00	450.00
Goblet, 10 oz, 5-1/2" h	.22.50	60.00	250.00
Iced Tea Tumbler, 14 oz, 5-3/4" h . .	.25.00	85.00	—
Juice Goblet, 5 oz, 4-3/4" h	.27.50	95.00	250.00
Juice Tumbler, 5 oz, 4" h	.20.00	60.00	200.00
Pitcher, 65 oz, 8" h †	.45.00	175.00	—
Pitcher, 65 oz, 8-1/2" h, ice lip	.75.00	135.00	50.00
Plate, 5-3/4" d, sherbet	.7.50	12.50	—
Plate, 6-3/4" d	—	—	—

Miss America, pink, 8-1/2" pitcher with ice lip.

Miss America, green plate and bowl.

Item	Crystal	Pink	Royal Ruby
Plate, 8-1/2" d, salad	9.00	32.00	150.00
Plate, 10-1/4" d, dinner	16.50	45.00	—
Plate, 10-1/4" d, grill	15.00	37.50	—
Platter, 12-1/4" l, oval	18.00	45.00	—
Relish, 8-3/4" l, 4 part	30.00	35.00	—
Relish, 11-3/4" d, divided	35.00	40.00	—
Salt and Pepper Shakers, pr †	35.00	65.00	—
Saucer	4.00	7.00	60.00
Sherbet	10.00	20.00	135.00
Sugar	12.00	24.00	175.00
Tumbler, 10 oz, 4-1/2" h, flat †	20.00	40.00	—
Tumbler, 5-3/4" h	28.00	—	—
Vegetable Bowl, 10" l, oval	18.00	47.50	—
Whiskey	24.00	—	—
Wine, 3 oz, 3-3/4" h	25.00	85.00	250.00

Miss America, close-up view of original label on pink tumbler.

Miss America, pink tumbler with original label.

Moderntone

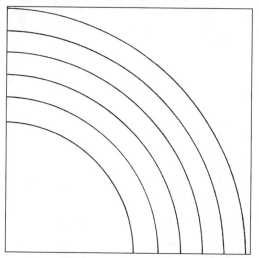

Manufactured by Hazel Atlas Glass Company, Clarksburg, W.V., and Zanesville, Ohio, from 1934 to 1942; also, in the late 1940s to early 1950s.

Made in amethyst, cobalt blue, crystal, pink and Platonite fired-on colors. Later period production saw plain white, as well as white with blue or red stripes, a Willow-type design in blue or red on white. Collector interest in crystal is limited and prices remain low, less than 50% of Platonite.

Item	Amethyst	White or White with Dec	Willow-Type Dec
Ashtray, 7-3/4" d, match holder center	—	—	—
Berry Bowl, 5" d, rim	25.00	5.00	15.00
Berry Bowl, 5" d, without rim	—	—	—
Berry Bowl, 8-3/4" d	42.00	7.50	28.00
Bowl, 8" d, no rim	—	—	—
Bowl, 8" d, rim	—	6.00	28.00
Butter Dish, metal cov	—	—	—
Cereal Bowl, 5" d, deep, no white	—	—	—
Cereal Bowl, 5" d, deep, with white	—	4.50	—
Cereal Bowl, 6-1/2" d	70.00	—	—
Cheese Dish, 7" d, metal cov	—	—	—
Cream Soup, 4-3/4" d	22.00	7.00	24.00
Cream Soup, 5" d, ruffled	30.00	—	—
Creamer	18.00	4.50	20.00
Cup	12.00	2.50	22.00
Custard Cup	18.00	—	—
Mug, 4" h, 8 oz	—	8.50	—
Mustard, metal lid	—	—	—
Plate, 5-7/8" d, sherbet	10.00	—	—
Plate, 6-3/4" d, salad	12.50	6.00	10.00
Plate, 7-3/4" d, luncheon	10.00	—	—
Plate, 8-7/8" d, dinner	13.50	4.00	20.00
Platter, 11" l, oval	40.00	14.00	30.00
Platter, 12" l, oval	48.00	10.00	35.00
Salt and Pepper Shakers, pr	45.00	12.00	—

Item	Amethyst	White or White with Dec	Willow-Type Dec
Sandwich Plate, 10-1/2" d	35.00	12.50	—
Saucer	4.50	2.50	4.50
Sherbet	13.00	4.50	14.00
Soup Bowl, 7-1/2" d	95.00	—	—
Sugar	18.00	4.50	20.00
Tumbler, 5 oz	40.00	—	—
Tumbler, 9 oz	30.00	—	—
Tumbler, 12 oz	85.00	—	—
Tumbler, cone, ftd	—	4.00	—
Whiskey, 1-1/2 oz	—	—	—

Moderntone, cobalt blue creamer & sugar bowl, salt and pepper shakers.

Item	Cobalt Blue	Platonite, Darker Shades	Platonite, Pastel Shades
Ashtray, 7-3/4" d, match holder center 165.00		—	—
Berry Bowl, 5" d, rim 27.50		—	5.00
Berry Bowl, 5" d, without rim ... —		12.50	25.00
Berry Bowl, 8-3/4" d 55.00		—	—
Bowl, 8" d, no rim .... —		40.00	50.00
Bowl, 8" d, rim .... —		—	15.00
Butter Dish, metal cov ...... —		—	—
Cereal Bowl, 5" d, deep, no white .... —		17.50	10.00
Cereal Bowl, 5" d, deep, with white .... —		—	9.00
Cereal Bowl, 6-1/2" d 70.00		—	—
Cheese Dish, 7" d, metal cov .460.00		—	—
Cream Soup, 4-3/4" d 24.00		—	12.00
Cream Soup, 5" d, ruffled 48.00		—	—
Creamer 12.00		12.00	5.50
Cup 16.00		9.00	3.50
Custard Cup 22.00		—	—
Mug, 4" h, 8 oz .... —		—	—
Mustard, metal lid 25.00		—	—
Plate, 5-7/8" d, sherbet 12.50		—	—
Plate, 6-3/4" d, salad 15.00		12.00	9.00
Plate, 7-3/4" d, luncheon 18.00		—	—
Plate, 8-7/8" d, dinner 22.00		15.00	7.00

Item	Cobalt Blue	Platonite, Darker Shades	Platonite, Pastel Shades
Platter, 11" l, oval	55.00	—	—
Platter, 12" l, oval	72.00	32.00	15.00
Salt and Pepper Shakers, pr	50.00	—	10.00
Sandwich Plate, 10-1/2" d	75.00	—	20.00
Saucer	5.00	7.50	2.00
Sherbet	15.00	12.00	8.00

Moderntone, cobalt blue cup and saucer, sherbet (on pedestal), salad plate, dinner plate and cream soup.

Item	Cobalt Blue	Platonite, Darker Shades	Platonite, Pastel Shades
Soup Bowl, 7-1/2" d	135.00	—	—
Sugar	12.50	12.00	6.00
Tumbler, 5 oz	55.00	—	—
Tumbler, 9 oz	40.00	45.00	12.00
Tumbler, 12 oz	95.00	—	—
Tumbler, cone, ftd	—	—	—
Whiskey, 1-1/2 oz	45.00	—	18.50

Children's

Hazel Atlas also manufactured children's sets in the early 1950s, known as Little Hostess Party Dishes. The original box adds to the value. Colorful combinations were found. Note: "Other Colors" in listings include: Lemon, Beige, Pink, Black, White, Aqua, Pastel Pink, Pastel Green, Pastel Blue and Yellow.

Item	Gray/ Rust/ Gold	Green/ Gray/ Chartruse	Other Colors
Creamer, 1-3/4"	17.50	16.00	15.00
Cup, 3/4"	15.00	12.00	12.00
Plate, 5-1/4" d	15.00	12.00	12.00
Saucer, 3-7/8" d	8.00	7.00	12.50
Sugar, 1-3/4"	12.00	15.00	20.00
Teapot, 3-1/2" d	125.00	115.00	95.00

Moondrops

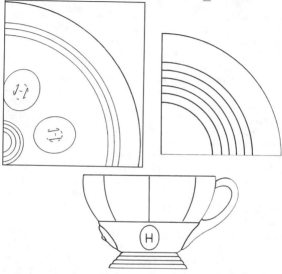

Manufactured by New Martinsville Glass Company, New Martinsville, W.V., from 1932 to 1940.

Made in amber, amethyst, black, cobalt blue, crystal, dark green, green, ice blue, Jade-ite, light green, pink, red and smoke.

Crystal production was limited to 5-1/4" h candlesticks ($65), cup and saucer ($10), and sherbet ($10).

Item	Cobalt Blue	Other Colors	Red
Ashtray	30.00	18.00	30.00
Berry Bowl, 5-1/4" d	20.00	12.00	20.00
Bowl, 8-1/2" d, ftd, concave top	40.00	25.00	40.00
Bowl, 9-1/2" d, 3 legs, ruffled	60.00	—	60.00
Bowl, 9-3/4" l, oval, handles	50.00	30.00	50.00
Butter Dish, cov	425.00	275.00	295.00
Candlesticks, pr, 2" h, ruffled	40.00	25.00	40.00
Candlesticks, pr, 4" h, sherbet style . .	30.00	18.00	30.00
Candlesticks, pr, 5" h, ruffled	32.00	22.00	32.00
Candlesticks, pr, 5" h, wings	90.00	60.00	90.00
Candlesticks, pr, 5-1/4" h, triple light	100.00	65.00	100.00
Candlesticks, pr, 8-1/2" h, metal stem	40.00	32.00	40.00
Candy Dish, 8" d, ruffled	40.00	20.00	40.00
Casserole, cov, 9-3/4" d	185.00	100.00	185.00
Celery Bowl, 11" l, boat-shape	30.00-	24.00	30.00
Cocktail Shaker, metal top	60.00	35.00	60.00
Comport, 4" d	25.00	15.00	25.00
Comport, 11-1/2" d	60.00	30.00	60.00
Console Bowl, 12" d, round, 3 ftd	—	40.00	—
Console Bowl, 13" d, wings	—	80.00	120.00
Cordial, 3/4 oz, 2-7/8" h	—	25.00	48.00
Cream Soup, 4-1/4" d	90.00	35.00	90.00
Creamer, 2-3/4" h	15.00	10.00	18.00
Creamer, 3-3/4" h	12.00	12.00	16.00
Cup	14.00	10.00	16.00
Decanter, 7-3/4" h	70.00	40.00	70.00
Decanter, 8-1/2" h	72.00	45.00	72.00

Item	Cobalt Blue	Other Colors	Red
Decanter, 10-1/4" h, rocket-shape	425.00	375.00	425.00
Decanter, 11-1/4" h	100.00	50.00	110.00
Goblet, 5 oz, 4-3/4" h	25.00	15.00	22.00
Goblet, 8 oz, 5-3/4" h	35.00	20.00	33.00
Goblet, 9 oz, 6-1/4" h, metal stem	15.00	17.50	15.00
Gravy Boat	120.00	90.00	125.00
Juice Tumbler, 3 oz, 3-1/4" h, ftd	15.00	10.00	15.00
Mayonnaise, 5-1/4" h	32.50	30.00	32.50
Mug, 12 oz, 5-1/8" h	40.00	24.00	42.00
Perfume Bottle, rocket-shape	200.00	150.00	210.00
Pickle, 7-1/2" d	25.00	15.00	25.00
Pitcher, 22 oz, 6-7/8" h	175.00	90.00	175.00
Pitcher, 32 oz, 8-1/8" h	195.00	110.00	195.00
Pitcher, 50 oz, 8" h, lip	200.00	115.00	200.00

Moondrops, ruby sugar and creamer.

Item	Cobalt Blue	Other Colors	Red
Pitcher, 53 oz, 8-1/8" h	195.00	120.00	195.00
Plate, 5-7/8" d	12.00	7.50	12.00
Plate, 6" d, round, off center indent	12.50	10.00	12.50
Plate, 6-1/8" d, sherbet	8.00	6.00	8.00
Plate, 7-1/8" d, salad	12.00	10.00	12.00
Plate, 8-1/2" d, luncheon	15.00	12.00	15.00
Plate, 9-1/2" d, dinner	25.00	15.00	25.00
Platter, 12" l, oval	35.00	20.00	35.00
Powder Jar, 3 ftd	175.00	100.00	185.00
Relish , 8-1/2" d, 3 ftd, divided	30.00	20.00	30.00
Sandwich Plate, 14" d	40.00	20.00	40.00
Sandwich Plate, 14" d, w handles	44.00	24.00	45.00
Saucer	6.00	4.00	6.50
Sherbet, 2-5/8" h	15.00	11.00	20.00
Sherbet, 3-1/2" h	25.00	15.00	25.00
Shot Glass, 2 oz, 2-3/4" h	17.50	12.00	17.50
Shot Glass, 2 oz, 2-3/4" h, handle	17.50	15.00	17.50
Soup Bowl, 6-3/4" d	80.00	—	80.00
Sugar, 2-3/4" h	10.00	10.00	18.00
Tray, 7-1/2" l	15.00	20.00	16.00
Tumbler, 5 oz, 3-5/8" h	15.00	10.00	15.00
Tumbler, 7 oz, 4-3/8" h	17.50	10.00	18.00
Tumbler, 8 oz, 4-3/8" h	17.50	12.00	22.00
Tumbler, 9 oz, 4-7/8" h, handle	30.00	15.00	28.00
Tumbler, 9 oz, 4-7/8" h	20.00	15.00	19.00
Tumbler, 12 oz, 5-1/8" h	30.00	15.00	33.00
Vase, 7-1/4" h, flat, ruffled	60.00	60.00	60.00

Item	Cobalt Blue	Other Colors	Red
Vase, 8-1/2" h, bud, rocket-shape	245.00	185.00	245.00
Vase, 9-1/4" h, rocket-shape	240.00	125.00	240.00
Vegetable Bowl, 9-3/4" l, oval	48.00	24.00	48.00
Wine, 3 oz, 5-1/2" h, metal stem	17.50	12.00	16.00
Wine, 4-3/4" h, rocket-shape	27.50	30.00	85.00
Wine, 4 oz, 4" h	24.00	12.00	24.00
Wine, 4 oz, 5-1/2" h, metal stem	20.00	12.00	18.00

Moondrops, pink cup and saucer.

Moonstone

Manufactured by Anchor Hocking Glass Company, Lancaster, Ohio, from 1941 to 1946.

Made in crystal with opalescent hobnails and Ocean Green with opalescent hobnails.

Item	Crystal	Ocean Green
Berry Bowl, 5-1/2" d	18.00	—
Bonbon, heart shape, handle	16.00	—
Bowl, 6-1/2" d, crimped, handle	20.00	—
Bowl, 7-1/4" d, flat	18.00	—
Bowl, 9-1/2" d, crimped	27.50	—
Bud Vase, 5-1/2" h	15.00	—
Candleholder, pr	25.00	—
Candy Jar, cov, 6" h	30.00	—
Cigarette Box, cov	25.00	—
Creamer	10.00	9.50
Cup	8.00	10.00
Dessert Bowl, 5-1/2" d, crimped	12.50	—

Moonstone, crystal covered candy dish with opalescent hobnails.

Moonstone, crystal puffbox, covered.

Item	Crystal	Ocean Green
Goblet, 10 oz	28.00	24.00
Plate, 6-1/4" d, sherbet	7.00	9.00
Plate, 8-3/8" d, luncheon	17.50	17.50
Puff Box, cov, 4-3/4" d, round	25.00	—
Relish, 7-1/4" d, divided	12.50	—
Relish, cloverleaf	14.00	—
Sandwich Plate, 10-3/4" d	45.00	—
Saucer	6.00	6.00
Sherbet, ftd	8.00	7.00
Sugar, ftd	10.00	12.50
Vase, 6-1/2" h, ruffled	12.00	—

Moonstone, crystal ruffled plate with opalescent hobnails.

Moroccan
Amethyst

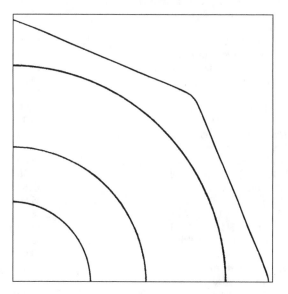

Manufactured by Hazel Ware, division of Continental Can, 1960s.
Made in amethyst.

Item	Amethyst
Ashtray, 3-1/4" round or triangular	.5.75
Ashtray, 6-7/8" w, triangular	.12.50
Ashtray, 8" w, square	.14.00
Bowl, 5-3/4" w, deep, square	.12.00
Bowl, 6" d, round	.12.50
Bowl, 7-3/4" l, oval	.18.50
Bowl, 7-3/4" l, rectangular	.15.00
Bowl, 7-3/4" l, rectangular, metal handle	.17.50
Bowls, 10-3/4" d	.30.00
Candy, cov, short	.35.00
Candy, cov, tall	.32.00
Chip and Dip, 10-3/4" and 5-3/4" bowls in metal frame	.40.00
Cocktail Shaker, chrome lid	.30.00
Cocktail, stirrer, 16 oz, 6-1/4" h, lip	.30.00
Cup and Saucer	.10.00
Fruit Bowl, 4-3/4" d, octagonal	.9.50
Goblet, 9 oz, 5-1/2" h	.12.50
Ice Bucket, 6" h	.35.00
Iced Tea Tumbler, 16 oz, 6-1/2" h	.18.50
Juice Goblet, 5-1/2 oz, 4-3/8" h	.12.00
Juice Tumbler, 4 oz, 2-1/2" h	.12.50
Old Fashioned Tumbler, 8 oz, 3-1/4" h	.15.00
Plate, 5-3/4" d, sherbet	.4.50
Plate, 7-1/4" d, salad	.4.75
Plate, 9-3/4" d, dinner	.7.00
Punch Bowl	.85.00
Punch Bowl Set, bowl, base, 12 cups	.145.00

Item	*Amethyst*
Punch Cup 6.00	
Relish, 7-3/4" l 14.00	
Salad Fork and Spoon 12.00	
Sandwich Plate, 12" d, metal handle 15.00	
Sherbet, 7-1/2 oz, 4-1/4" h 8.00	
Snack Plate, 10" l, fan shaped, cup rest 8.00	
Snack Set, square plate, cup 12.00	
Tumbler, 9 oz 12.50	
Tumbler, 11 oz, 4-1/4" h, crinkled bottom 12.00	
Tumbler, 11 oz, 4-5/8" h 12.00	
Vase, 8-1/2" h, ruffled 40.00	
Wine, 4-1/2 oz, 4" h 12.50	

*Moroccan Amethyst,
cup and saucer.*

Mt. Pleasant
Double Shield

Manufactured by L.E. Smith, Mt. Pleasant, Pa., from the 1920s to 1934.

Made in amethyst, black, cobalt blue, crystal, green, pink and white.

Item	Amethyst or Cobalt Blue	Black	Green or Pink
Bonbon, 7" d, rolled edge 24.00	24.00	24.50	16.00
Bowl, 6" d, 3 legs .... —	—	25.00	—
Bowl, 6" w, sq, 2 handles 27.50	27.50	18.00	15.00
Bowl, 7" d, 3 ftd, rolled out edge ...18.50	18.50	24.50	17.50
Bowl, 8" d, scalloped, 2 handles 37.50	37.50	35.00	20.00
Bowl, 8" d, sq, 2 handles 38.00	38.00	40.00	20.00
Bowl, 9" d, scalloped, 1-3/4" deep, ftd 30.00	30.00	32.00	—
Bowl, 10" d, 2 handles, turned-up edge 32.00	32.00	34.00	—
Cake Plate, 10-1/2" d, 1-1/4" h, ftd ..45.00	45.00	47.00	—
Cake Plate, 10-1/2" d, 2 handles 26.00	26.00	40.00	17.50
Candlesticks, pr, single light 28.00	28.00	42.50	24.00
Candlesticks, pr, two light 50.00	50.00	55.00	30.00
Creamer 21.00	21.00	20.00	20.00
Cup 15.00	15.00	15.00	12.50
Fruit Bowl, 4-7/8" sq 16.00	16.00	20.00	12.00
Fruit Bowl, 9-1/4" sq 30.00	30.00	50.00	20.00
Fruit Bowl, 10" d, scalloped 40.00	40.00	40.00	—
Leaf, 8" l 12.50	12.50	17.50	—
Leaf, 11-1/4" l 25.00	25.00	30.00	—
Mayonnaise, 5-1/2" h, 3 ftd 25.00	25.00	28.00	17.50
Mint, 6" d, center handle 25.00	25.00	26.50	16.00
Plate, 7" h, 2 handles, scalloped 15.00	15.00	16.00	12.50
Plate, 8" d, scalloped 16.00	16.00	15.00	12.50
Plate, 8" d, scalloped , 3 ftd 17.50	17.50	27.00	12.50
Plate, 8" w, sq 17.50	17.50	25.00	12.50

Item	Amethyst or Cobalt Blue	Black	Green or Pink
Plate, 8-1/4" w, sq, indent for cup	17.50	19.00	—
Plate, 9" d, grill	20.00	20.00	—
Plate, 12" d, 2 handles	35.00	35.00	20.00
Rose Bowl, 4" d	25.00	30.00	20.00
Salt and Pepper Shakers, pr	50.00	50.00	25.00
Sandwich Server, center handle	40.00	37.50	—
Saucer	5.00	5.00	3.50
Sherbet	15.00	16.50	12.50
Sugar	9.00	20.00	20.00
Tumbler, ftd	25.00	27.50	—
Vase, 7-1/4" h	30.00	35.00	—

Mt. Pleasant, black creamer, sugar (on pedestal), cup and bowl.

Mt. Pleasant, black scalloped fruit bowl.

New Century

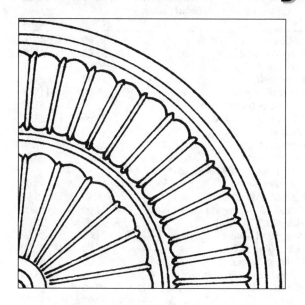

Manufactured by Hazel Atlas Company, Clarksburg, W.V., and Zanesville, Ohio, from 1930 to 1935.

Made in crystal and green, with limited production in amethyst, cobalt blue and pink.

Item	Amethyst, Cobalt Blue or Pink	Crystal	Green
Ashtray/Coaster, 5-3/8" d	—	30.00	30.00
Berry Bowl, 4-1/2" d	—	35.00	35.00
Berry Bowl, 8" d	—	30.00	30.00
Butter Dish, cov	—	75.00	75.00
Casserole, cov, 9" d	—	115.00	115.00
Cocktail, 3-1/4 oz	—	42.00	42.00
Cream Soup, 4-3/4" d	—	25.00	25.00
Creamer	—	12.00	14.00
Cup and Saucer	27.50	15.00	17.50
Decanter, stopper	—	90.00	90.00
Pitcher, with or without ice lip, 60 oz or 80 oz	55.00	45.00	48.00
Plate, 6" d, sherbet	—	5.50	6.50
Plate, 7-1/8" d, breakfast	—	12.00	12.00
Plate, 8-1/2" d, salad	—	12.00	12.00
Plate, 10" d, dinner	—	24.00	24.00
Plate, 10" d, grill	—	15.00	18.00
Platter, 11" l, oval	—	30.00	30.00
Salt and Pepper Shakers, pr	—	45.00	45.00
Sherbet, 3" h	—	9.00	9.00
Sugar, cov	—	40.00	45.00
Tumbler, 5 oz, 3-1/2" h	12.00	15.00	18.00
Tumbler, 5 oz, 4" h, ftd	—	30.00	32.50
Tumbler, 8 oz, 3-1/2" h	—	25.00	27.50
Tumbler, 9 oz, 4-1/4" h	14.00	17.50	18.00

Item	Amethyst, Cobalt Blue or Pink	Crystal	Green
Tumbler, 9 oz, 4-7/8" h, ftd	—	20.00	20.00
Tumbler, 10 oz, 5" h	16.00	17.50	17.50
Tumbler, 12 oz, 5-1/4" h	25.00	30.00	32.50
Whiskey, 2-1/2" h, 1-1/2 oz	—	18.00	20.00
Wine, 2-1/2 oz	—	35.00	40.00

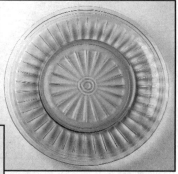

*New Century,
green plate.*

*New Century, green salt
and pepper shakers.*

Newport

Hairpin

Manufactured by Hazel Atlas Glass Company, Clarksburg, W.V., and Zanesville, Ohio, from 1936 to the early 1950s.

Made in amethyst, cobalt blue, pink (from 1936 to 1940), Platonite white and fired-on colors (from the 1940s to early 1950s).

Note: *Platonite values are 50% less than pink values.*

Item	Amethyst or Cobalt Blue	Fired-On Color	Pink
Berry Bowl, 4-3/4" d	25.00	9.00	10.00
Berry Bowl, 8-1/4" d	50.00	16.00	25.00
Cereal Bowl, 5-1/4" d	42.00	—	20.00
Cream Soup, 4-3/4" d	25.00	10.00	17.50
Creamer	22.00	8.50	10.00
Cup	15.00	9.00	6.00
Plate, 6" d, sherbet	10.00	5.00	3.50
Plate, 8-1/2" d, luncheon	22.00	9.00	8.00
Plate, 8-13/16" d, dinner	35.00	15.00	15.00
Platter, 11-3/4" l, oval	48.00	18.00	20.00
Salt and Pepper Shakers, pr	65.00	32.00	30.00
Sandwich Plate, 11-1/2" d	50.00	15.00	24.00
Saucer	6.00	3.00	2.50
Sherbet	18.50	10.00	8.00
Sugar	22.00	9.50	10.00
Tumbler, 9 oz, 4-1/2" h	48.00	15.00	20.00

*Newport,
amethyst plate,
sugar, creamer
and soup bowl.*

Normandie
Bouquet and Lattice

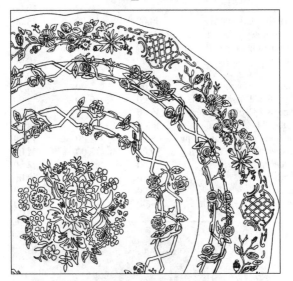

Manufactured by Federal Glass Company, Columbus, Ohio, from 1933 to 1940.

Made in amber, crystal, iridescent and pink.

Note: *Crystal values are 50% less than pink prices shown.*

Item	*Amber*	*Iridescent*	*Pink*
Berry Bowl, 5" d 9.50	6.50		12.00
Berry Bowl, 8-1/2" d 35.00	30.00		80.00
Cereal Bowl, 6-1/2" d 30.00	10.00		35.00
Creamer, ftd 20.00	8.00		18.00
Cup and Saucer 12.00	10.00		20.00
Iced Tea Tumbler, 12 oz, 5" h . .40.00	—		—
Juice Tumbler, 5 oz, 4" h 38.00	—		—
Pitcher, 80 oz, 8" h 115.00	—		245.00
Plate, 7-3/4" d, salad 10.00	55.00		14.00
Plate, 9-1/4" d, luncheon 12.50	16.50		100.00
Plate, 11" d, dinner 32.00	10.00		18.00
Plate, 11" d, grill 15.00	8.50		25.00
Platter, 11-3/4" l 24.00	12.00		80.00
Salt and Pepper Shakers, pr . . .50.00	—		4.00
Sherbet and Underplate 14.00	12.00		16.00
Sugar .8.00	7.00		12.00
Tumbler, 9 oz, 4-1/4" h 25.00	—		50.00
Vegetable Bowl, 10" l, oval 27.50	25.00		40.00

Normandi, Iridescent cup and saucer.

Old Café

Manufactured by Hocking Glass Company, Lancaster, Ohio, from 1936 to 1940.

Made in crystal, pink and royal ruby.

Item	Crystal	Pink	Royal Ruby
Berry Bowl, 3-3/4" d 4.50		5.00	6.00
Bowl, 5" d 5.00		6.00	
Bowl, 9" d, closed handles 10.00		10.00	15.00
Candy Dish, 8" d, low 8.00		12.00	16.00
Candy Jar, 5-1/2" d, crystal with ruby cover . . . . —		—	20.00
Cereal Bowl, 5-1/2" d 9.00		9.00	12.00
Cup and Saucer 10.00		10.00	22.00
Juice Tumbler, 3" h 10.00		10.00	12.00
Lamp 24.00		24.00	35.00
Olive Dish, 6" l, oblong 7.50		8.50	—
Pitcher, 36 oz, 6" h 85.00		85.00	—
Pitcher, 80 oz 120.00		120.00	—
Plate, 6" d, sherbet 4.00		4.00	—
Plate, 10" d, dinner 35.00		35.00	—
Sherbet, low, ftd 7.00		7.00	12.00
Tumbler, 4" h 12.00		12.00	18.00
Vase, 7-1/4" h 35.00		40.00	45.00

Old Café, ruby bowl.

Old Café, clear vase.

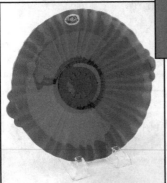

Old Café, close-up view of original label on ruby bowl with handles.

Old Café, ruby bowl with handles and original label.

Old Colony

Lace Edge, Open Lace

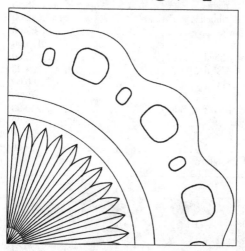

Manufactured by Hocking Glass Company, Lancaster, Ohio, from 1935 to 1938.

Made in crystal and pink.

Crystal Old Colony pieces are valued at about 50% of pink, as are frosted or satin finish prices. Many other companies made a look-alike to Old Colony, so care must be exercised.

Item	Pink
Bonbon, cov	.65.00
Bowl, 9-1/2" d, plain	.38.50
Bowl, 9-1/2" d, ribbed	.32.00
Butter Dish, cov	.65.00
Candlesticks, pr	.125.00
Candy Jar, cov, ribbed	.65.00
Cereal Bowl, 6-3/8" d	.24.00
Comport, 7" d, cov	.60.00
Comport, 9" d	.675.00
Console Bowl, 10-1/2" d, 3 legs	.250.00
Cookie Jar, cov	.75.00
Creamer	.25.00
Cup	.24.00
Flower Bowl, crystal frog	.30.00

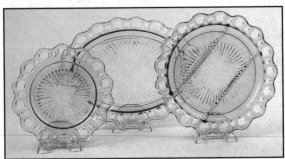

Old Colony Lace Edge, pink plate, platter and divided relish.

Item	Pink
Plate, 7-1/4" d, salad	27.50
Plate, 8-1/4" d, luncheon	32.00
Plate, 10-1/2" d, dinner	36.00
Plate, 10-1/2" d, grill	28.00
Plate, 13" d, 4 part, solid lace	65.00
Plate, 13" d, solid lace	65.00
Platter, 12-3/4" l	42.00
Platter, 12-3/4" l, 5 part	40.00
Relish Dish, 7-1/2" d, 3 part, deep	60.00
Relish Plate, 10-1/2" d, 3 part	25.00
Salad Bowl, 7-3/4" d, ribbed	60.00
Saucer	15.00
Sherbet, ftd	112.00
Sugar	25.00
Tumbler, 5 oz, 3-1/2" h, flat	120.00
Tumbler, 9 oz, 4-1/2" h, flat	22.00
Tumbler, 10-1/2 oz, 5" h, ftd	95.00
Vase, 7" h	495.00

*Old Colony Lace Edge, pink
satin-finish candleholder.*

Old English
Threading

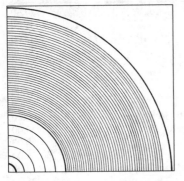

*Old English,
green compote.*

Manufactured by Indiana Glass Company, Dunkirk, Ind., late 1920s.

Made in amber, crystal, green and pink.

Item	Amber or Pink	Crystal	Green
Bowl, 4" d, flat	20.00	18.00	22.00
Bowl, 9-1/2" d, flat	35.00	25.00	35.00
Candlesticks, pr, 4" h	35.00	25.00	35.00
Candy Dish, cov, flat	50.00	40.00	50.00
Candy Jar, cov	55.00	45.00	55.00
Cheese Compote, 3-1/2" h	17.50	12.00	17.50
Cheese Plate, indent	20.00	10.00	20.00
Compote, 3-1/2" h, 6-3/8" w, 2 handles	24.00	12.00	24.00
Compote, 3-1/2" h, 7" w	24.00	12.00	24.00
Creamer	18.00	10.00	18.00
Egg Cup	—	10.00	—
Fruit Bowl, 9" d, ftd	30.00	20.00	30.00
Fruit Stand, 11" h, ftd	40.00	18.00	40.00
Goblet, 8 oz, 5-3/4" h	30.00	15.00	30.00
Pitcher	70.00	35.00	70.00
Pitcher, cov	125.00	55.00	125.00
Sandwich Server, center handle	60.00	—	60.00
Sherbet	20.00	10.00	20.00
Sugar, cov	38.00	14.00	38.00
Tumbler, 4-1/2" h, ftd	24.00	12.00	28.00
Tumbler, 5-1/2" h, ftd	35.00	17.50	35.00
Vase, 5-3/8" h, 7" w, fan-shape	48.00	24.00	48.00
Vase, 8" h, 4-1/2" w, ftd	45.00	20.00	45.00
Vase, 8-1/4" h, 4-1/4" w, ftd	45.00	20.00	45.00
Vase, 12" h, ftd	60.00	32.00	60.00

Ovide

Manufactured by Hazel Atlas Glass Company, Clarksburg, W.V., and Zanesville, Ohio, 1930 to 1935 and in the 1950s.

Made in black, green, white Platonite with fired-on colors in the 1950s.

Item	Black	Green	Platonite
Berry Bowl, 4-3/4" d	—	—	10.00
Berry Bowl, 8" d	—	—	22.00
Candy Dish, cov	45.00	24.00	35.00
Cereal Bowl, 5-1/2" d	10.00	—	12.00
Creamer	7.00	6.00	18.00
Cup	6.50	4.50	15.00
Egg Cup	—	—	22.00
Fruit Cocktail, ftd	5.00	4.50	—
Plate, 6" d, sherbet	—	2.50	6.00
Plate, 8" d, luncheon	—	3.50	15.00
Plate, 9" d, dinner	—	—	25.00
Platter, 11" d	—	—	24.00
Salt and Pepper Shakers, pr	28.00	28.00	25.00
Saucer	3.50	4.50	6.00
Sherbet	6.50	3.50	15.00
Sugar, open	9.00	7.00	20.00
Tumbler	18.00	—	20.00

*Ovide, informed
pink and gray plate.*

Oyster & Pearl

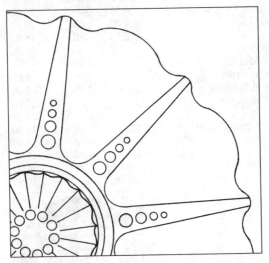

Manufactured by Anchor Hocking Glass Corporation, from 1938 to 1940.

Made in crystal, pink, royal ruby and white with fired-on green or pink.

Item	Crystal	Pink or Royal Ruby	White, Fired-On
Bowl, 5-1/2" d, handle 8.00		15.00	—
Bowl, 5-1/4" w, handle, heart-shape 12.00		21.00	10.00
Bowl, 6-1/2" d, handle 12.00		15.00	—
Candle Holders, pr, 3-1/2" h . . .24.00		45.00	15.00
Fruit Bowl, 10-1/2" d, deep . . .20.00		25.00	15.00
Relish Dish, 10-1/4" l, divided .10.00		12.00	—
Sandwich Plate, 13-1/2" d 20.00		34.00	—

Oyster and Pearl, ruby plate.

Oyster and Pearl, pink relish.

Parrot

Sylvan

*Parrot, amber jam dish
and green sherbet plate.*

Manufactured by Federal Glass Company, Columbus, Ohio, from 1931 to 1932.

Made in amber and green, with limited production in blue and crystal.

Item	*Amber*	*Green*
Berry Bowl, 5" d	22.50	25.00
Berry Bowl, 8" d	75.00	80.00
Butter Dish, cov	1,250.00	475.00
Creamer, ftd	65.00	55.00
Cup	35.00	35.00
Hot Plate, 5" d, pointed	875.00	900.00
Hot Plate, round	—	950.00
Jam Dish, 7" d	35.00	—
Pitcher, 80 oz, 8-1/2" h	—	2,500.00
Plate, 5-3/4" d, sherbet	24.00	35.00
Plate, 7-1/2" d, salad	—	40.00
Plate, 9" d, dinner	50.00	50.00
Plate, 10-1/2" d, grill, round	35.00	—
Plate, 10-1/2" d, grill, square	—	30.00
Platter, 11-1/4" l, oblong	65.00	70.00
Salt and Pepper Shakers, pr	—	270.00
Saucer	18.00	18.00
Sherbet, ftd, cone	30.00	27.50
Soup Bowl, 7" d	35.00	45.00
Sugar, cov	450.00	175.00
Tumbler, 10 oz, 4-1/4" h	100.00	130.00
Tumbler, 10 oz, 5-1/2" h, ftd, Madrid mold	145.00	—
Tumbler, 12 oz, 5-1/2" h	115.00	160.00
Tumbler, 5-3/4" h, ftd, heavy	100.00	120.00
Vegetable Bowl, 10" l, oval	75.00	65.00

Patrician

Spoke

Manufactured by Federal Glass Company, Columbus, Ohio, from 1933 to 1937.

Made in amber (also called Golden Glo), crystal, green and pink.

Note: *Values for amber and green Patrician are generally the same. However, the cookie jar is rare in green, so its value jumps to $500. The dinner plates in green are valued at $32.*

Item	Amber or Green	Crystal	Pink
Berry Bowl, 5" d	12.50	10.00	18.50
Berry Bowl, 8-1/2" d	50.00	15.00	35.00
Butter Dish, cov	95.00	100.00	225.00
Cereal Bowl, 6" d	32.00	27.50	25.00
Cookie Jar, cov	90.00	80.00	—
Cream Soup, 4-3/4" d	28.00	25.00	22.00
Creamer, ftd	12.50	9.00	12.50
Cup	12.50	10.00	12.50
Jam Dish	30.00	25.00	30.00
Mayonnaise, three toes	—	—	165.00
Pitcher, 75 oz, 8" h, molded handle	125.00	125.00	115.00
Pitcher, 75 oz, 8-1/4" h, applied handle	150.00	140.00	145.00
Plate, 6" d, sherbet	10.00	8.50	10.00
Plate, 7-1/2" d, salad	17.50	15.00	15.00
Plate, 9" d, luncheon	14.00	12.50	12.50
Plate, 10-1/2" d, grill	20.00	13.50	20.00
Plate, 10-1/2 d, dinner	10.00	12.75	36.00
Platter, 11-1/2" l, oval	32.50	30.00	28.00
Salt and Pepper Shakers, pr	65.00	65.00	85.00
Saucer	10.00	9.25	9.50
Sherbet	14.00	10.00	16.00
Sugar	12.50	9.00	12.50
Sugar Lid	55.00	50.00	60.00
Tumbler, 5 oz, 4" h	30.00	28.50	32.00

Item	Amber or Green	Crystal	Pink
Tumbler, 8 oz, 5-1/4" h, ftd	50.00	42.00	—
Tumbler, 9 oz, 4-1/4" h	32.00	28.50	28.00
Tumbler, 12 oz	45.00	—	—
Tumbler, 14 oz, 5-1/2" h	42.00	38.00	46.00
Vegetable Bowl, 10" l, oval	38.00	30.00	30.00

Patrician, amber bowl, sherbet and cup.

Patrick

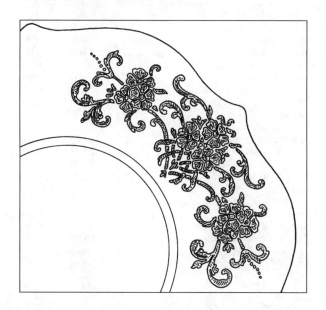

Manufactured by Lancaster Glass Company, Lancaster, Ohio, early 1930s.

Made in pink and yellow.

Item	Pink	Yellow
Candlesticks, pr	200.00	160.00
Candy Dish, 3 ftd	175.00	175.00
Cheese and Cracker Set	150.00	130.00
Cocktail, 4" h	85.00	85.00
Console Bowl, 11" d	150.00	150.00
Creamer	75.00	40.00
Cup	70.00	40.00
Fruit Bowl, 9" d, handle	175.00	130.00
Goblet, 10 oz, 6" h	85.00	75.00
Juice Goblet, 6 oz, 4-3/4" h	85.00	75.00
Mayonnaise, 3 piece	200.00	140.00
Plate, 7" d, sherbet	20.00	15.00
Plate, 7-1/2" d, salad	25.00	20.00
Plate, 8" d, luncheon	45.00	30.00
Saucer	20.00	12.00
Sherbet, 4-3/4" d	72.00	60.00
Sugar	75.00	40.00
Tray, 11" d, center handle	165.00	120.00
Tray, 11" d, two handles	80.00	65.00

Patrick, yellow luncheon plate.

Petalware

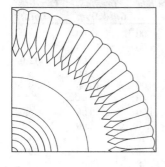

Petalware, Monax plate.

Manufactured by MacBeth-Evans Glass Company, Charleroi, Pa., from 1930 to 1940.

Made in cobalt blue, Cremax, crystal, fired-on red, blue, green and yellow, Monax and pink. Florette is the name given to a floral dec with a pointed petal. There are other patterns, such as red flower with a red rim, fruit and other floral patterns.

Crystal values are approximately 50% less than those listed for Cremax. Cobalt blue production was limited, the mustard is currently valued at $15 when complete with its metal lid. Monax Regency is priced the same as Monax Florette.

Item	Cremax	Cremax, Gold Trim	Fired-On Colors
Berry Bowl, 9" d	30.00	32.00	—
Cereal Bowl, 5-1/4" d	15.00	17.50	8.50
Cream Soup, 4-1/2" d	12.50	12.00	12.00
Creamer, ftd	12.50	15.00	8.50
Cup	8.00	10.00	9.50
Lamp Shade, 9" d	17.00	—	—
Plate, 6" d, sherbet	4.50	50.00	6.00
Plate, 8" d, salad	8.00	8.00	7.50
Plate, 9" d, dinner	15.50	14.00	8.50
Platter, 13" l, oval	25.00	20.00	20.00
Salver, 11" d	14.00	17.00	14.00
Salver, 12" d	—	—	—
Saucer	3.50	4.00	4.00
Sherbet, 4-1/2" h, low ftd	15.00	12.00	8.00
Soup Bowl, 7" d	65.00	60.00	70.00
Sugar, ftd	7.50	11.00	12.00

Petalware, pink sugar, creamer and two plates.

Item	Monax, Florette	Monax, Plain	Pink
Berry Bowl, 9" d	35.50	18.00	25.00
Cereal Bowl, 5-1/4" d	15.50	9.00	13.00
Cream Soup, 4-1/2" d	15.00	11.25	17.00
Creamer, ftd	12.00	10.00	10.00
Cup	8.00	4.50	10.00
Lamp Shade, 9" d	14.00	18.00	—
Plate, 6" d, sherbet	6.00	2.50	4.50
Plate, 8" d, salad	10.00	4.50	10.00
Plate, 9" d, dinner	16.50	10.00	16.00
Platter, 13" l, oval	25.00	20.00	17.50
Salver, 11" d	27.50	14.00	20.00
Salver, 12" d	—	24.00	20.00
Saucer	5.00	4.50	5.00
Sherbet, 4-1/2" h, low ftd	12.00	10.00	8.50
Soup Bowl, 7" d	65.00	60.00	—
Sugar, ftd	12.00	10.00	10.00

Petalware, pink plate, sugar and creamer.

Philbe (Fire-King)

Philbe (Fire-King) green creamer.

Manufactured by Anchor-Hocking, from 1937 to 1938.

Made in blue, crystal, green and pink.

Note: *The short production time of this pattern has caused some rare forms. The covered cookie jar can be hard to find. Expect to pay $1,850 for blue, $650 for crystal, and $995 for green or pink. Also the 8-1/2" h 56 oz pitcher can command $1,450 in blue, $625 in crystal, and $1,200 for green or pink.*

Item	Blue	Crystal	Green or Pink
Candy Jar, cov, 4" d, low 900.00		350.00	850.00
Cereal Bowl, 5-1/2" d 70.00		25.00	45.00
Creamer, 3-1/4", ftd 145.00		50.00	135.00
Cup 160.00		85.00	115.00
Goblet, 9 oz, 7-1/4" h 225.00		80.00	175.00
Iced Tea Tumbler, 15 oz, 6-1/2" h, ftd	85.00	45.00	75.00
Juice Tumbler, 3-1/2" h, ftd 175.00		45.00	150.00
Pitcher, 36 oz, 6" h 900.00		300.00	625.00
Plate, 6" d, sherbet 75.00		35.00	60.00
Plate, 8" d, luncheon 50.00		22.00	40.00
Plate, 10-1/2" d, grill 75.00		25.00	65.00
Platter, 12" l, closed handles 200.00		65.00	175.00
Refrigerator Dish, 4" x 5" 45.00		—	—
Refrigerator Dish, 5" x 9" 50.00		—	—
Salad Bowl, 7-1/4" d 85.00		30.00	50.00
Salver, 10-1/2" d 80.00		25.00	55.00
Salver, 11-5/8" d 95.00		25.00	65.00
Sandwich Plate, 10" d 150.00		60.00	95.00
Saucer, 6" d 75.00		35.00	60.00
Sugar, 3-1/4", ftd 145.00		50.00	135.00
Tumbler, 9 oz, 4" h, flat 125.00		40.00	100.00
Tumbler, 10 oz, 5-1/4" h 95.00		35.00	75.00
Vegetable Bowl, 10" l, oval 165.00		75.00	115.00

Pineapple & Floral

No. 618

Manufactured by Indiana Glass Company, Dunkirk, Ind., from 1932 to 1937.

Made in amber, avocado (late 1960s), cobalt blue (1980s), crystal, fired-on green, fired-on red and pink (1980s).

Reproductions: † Salad bowl and diamond-shaped comport have been reproduced in several different colors, including crystal, pink and avocado green.

Item	Amber	Crystal	Red
Ashtray, 4-1/2" d	20.00	17.50	20.00
Berry Bowl, 4-3/4" d	24.00	20.00	22.00
Cereal Bowl, 6" d	24.00	30.00	22.00
Comport, diamond shape	10.00	5.00	10.00
Creamer, diamond shape	10.00	7.50	10.00
Cream Soup	16.50	18.00	16.50
Cup and Saucer	17.50	16.00	17.50
Plate, 6" d, sherbet	8.00	6.50	8.00
Plate, 8-3/8" d, salad	12.00	10.00	12.00
Plate, 9-3/8" d, dinner	17.50	15.00	17.50
Plate, 9-3/4" d, indentation	—	25.00	—
Plate, 11" d, closed handles	24.00	20.00	24.00

Pineapple & Floral, amber cream soup.

Item	Amber	Crystal	Red
Plate, 11-1/2" d, indentation	—	25.00	—
Platter, 11" l, closed handles 20.00		18.00	20.00
Relish, 11-1/2" d, divided 24.00		20.00	24.00
Salad Bowl, 7" d † 10.00		5.00	10.00
Sandwich Plate, 11-1/2" d 24.00		20.00	24.00
Sherbet, ftd 24.00		20.00	24.00
Sugar, diamond-shape 10.00		7.50	10.00
Tumbler, 8 oz, 4-1/4" h 40.00		40.00	40.00
Tumbler, 12 oz, 5" h 48.00		47.50	48.00
Vase, cone shape 45.00		42.50	45.00
Vegetable Bowl, 10" l, oval 32.00		30.00	32.00

Pineapple & Floral, clear sugar and creamer.

Pioneer

Manufactured by Federal Glass Co., Columbus, Ohio, starting in the 1940s.

Originally made in pink, crystal was added later. The crystal 11" fluted bowl and 12" dinner plate were made until 1973.

Item	Crystal	Pink
Bowl, 7" d, low, fruits center	8.00	10.00
Bowl, 7-3/4" d, ruffled, fruits center	10.00	12.00
Bowl, 10-1/2" d, fruits center	12.00	14.00
Bowl, 10-1/2" d, plain center	10.00	12.00
Bowl, 11" d, ruffled, fruits center	15.00	18.00
Bowl, 11" d, ruffled, plain center	12.00	15.00
Nappy, 5-3/8" d, fruits center	8.00	10.00
Nappy, 5-3/8" d, plain center	6.00	8.00
Plate, 8" d, luncheon, fruits center	6.00	8.00
Plate, 12" d	10.00	12.00

Pioneer, pink plate with fruit center.

Pretzel

No. 622

Manufactured by Indiana Glass Company, Dunkirk, Ind., from late 1930s to 1960s.

Made in avocado, crystal and teal. Some crystal pieces have a fruit decoration. Recent amber, blue and opaque white issues. A teal cup and saucer is valued at $165.

Item	Crystal, Plain	Crystal, Fruits
Berry Bowl, 9-3/8" d	18.00	—
Bowl, 8" d	7.00	—
Celery Tray, 10-1/4" l	7.50	—
Creamer	6.00	—
Cup and Saucer	10.00	—
Fruit Cup, 4-1/2" d	7.50	—
Iced Tea Tumbler, 12 oz, 5-1/2" h	70.00	—
Juice Tumbler	35.00	—
Olive, 7" l, leaf-shape	7.00	—
Pickle, 8-1/2" d, two handles	4.00	—
Pitcher, 39 oz	250.00	—
Plate, 6" d	2.50	3.50
Plate, 6" d, tab handle	7.00	—

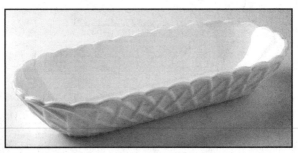

Pretzel, milk white celery tray.

Item	Crystal, Plain	Crystal, Fruits
Plate, 7" sq, wings	9.00	—
Plate, 7-1/4" w, sq, indent	8.00	—
Plate, 7-1/4" w, sq, indent, 3 part	10.00	—
Plate, 8-3/8" d, salad	6.00	4.00
Plate, 9-3/8" d, dinner	10.00	12.00
Plate, 10" d, dinner	10.00	15.00
Relish, 7", 3 part	9.00	—
Sandwich Plate, 11-1/2" d	11.00	12.00
Soup Bowl, 7-1/2" d	15.00	10.00
Sugar	6.00	—
Tumbler, 5 oz, 3-1/2" h	50.00	—
Tumbler, 9 oz, 4-1/2" h	55.00	—

Pretzel, creamer and clear sugar.

Primo

Paneled Aster

Manufactured by U.S. Glass Company, Pittsburgh, Pa., early 1930s.
Made in green and yellow.

Item	Green	Yellow
Bowl, 4-1/2"d	17.50	19.50
Bowl, 7-3/4" d	25.00	25.00
Cake Plate, 10" d, 3 ftd	25.00	25.00
Coaster/Ashtray	8.75	8.75
Creamer	12.00	15.00
Cup	14.50	14.50
Plate, 7-1/2" d	10.25	12.00
Plate, 10" d, dinner	22.50	24.00
Plate, 10" d, grill	12.00	15.00
Saucer	3.25	3.25
Sherbet	14.25	14.50
Sugar	12.00	12.00
Tumbler, 9 oz, 5-3/4" h, ftd	22.00	25.00

Primo, yellow cup.

Princess

Manufactured by Hocking Glass Company, Lancaster, Ohio, from 1931 to 1935.

Made in apricot yellow, blue, green, pink and topaz yellow. Original production in blue was limited to: covered cookie jar ($875), cup ($115), 5-1/2" d plate ($65), grill plate ($65), 9-1/2" grill plate ($115), and 6" sq. saucer ($65).

Reproductions: † The candy dish and salt and pepper shakers have been reproduced in blue, green and pink.

Item	Apricot or Topaz	Green	Pink
Ashtray, 4-1/2" d	100.00	70.00	80.00
Berry Bowl, 4-1/2" d	55.00	30.00	32.00
Butter Dish, cov	650.00	110.00	95.00
Cake Plate, 10" d, ftd	—	37.50	100.00
Candy Dish, cov †	—	70.00	85.00
Cereal Bowl, 5" d	—	40.00	35.00
Coaster	100.00	35.00	65.00
Cookie Jar, cov	—	65.00	75.00
Creamer, oval	25.00	15.00	17.50
Cup	7.50	14.00	15.50
Hat-Shaped Bowl, 9-1/2" d	125.00	45.00	50.00
Iced Tea Tumbler, 13 oz, 5-1/2" h . . .	45.00	125.00	115.00
Juice Tumbler, 5 oz, 3" h	28.00	25.00	28.00
Pitcher, 24 oz, 7-3/8" h, ftd	—	550.00	75.00
Pitcher, 37 oz, 6" h	565.00	55.00	62.00
Pitcher, 60 oz, 8" h	95.00	65.00	80.00
Plate, 5-1/2" d, sherbet	4.75	12.00	12.00
Plate, 8" d, salad	10.00	15.00	15.00
Plate, 9-1/2" d, dinner	25.00	33.50	45.00
Plate, 9-1/2" d, grill	10.00	15.00	15.00
Plate, 10-1/2" d, grill, closed handles	10.00	15.00	15.00
Platter, 12" l, closed handles	60.00	25.00	25.00
Relish, 7-1/2" l, divided, 4 part	100.00	35.00	30.00
Relish, 7-1/2" l, plain	160.00	115.00	175.00
Salad Bowl, 9" d, octagonal	125.00	46.00	40.00

Item	Apricot or Topaz	Green	Pink
Salt and Pepper Shakers, pr, 4-1/2" h †	75.00	60.00	65.00
Sandwich Plate, 10-1/4" d, 2 closed handles	165.00	20.00	35.00
Saucer, 6" sq	2.75	10.00	10.00
Sherbet, ftd	40.00	28.00	25.00
Spice Shakers, pr, 5-1/2" h	—	20.00	—
Sugar, cov	30.00	35.00	45.00
Tumbler, 9 oz, 4" h	25.00	28.00	25.00
Tumbler, 9 oz, 4-3/4" h, sq, ftd	—	65.00	25.00
Tumbler, 10 oz, 5-1/4" h, ftd	28.00	35.00	32.00
Tumbler, 12-1/2 oz, 6-1/2" h, ftd	25.00	115.00	95.00
Vase, 8" h	—	45.00	50.00
Vegetable Bowl, 10" l, oval	60.00	30.00	30.00

Princess, green bowl and cookie jar.

Pyramid

No. 610

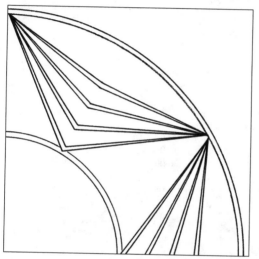

Manufactured by Indiana Glass Company, Dunkirk, Ind., from 1926 to 1932.

Made in crystal, green, pink, white and yellow. Later production in 1974 to 1975 by Tiara produced black and blue pieces. Production limited in blue and white. Prices for black not firmly established in secondary market at this time.

Item	Crystal	Green	Pink	Yellow
Berry Bowl, 4-3/4" d	12.00	25.00	20.00	40.00
Berry Bowl, 8-1/2" d	20.00	65.00	40.00	65.00
Bowl, 9-1/2" l, oval	25.00	45.00	35.00	55.00
Creamer	17.50	35.00	35.00	40.00
Ice Tub	95.00	145.00	155.00	225.00
Pickle Dish, 9-1/2" l, 5-3/4" w	20.00	35.00	35.00	65.00
Pitcher	375.00	225.00	400.00	450.00
Relish, handles	25.00	60.00	50.00	65.00
Sugar	17.50	35.00	35.00	40.00
Tray for creamer and sugar	25.00	30.00	30.00	35.00
Tumbler, 8 oz, ftd	55.00	50.00	55.00	75.00
Tumbler, 11 oz, ftd	70.00	75.00	50.00	95.00

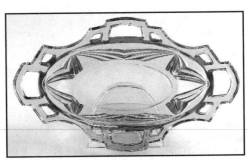

Pyramid, green relish.

Queen Mary

Prismatic Line, Vertical Ribbed

Manufactured by Hocking Glass Company, Lancaster, Ohio, from 1936 to 1948.

Made in crystal, pink and royal ruby. Royal ruby production limited to ashtray ($5), and candlesticks ($70).

Item	Crystal	Pink
Ashtray	4.00	5.50
Berry Bowl, 4-1/2" d	3.00	5.00
Berry Bowl, 5" d	5.00	10.00
Berry Bowl, 8-3/4" d	10.00	17.50
Bowl, 4" d, one handle	4.00	12.50
Bowl, 5-1/2" d, two handles	6.00	15.00
Bowl, 7" d	7.50	35.00
Butter Dish, cov	42.00	125.00
Candlesticks, pr, 2 light, 4-1/2" h	24.00	—
Candy Dish, cov	30.00	42.00
Celery Tray, 5" x 10"	10.00	24.00
Cereal Bowl, 6" d	8.00	24.00
Cigarette Jar, 2" x 3" oval	6.50	7.50
Coaster	4.00	5.00
Comport, 5-3/4"	9.00	14.00
Creamer, ftd	6.00	40.00

Queen Mary, crystal bowl and candlesticks.

Item	Crystal	Pink
Creamer, oval	6.00	12.00
Cup, large	6.50	10.00
Cup, small	8.50	12.50
Juice Tumbler, 5 oz, 3-1/2" h	9.50	15.00
Pickle Dish, 5" x 10"	10.00	24.00
Plate, 6" d, sherbet	4.00	5.00
Plate, 6-1/2" d, bread and butter	6.00	—
Plate, 8-1/4" d, salad	6.00	—
Plate, 9-1/2" d, dinner	15.00	60.00
Preserve, cov	30.00	125.00
Relish, clover-shape	15.00	17.50
Relish, 12" d, 3 part	10.00	15.00
Relish, 14" d, 4 part	15.00	17.50
Salt and Pepper Shakers, pr	25.00	—

Queen Mary, pink
10 oz. tumbler, 5" h.

Item	*Crystal*	*Pink*
Sandwich Plate, 12" d .20.00		17.50
Saucer 2.00		5.00
Serving Tray, 14" d 15.00		9.00
Sherbet, ftd 6.50		10.00
Sugar, ftd . . . . —		40.00
Sugar, oval 6.00		12.00
Tumbler, 9 oz, 4" h 6.00		19.50
Tumbler, 10 oz, 5" h, ftd 35.00		70.00

Queen Mary,
cup and saucer.

Radiance

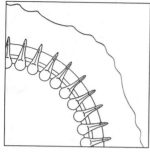

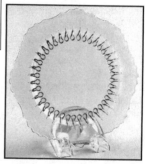

Radiance,
blue plate.

Manufactured by New Martinsville Glass Company, New Martinsville, W.V., from 1936 to 1939.

Made in amber, cobalt blue, crystal, emerald green, ice blue, pink and red. Some pieces are found with an etched design. This adds slightly to the value.

Note: *Production was limited in cobalt blue, emerald green, and pink.*

Item	Amber	Crystal	Ice Blue or Red
Bonbon, 6" d	16.00	8.00	32.00
Bonbon, 6" d, cov	48.00	24.00	95.00
Bonbon, 6" d, ftd	18.00	9.00	35.00
Bowl, 6" d, ruffled	—	—	—
Bowl, 6-1/2" d, ftd, metal holder	—	—	—
Bowl, 10" d, crimped	28.00	14.00	48.00
Bowl, 10" d, flared	22.00	11.00	—
Bowl, 12" d, crimped	30.00	15.00	50.00
Bowl, 12" d, flared	28.00	14.00	50.00
Butter Dish, cov	210.00	100.00	460.00
Butter Dish, chrome lid	40.00	37.50	—
Cake Salver	—	—	175.00
Candlesticks, pr, 2 light	75.00	37.50	120.00
Candlesticks, pr, 6" h, ruffled	85.00	40.00	175.00
Candlesticks, pr, 8" h	60.00	30.00	110.00
Candy Dish, cov, 3 part	—	—	125.00
Celery Tray, 10" l	18.00	9.00	32.00
Cheese and Cracker Set, 11" d plate	45.00	20.00	195.00
Comport, 5" h	18.00	9.00	30.00
Comport, 6" h	24.00	12.00	35.00
Condiment Set, 4 pc, tray	160.00	85.00	295.00
Cordial, 1 oz	30.00	15.00	45.00
Creamer	15.00	10.00	35.00
Cruet, individual	40.00	20.00	26.00
Cup, ftd	15.00	8.00	18.00
Decanter, stopper, handle	90.00	45.00	175.00

Item	Amber	Crystal	Ice Blue or Red
Lamp, 12" h	60.00	30.00	115.00
Mayonnaise, 3 pc set	37.50	19.00	85.00
Nut Bowl, 5" d, 2 handles	12.00	6.50	20.00
Pickle, 7"d	16.00	8.00	25.00
Pitcher, 64 oz	150.00	95.00	225.00
Pitcher, silver overlay	—	—	—
Plate, 8" d, luncheon	10.00	5.00	12.00
Punch Bowl, 9" d	110.00	65.00	185.00
Punch Bowl Liner, 14" d	48.00	24.00	85.00
Punch Cup	8.00	5.00	15.00
Punch Ladle	100.00	45.00	120.00
Relish, 7" d, two part	18.00	9.00	32.00
Relish, 8" d, three part	28.00	14.00	35.00
Salt and Pepper Shakers, pr	50.00	25.00	90.00
Saucer	6.00	3.50	7.50
Sugar	16.00	8.00	30.00
Tray, oval	25.00	15.00	32.00
Tumbler, 9" oz	22.50	12.00	30.00
Vase, 10" h, crimped	48.00	24.00	60.00
Vase, 10" h, flared	48.00	24.00	60.00
Vase, 12" h, crimped	60.00	30.00	55.00
Vase, 12" h, flared	60.00	30.00	55.00

Raindrops

Optic Design

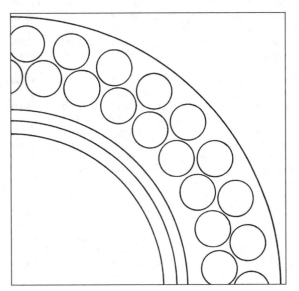

Manufactured by Federal Glass Company, Columbus, Ohio, from 1929 to 1933.

Made in crystal and green.

Item	Crystal	Green
Berry Bowl, 7-1/2" d	30.00	45.00
Cereal Bowl, 6" d	10.00	15.00
Creamer	8.00	10.00
Cup	8.50	6.50
Fruit Bowl, 4-1/2" d	5.00	11.00
Plate, 6" d, sherbet	1.50	3.00
Plate, 8" d, luncheon	4.00	7.50
Salt and Pepper Shakers, pr	150.00	315.00
Saucer	3.00	3.50
Sherbet	4.50	7.50
Sugar, cov	7.50	15.00
Tumbler, 2 oz, 2-1/8" h	4.00	7.00
Tumbler, 4 oz, 3" h	4.00	7.00
Tumbler, 5 oz, 3-7/8" h	5.50	9.50
Tumbler, 9-1/2 oz, 4-1/8" h	6.00	12.00
Tumbler, 10 oz, 5" h	6.00	12.00
Tumbler, 14 oz, 5-3/8" h	7.50	15.00
Whiskey, 1 oz, 1-7/8" h	7.50	10.00

Raindrops, green salad plate.

Ribbon

Manufactured by Hazel Atlas Glass Company, Clarksburg, W.V., and Zanesville, Ohio, early 1930s.

Made in black, crystal, green and pink. Production in pink was limited to salt and pepper shakers, valued at $40.

Item	Black	Crystal	Green
Berry Bowl, 4" d	—	20.00	22.00
Berry Bowl, 8" d	—	27.50	30.00
Bowl, 9" d, wide bands	—	—	35.00
Candy Dish, cov	42.50	32.00	38.00
Cereal Bowl, 5" d	—	20.00	25.00
Creamer, ftd	—	10.00	15.00
Cup and Saucer	—	6.50	9.50
Plate, 6-1/4" d, sherbet	—	3.50	4.50
Plate, 8" d, luncheon	15.00	5.00	8.00
Salt and Pepper Shakers, pr	45.00	22.00	32.00
Sherbet	—	6.00	8.00
Sugar, ftd	—	10.00	14.00
Tumbler, 10 oz, 6" h	—	27.00	30.00

Ribbon, green cup.

Ribbon, green cramer.

Ring

Banded Rings

Manufactured by Hocking Glass Company, Lancaster, Ohio, from 1927 to 1933.

Made in crystal, crystal with rings of black, blue, pink, red, orange, silver and yellow; green, Mayfair blue, pink and red. Prices for decorated pieces are quite similar to each other.

Item	Crystal	Decor-ated	Green
Berry Bowl, 5" d 4.00		9.00	8.00
Berry Bowl, 8" d 7.50		16.00	16.00
Bowl, 5-1/4" d, divided 12.50		—	—
Butter Tub .24.00		25.00	20.00
Cereal Bowl . . . . —		5.00	8.00
Cocktail Shaker 20.00		30.00	27.50
Cocktail, 3-1/2 oz, 3-3/4" h 12.00		18.00	18.00
Creamer, ftd .5.00		10.00	10.00
Cup and Saucer 6.50		5.50	7.50
Decanter, stopper 25.00		35.00	32.00
Goblet, 9 oz, 7-1/4" h 7.00		14.00	14.00
Ice Bucket .20.00		33.00	30.00
Ice Tub 24.00		25.00	20.00
Iced Tea Tumbler, 6-1/2" h 8.00		15.00	15.00
Juice Tumbler, 3-1/2" h, ftd 6.50		10.00	15.00
Old Fashioned Tumbler, 8 oz, 4" h . .15.00		17.50	17.50

Ring, green ice tub.

Item	Crystal	Decor-ated	Green
Pitcher, 60 oz, 8" h 22.00		25.00	25.00
Pitcher, 80 oz, 8-1/2" h 25.00		30.00	36.00
Plate, 6-1/2" d, off-center ring 5.00		8.50	8.00
Plate, 8" d, luncheon 3.00		7.00	9.00
Salt and Pepper Shakers, pr, 3" h . . .20.00		40.00	42.00
Sandwich Plate, 11-3/4" d 8.00		15.00	15.00
Sandwich Server, center handle 15.00		27.50	27.50
Sherbet, 6-1/4" d underplate 8.00		14.50	16.00
Sherbet, flat, 6-1/2" d underplate . . .12.00		18.00	21.00
Soup Bowl, 7" d 10.00		9.00	8.00
Sugar, ftd .5.00		10.00	3.00
Tumbler, 4 oz, 3" h 4.00		6.50	6.00
Tumbler, 5-1/2" h, ftd 6.00		10.00	10.00
Tumbler, 5 oz, 3-1/2" h 6.50		6.50	12.00
Tumbler, 9 oz, or 10 oz 8.50		7.00	9.00
Tumbler, 12 oz, 5-1/8" h, ftd 10.00		12.00	20.00
Vase, 8" h 20.00		35.00	37.50
Whiskey, 1-1/2 oz, 2" h 8.50		10.00	12.00
Wine, 3-1/2 oz, 4-1/2" h 17.50		20.00	24.00

Ring, crystal sandwich server.

Rock Crystal

Early American Rock Crystal

Manufactured by McKee Glass Company, Pittsburgh, Pa., in the 1920s and colors in 1930s.

Made in amber, amberina red, amethyst, aquamarine, blue frosted, cobalt blue, crystal, crystal with goofus dec, crystal with gold dec, dark red, four shades of green, milk glass, pink and frosted pink, red, red slag, Vaseline and yellow.

Note: *A butter dish is only known in crystal ($345).*

Item	Crystal	Colors	Red
Banana Split Dish 75.00		—	—
Bonbon, 7-1/2" d, scalloped edge . . .22.00		35.00	55.00
Bowl, 4" d, or 4-1/2" d, scalloped edge 15.00		24.00	35.00
Bowl, 5" d, plain or scalloped edge .20.00		26.00	45.00
Bowl, 8-1/2" d, center handle . . . . —		—	150.00
Bowl, 12-1/2" d, pedestal 80.00		125.00	300.00
Cake Stand, 11" d, 2-3/4" h, ftd 40.00		55.00	135.00
Candelabra, pr, 2-light 50.00		110.00	250.00
Candelabra, pr, 3-light 70.00		135.00	350.00
Candlesticks, pr, 5-1/2" h, low 45.00		70.00	175.00
Candlesticks, pr, 8" h 95.00		70.00	400.00
Candy Dish, cov, ftd, 9-1/2" d 55.00		95.00	225.00
Candy Dish, cov, round 50.00		75.00	175.00
Celery Tray, 12" l, oblong 30.00		40.00	85.00
Center Bowl, 12-1/2" d, ftd 98.00		135.00	310.00
Champagne, 6 oz, ftd 20.00		25.00	35.00
Claret, 3 oz . . . . —		65.00	—
Cocktail, 3-1/2 oz, ftd 17.50		24.00	45.00
Comport, 7" d 35.00		50.00	90.00
Cordial, 1 oz, ftd 25.00		45.00	65.00
Creamer, 9 oz, ftd 20.00		35.00	75.00
Creamer, flat, scalloped edge 40.00		—	—
Cruet, stopper, 6 oz, ...95.00		—	—
Cup, 7 oz, and Saucer 25.00		30.00	90.00
Deviled Egg Plate 50.00		—	—

Item	Crystal	Colors	Red
Egg Cup, 3-1/2 oz, ftd	22.50	20.00	65.00
Finger Bowl, 5" d bowl, 7" d plate, pie-crust edge	35.00	48.00	60.00
Goblet, 8 oz, ftd	22.50	30.00	65.00
Ice Dish	35.00	—	—
Iced Tea Goblet, 11 oz	25.00	35.00	70.00
Jelly, 5" d, ftd, scalloped edge	18.00	30.00	50.00
Juice Tumbler, 5 oz	24.00	30.00	50.00
Lamp, electric	225.00	375.00	650.00
Old Fashioned Tumbler, 5 oz	20.00	30.00	60.00
Parfait, 3-1/2 oz, low, ftd	27.50	40.00	75.00
Pickle, 7" l	20.00	40.00	65.00
Pitcher, covered, 9" h	175.00	350.00	675.00
Pitcher, half gallon, 7-1/2" h	100.00	165.00	—
Pitcher, quart, scalloped edge	150.00	220.00	—
Pitcher, tankard	190.00	650.00	900.00
Plate, 6" d, bread & butter, scalloped edge	6.50	9.50	20.00
Plate, 7-1/2" d, pie-crust or scalloped edge	8.00	12.00	22.00
Plate, 8-1/2" d, pie-crust or scalloped edge	9.00	12.00	30.00
Plate, 9" d, scalloped edge	18.50	24.00	55.00
Plate, 10-1/2" d, center design, scalloped edge	47.50	75.00	175.00
Plate, 10-1/2" d, scalloped edge	27.50	35.00	65.00

Item	Crystal	Colors	Red
Plate, 11-1/2" d, scalloped edge 20.00		30.00	60.00
Punch Bowl and Stand, 14" 555.00		—	—
Relish, 11-1/2" d, 2 part 35.00		50.00	75.00
Relish, 12-1/2" d, 5 part 45.00		—	—
Relish, 14" d, 6 part 45.00		65.00	—
Roll Tray, 13" d 35.00		60.00	125.00
Salad Bowl, 7" d, scalloped edge . . .25.00		40.00	65.00
Salad Bowl, 8" d, scalloped edge . . .32.00		42.00	67.50
Salad Bowl, 9" d, scalloped edge . . .35.00		50.00	85.00
Salad Bowl, 10-1/2" d, scalloped edge 25.00		50.00	90.00
Salt and Pepper Shakers, pr 80.00		135.00	—
Salt Dip .35.00		—	—
Sandwich Server, center handle . . .32.00		40.00	140.00
Sherbet, 3-1/2 oz, ftd 15.00		20.00	25.00
Spoon Tray, 7" l 20.00		40.00	65.00
Spooner .42.00		—	—
Sugar, cov 50.00		65.00	155.00
Sugar, 10 oz, open 18.00		20.00	45.00
Sundae, 6 oz, low, ftd 10.00		15.00	35.00
Syrup, lid 165.00		—	—
Tray, 5-3/8" x 7-3/8", 7/8" h 70.00		—	—
Tumbler, 9 oz, concave or straight sides 15.00		26.00	30.00
Tumbler, 12 oz, concave or straight sides 35.00		40.00	70.00

Item	*Crystal*	*Colors*	*Red*
Vase, 11" h, ftd 75.00		95.00	170.00
Vase, cornucopia 70.00		95.00	—
Whiskey, 2-1/2 oz 25.00		35.00	65.00
Wine, 2 oz or 3 oz 22.50		30.00	50.00

Rock Crystal, amber plate.

Rose Cameo

Manufactured by Belmont Tumbler Company, Bellaire, Ohio, in 1931.

Made in green.

Item	*Green*
Berry Bowl, 4-1/2" d	.12.00
Cereal Bowl, 5" d	.27.50
Bowl, 6" d, straight sides	.25.00
Plate, 7" d, salad	.16.00
Sherbet	.16.00
Tumbler, 5" h, ftd	.22.50
Tumbler, 5" h, ftd, sterling silver trim	.25.00

Rose Cameo,
green tumbler.

Rosemary

Dutch Rose

Manufactured by Federal Glass Company, Columbus, Ohio, from 1935 to 1937.

Made in amber, green and pink.

Item	Amber	Green	Pink
Berry Bowl, 5" d 7.00		17.50	17.50
Cereal Bowl, 6" d 30.00		32.00	35.00
Cream Soup, 5" d 18.00		25.00	30.00
Creamer, ftd 10.00		16.00	20.00
Cup 9.00		12.50	15.00
Plate, 6-3/4" d, salad 6.50		12.00	12.50
Plate, 9-1/2" d, dinner 10.00		15.00	22.00
Plate, 9-1/2" d, grill 12.00		15.00	22.00
Platter, 12" l, oval 18.50		24.00	35.00
Saucer 4.00		6.50	6.50
Sugar, ftd 10.00		16.00	20.00
Tumbler, 9 oz, 4-1/4" h 35.00		38.00	50.00
Vegetable Bowl, 10" l, oval 18.00		40.00	45.00

Rosemary, amber vegetable bowl and berry bowl.

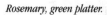

Rosemary, green platter.

Roulette

Many Windows

Manufactured by Hocking Glass Company, Lancaster, Ohio, from 1935 to 1939.

Made in crystal, green and pink.

Item	Crystal	Green	Pink
Cup	35.00	8.00	8.50
Fruit Bowl, 9" d	12.00	18.00	18.00
Iced Tea Tumbler, 12 oz, 5-1/8" h	24.00	40.00	35.00
Juice Tumbler, 5 oz, 3-1/4" h	10.00	20.00	24.00
Old Fashioned Tumbler, 7-1/2 oz, 3-1/4" h	24.00	40.00	40.00
Pitcher, 65 oz, 8" h	30.00	35.00	45.00
Plate, 6" d, sherbet	3.50	4.50	5.00
Plate, 8-1/2" d, luncheon	7.00	8.00	6.00
Sandwich Plate, 12" d	15.00	18.50	20.00
Saucer	2.50	4.00	3.00
Sherbet	8.00	10.00	12.00
Tumbler, 9 oz, 4-1/8" h	15.00	20.00	22.00
Tumbler, 10 oz, 5-1/2" h, ftd	18.00	30.00	35.00
Whiskey, 1-1/2 oz, 2-1/2" h	10.00	18.00	18.00

*Roulette, green
plate and sherbet.*

Round Robin

Unknown maker, early 1930s.

Made in crystal, iridescent and green. Crystal, produced as the base for iridescent pieces, is found occasionally.

Item	Iridescent	Green
Berry Bowl, 4" d	5.00	6.00
Creamer, ftd	7.50	8.50
Cup	7.50	8.00
Domino Tray	—	40.00
Plate, 6" d, sherbet	4.00	5.00
Plate, 8" d, luncheon	9.00	12.00
Sandwich Plate, 12" d	15.00	17.50
Saucer	2.50	2.00
Sherbet	8.50	10.00
Sugar	7.50	8.50

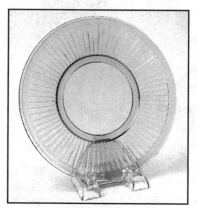

Round Robin, green plate.

Roxana

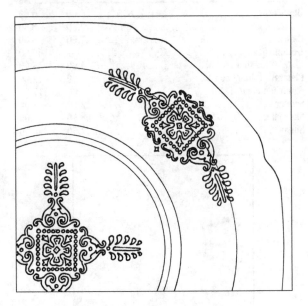

Manufactured by Hazel Atlas Glass Company, Clarksburg, W.V., and Zanesville, Ohio, in 1932.

Made in crystal, golden topaz and white. Production in white was limited to a 4-1/2" bowl, valued at $15.

Item	Crystal	Gold Topaz
Berry Bowl, 5" d	6.50	12.00
Bowl, 4-1/2" x 2-3/8"	6.00	12.00
Cereal Bowl, 6" d	7.50	15.00
Plate, 5-1/2" d	4.50	9.00
Plate, 6" d, sherbet	4.00	8.50
Sherbet, ftd	6.00	12.50
Tumbler, 9 oz, 4-1/4" h	8.50	18.00

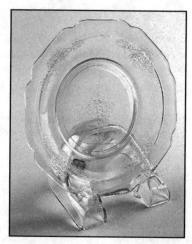

Roxana, yellow saucer.

Royal Lace

Manufactured by Hazel Atlas Glass Company, Clarksburg, W.V., and Zanesville, Ohio, from 1934 to 1941.

Made in cobalt (Ritz) blue, crystal, green, pink and some amethyst.

Reproductions: † Reproductions include a 5 oz, 3-1/2" h tumbler, found in a darker cobalt blue. A cookie jar has also been reproduced in cobalt blue.

Note: *Values for crystal Royal Lace pieces generally are 50% less than green values. However, collector demand is driving the crystal prices upward for some scarce forms.*

Note: *The nut bowl is scarce and is valued at $1,500 in cobalt blue and $400 in green or pink.*

Item	Cobalt Blue	Green	Pink
Berry Bowl, 5" d	35.00	30.00	35.00
Berry Bowl, 10" d	60.00	35.00	45.00
Bowl, 10" d, 3 legs, rolled edge	650.00	125.00	100.00
Bowl, 10" d, 3 legs, ruffled edge	675.00	125.00	100.00
Bowl, 10" d, 3 legs, straight edge	—	45.00	40.00
Butter Dish, cov	650.00	275.00	200.00
Candlesticks, pr, rolled edge	—	85.00	60.00
Candlesticks, pr, ruffled edge	—	70.00	60.00
Candlesticks, pr, straight edge	—	75.00	55.00
Cookie Jar, cov †	495.00	75.00	55.00
Cream Soup, 4-3/4" d	48.00	35.00	30.00
Creamer, ftd	60.00	25.00	20.00

Royal Lace, cookie jar with cover.

Item	Cobalt Blue	Green	Pink
Cup and Saucer	45.00	25.00	18.00
Pitcher, 48 oz, straight sides	150.00	110.00	85.00
Pitcher, 64 oz, 8" h	225.00	110.00	120.00
Pitcher, 68 oz, 8" h ice lip	240.00	—	95.00
Pitcher, 86 oz, 8" h	—	135.00	95.00
Pitcher, 96 oz, 9-1/2" h, ice lip	265.00	140.00	100.00

Royal Lace, clear plate.

Item	Cobalt Blue	Green	Pink
Plate, 6" d, sherbet	16.50	12.00	18.00
Plate, 8-1/2" d, luncheon	40.00	18.00	24.00
Plate, 9-7/8" d, dinner	42.00	30.00	27.50
Plate, 9-7/8" d, grill	40.00	25.00	22.50
Platter, 13" l, oval	60.00	45.00	48.00
Salt and Pepper Shakers, pr	250.00	130.00	80.00
Sherbet, ftd	50.00	25.00	18.00
Sherbet, metal holder	45.00	—	—
Sugar, cov	45.00	40.00	50.00
Sugar, open	—	25.00	22.00
Toddy or Cider Set	275.00	—	—
Tumbler, 5 oz, 3-1/2" h †	65.00	35.00	35.00
Tumbler, 9 oz, 4-1/8" h †	45.00	35.00	28.00
Tumbler, 10 oz, 4-7/8" h	100.00	60.00	60.00
Tumbler, 12 oz, 5-3/8" h	125.00	50.00	55.00
Vegetable Bowl, 11" l, oval	60.00	35.00	35.00

Royal Lace, 9 oz. tumbler.

Royal Ruby

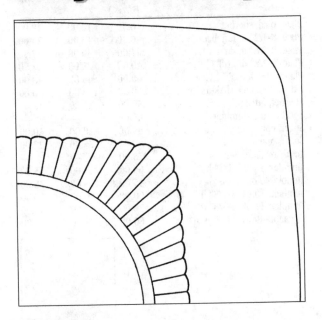

Manufactured by Anchor Hocking Glass Corporation, Lancaster, Pa., from 1938 to 1967.

Made only in Royal Ruby.

Item	*Royal Ruby*
Apothecary Jar, 8-1/2"h	22.00
Ashtray, 4-1/2", leaf	5.00
Ashtray, 5-7/8", sq	9.00
Ashtray, 7-3/4"	32.00
Beer Bottle, 7 oz	30.00
Beer Bottle, 12 oz	32.00
Beer Bottle, 16 oz	35.00
Beer Bottle, 32 oz	40.00
Berry, 4-5/8" d, small, square	9.50
Berry, 8-1/2" d, round	25.00
Bonbon, 6-1/2" d	20.00
Bowl, 7-3/8" w, sq	18.50
Bowl, 11" or 12"	50.00
Cereal Bowl, 5-1/4" d	12.00
Cigarette Box, card holder, 6-1/8" x 4"	90.00
Cocktail, 3-1/2 oz, Boopie	8.50

Royal Ruby, punch set, punch bowl and six cups.

Item	Royal Ruby
Cocktail, 3-1/2 oz, tumbler	10.00
Cordial, ftd	15.00
Creamer, flat or ftd	10.00
Cup, round or square	7.00
Dessert Bowl, 4-3/4" w, sq	9.00
Fruit Bowl, 4-1/4" d	6.50
Goblet, 9 oz	9.00
Goblet, 9-1/2 oz	14.00
Goblet, ball stem	12.00
Ice Bucket	55.00
Iced Tea Goblet, 14 oz, Boopie	20.00
Iced Tea Tumbler, 13 oz, 6" h, ftd	10.00
Ivy Ball, 4" h, Wilson	12.00
Juice Tumbler, 4 oz	7.00
Juice Tumbler, 5-1/2 oz	10.00
Juice Tumbler, 5 oz, flat or ftd	12.00
Juice Pitcher	39.00
Lamp	35.00
Marmalade, ruby top, crystal base	22.00
Pitcher, 3 qt	42.00
Pitcher, 42 oz	38.00
Pitcher, 86 oz, 8-1/2" upright	35.00
Plate, 6-1/4" d, sherbet	4.50
Plate, 7" d, salad	5.50
Plate, 7-3/4" w, sq, salad	7.50
Plate, 8-3/8" w, sq, luncheon	12.00
Plate, 9-1/8" d, dinner	14.00

Item	Royal Ruby
Plate, 13-3/4" d	35.00
Popcorn Bowl, 5-1/4" d	12.50
Popcorn Bowl, 10" d, deep	40.00
Puff Box, ruby top, crystal base, orig label	28.00
Punch Bowl and Stand	75.00
Punch Set, 14 pieces	200.00
Punch Cup	3.50
Relish, 3-3/4" x 8-3/4", tab handle	16.00
Salad Bowl, 8-1/2" d	19.00
Salad Bowl, 11-1/2" d	40.00
Saucer	4.00
Set, 50 pcs, orig labels, orig box	350.00
Sherbet, 6-1/2 oz, stemmed	7.50
Sherbet, 6 oz, Boopie	8.50
Shot Glass	4.50
Soup Bowl, 7-1/2" d	15.00
Sugar	8.00
Sugar Lid, notched	11.00
Tray, center handle, ruffled	16.50
Tumbler, 5 oz, 3-1/2" h	6.00
Tumbler, 9 oz, Windsor	8.50
Tumbler, 10 or 14 oz, 5" h	9.00
Tumbler, 15 oz, long boy	15.00
Vase, 3-3/4" h, Roosevelt	7.50
Vase, 4" h, Wilson, fancy edge	12.00
Vase, 6-3/8" h, Harding	15.00
Vase, 6-5/8" h, Coolidge	20.00

Item	Royal Ruby
Vase, 9" h, Hoover, plain	.20.00
Vase, 9" h, Hoover, white birds on branch dec	.25.00
Vase, 10" h, fluted, star base	.35.00
Vase, 10" h, ftd, Rachael	.50.00
Vegetable Bowl, 8" l, oval	.45.00
Wine, 2-1/2 oz, ftd	.12.50

Royal Ruby, sugar, creamer, (on pedestal), cup and saucer.

S-Pattern

Stippled Rose Band

Manufactured by MacBeth-Evans Glass Company, Charleroi, Pa., from 1930 to 1933.

Made in amber, crystal, crystal with amber, blue, green, pink or silver trims, fired-on red, green, light yellow and Monax.

Note: *Pieces with fired-on colors are valued at 50% more than crystal pieces with trim. However, fired-on forms are limited to creamer and sugars and cups.*

Item	Amber or Yellow	Crystal	Crystal with Trims
Berry Bowl, 8-1/2" d	8.50	12.00	—
Cake Plate, 11-3/4" d	50.00	48.00	55.00
Cake Plate, 13" d	80.00	65.00	75.00
Cereal Bowl, 5-1/2" d	6.00	4.00	6.00
Creamer, thick	7.50	6.50	8.00
Creamer, thin	7.50	6.50	8.00
Cup, thick	5.00	4.00	5.50
Cup, thin	5.00	4.00	5.50
Pitcher, 80 oz	—	65.00	—
Plate, 6" d, sherbet	3.50	3.00	4.00
Plate, 8-1/4" d, luncheon	5.00	7.00	9.50

S-Pattern, yellow tumbler.

Item	Amber or Yellow	Crystal	Crystal with Trims
Plate, 9-1/4" d, dinner	9.50	—	12.50
Plate, grill	8.50	6.50	9.00
Saucer	4.00	3.00	4.00
Sherbet, low, ftd	8.00	5.50	8.50
Sugar, thick	7.50	6.50	8.00
Sugar, thin	7.50	6.50	8.00
Tumbler, 5 oz, 3-1/2" h	6.50	5.00	6.50
Tumbler, 10 oz, 4-3/4" h	8.50	7.00	7.50
Tumbler, 12 oz, 5" h	15.00	10.00	17.50

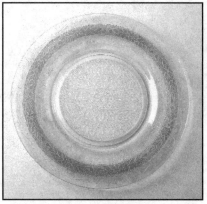

S-Pattern, crystal yellow-satin plate.

Sandwich

Hocking

Manufactured by Hocking Glass Company, and later Anchor Hocking Corporation, from 1939 to 1964.

Made in crystal, Desert Gold, 1961-64; Forest Green, 1956-1960s; pink, 1939-1940; Royal Ruby, 1938-1939; and white/ivory (opaque) 1957-1960s.

Reproductions: † The cookie jar has been reproduced in crystal.

* No cover is known for the cookie jar in Forest Green.

Note: *The secondary market for pink, royal ruby, and white is not yet established. Crystal remains the most popular color with collectors.*

Item	Crystal	Desert Gold	Forest Green
Bowl, 4-5/16" d, smooth	5.00	—	4.00
Bowl, 4-7/8" d, smooth	5.00	6.00	—
Bowl, 4-7/8" d, crimped	20.00	—	—
Bowl, 5-1/4" d, scalloped	5.00	6.00	—
Bowl, 5-1/4" d, smooth	—	—	—
Bowl, 6-1/2" d, scalloped	7.50	9.00	60.00
Bowl, 6-1/2" d, smooth	7.50	9.00	—
Bowl, 7-1/4" d, scalloped	8.00	—	—
Bowl, 8-1/4" d, oval	10.00	—	—
Bowl, 8-1/4" d, scalloped	10.00	—	80.00
Butter Dish, cov	45.00	—	—
Cereal Bowl, 6-3/4" d	32.00	12.00	—
Cookie Jar, cov † *	40.00	45.00	20.00
Creamer	6.50	—	30.00
Cup, coffee	2.00	12.00	24.00
Cup, tea	3.00	14.00	24.00
Custard Cup	7.00	—	4.00
Custard Cup Liner	5.50	—	1.50
Custard Cup, crimped	12.50	—	—
Dessert Bowl, 5" d, crimped	18.50	—	—
Juice Pitcher, 6" h	115.00	—	145.00
Juice Tumbler, 3 oz, 3-3/8" h	12.00	—	6.00
Juice Tumbler, 5 oz, 3-9/16" h	7.50	—	4.50
Pitcher, 1/2 gallon, ice lip	85.00	—	550.00
Plate, 6" d	5.00	—	—
Plate, 7" d, dessert	25.00	—	—

Item	Crystal	Desert Gold	Forest Green
Plate, 8" d, luncheon	18.00	—	—
Plate, 9" d, dinner	20.00	10.00	125.00
Plate, 9" d, indent for punch cup	12.00	—	—
Punch Bowl, 9-3/4" d	18.00	—	—
Punch Bowl and Stand	32.00	—	—
Punch Bowl Set, bowl, base, 12 cups	60.00	—	—
Punch Cup	3.00	—	—
Salad Bowl, 7" d	8.00	25.00	—
Salad Bowl, 7-5/8" d	—	—	60.00
Salad Bowl, 9" d	24.00	20.00	—
Sandwich Plate, 12" d	14.00	17.50	—
Saucer	3.50	5.00	15.00
Sherbet, ftd	8.00	8.00	—
Snack Set, plate and cup	9.00	—	—
Sugar, cov	30.00	—	—
Sugar, no cover	6.00	—	30.00

Sandwich Hocking, crystal oval bowl.

Item	Crystal	Desert Gold	Forest Green
Tumbler, 9 oz, ftd	.32.50	125.00	—
Tumbler, 9 oz, water	.9.00	—	7.00
Vase	—	—	27.50
Vegetable, 8-1/2" l, oval	.10.00	—	—

Sandwich Hocking, amber around bowl.

Sandwich

Indiana

Manufactured by Indiana Glass Company, Dunkirk, Ind., 1920s to 1980s.

Made in crystal, late 1920s to 1990s; amber, late 1920s to 1980s; milk white, mid 1950s; teal blue, 1950s to 1960s; red, 1933 and early 1970s; smoky blue, 1976 to 1977, green in the late 1960s and 1970s by Taira.

Reproductions: † Reproductions include a butter dish, decanter, and wine. Reproductions are found in dark amber, crystal, green and pink.

Note: *Because this pattern was in production for over sixty years, it is often difficult to tell new pieces from old. Look for signs of use and clearly-molded pattern details. Vintage red Indiana Sandwich was limited to creamer and sugar ($48 each), cup and saucer ($37.50), decanter ($90), and wine ($15).*

Item	Amber	Crystal	Teal Blue
Ashtray, club	3.25	4.00	—
Ashtray, diamond	3.25	4.00	—
Ashtray, heart	3.25	4.00	2.00
Ashtray, spade	3.25	4.00	—
Basket, 10" h	35.00	35.00	—
Berry Bowl, 4-1/4" d	3.50	5.00	—
Bowl, 6" w, hexagonal	5.50	6.00	15.00
Bowl, 8-1/2" d	10.00	11.00	—
Butter Dish, cov †	25.00	25.00	150.00
Candlesticks, pr, 3-1/2" h	18.00	20.00	—
Candlesticks, pr, 7" h	25.00	25.00	—
Celery Tray, 10-1/2" l	17.50	14.00	—
Cereal Bowl, 6" d	12.00	6.50	—
Cocktail, 3 oz, ftd	7.50	7.50	—
Comport, low, ruffled	15.00	—	—
Console Bowl, 9" d	17.50	17.50	—
Console Bowl, 11-1/2" d	20.00	20.00	—
Creamer	6.00	6.00	—
Creamer and Sugar, tray	18.00	18.00	35.00
Cruet, 6-1/2 oz, stopper	—	—	145.00
Cup	4.00	4.00	8.50
Decanter, stopper †	25.00	25.00	—
Fairy Lamp	15.00	—	—
Goblet, 9 oz	14.00	15.00	—
Iced Tea Tumbler, 12 oz, ftd	10.00	10.00	—
Mayonnaise, ftd	14.00	14.00	—

Item	Amber	Crystal	Teal Blue
Pitcher, 68 oz 24.00		24.00	—
Plate, 6" d, sherbet 3.50		3.50	7.50
Plate, 7" d, bread and butter 4.00		4.00	—
Plate, 8" d, oval, indent . . . . —		4.00	6.50
Plate, 8-3/8" d, luncheon 7.50		8.00	—
Plate, 10-1/2" d, dinner 9.00		8.50	20.00
Puff Box .18.00		18.00	—
Salt and Pepper Shakers, pr 18.00		18.00	—
Sandwich Plate, 13" d 14.50		14.50	25.00
Sandwich Server, center handle 20.00		20.00	—
Saucer 3.50		2.50	7.00
Sherbet, 3-1/4" h 6.00		5.50	12.00
Sugar, cov, large 20.00		20.00	—
Tumbler, 8 oz, ftd, water 10.00		10.00	—
Wine, 3" h, 4 oz † 10.00		12.00	—

Sandwich, Indiana, crystal creamer, sugar and tray.

Sandwich

Line #41

Manufactured by Duncan & Miller Glass Company, Washington, Pa., from 1924 to 1955.

Made in crystal with limited production in amber, cobalt blue, green, pink and red. The molds were sold to Lancaster Colony, which continues to produce some glass in this pattern, but in newer brighter colors, such as amberina, blue and green.

Item	Crystal
Almond Bowl, 2-1/2" d	12.00
Ashtray, 2-1/2" x 3-3/4"	10.00
Ashtray, 2-3/4" sq	8.50
Basket, 6-1/2", loop handle	135.00
Basket 10", loop handle, crimped	185.00
Basket, 10", loop handle, oval	185.00
Basket, 11-1/2", loop handle	225.00
Bonbon, 5" w, heart shape	15.00
Bonbon, 6" w, heart shape, ring handle	20.00
Bonbon, cov, 7-1/2" d, ftd	45.00
Bowl, 5-1/2" d, handle	15.00
Butter, cov, quarter pound	40.00
Cake Stand, 11-1/2" d, ftd	95.00
Cake Stand, 12" d, ftd	115.00
Cake Stand, 13" d, ftd	125.00
Candelabra, with bobeche and prisms, 10" h, 3-lite	200.00
Candelabra, with bobeche and prisms, 10" h, 1-lite	95.00
Candelabra, with bobeche and prisms, 16" h, 3-lite	225.00
Candlesticks, pr, 4" h	30.00
Candlesticks, pr, 5" h, 3-lite	90.00
Candy Box, cov, 5" d, flat	42.00
Candy Comport, 3-1/4" d, low, ftd or flared	25.00
Candy Dish, 6" sq	375.00
Candy Jar, cov, 8-1/2" d, flat	60.00
Celery Tray, 10" l, oval	30.00
Champagne, 5 oz	25.00

Item	*Crystal*
Cheese Comport, 13" d underplate	.60.00
Cheese Dish, cov	.125.00
Cigarette Box, cov, 3-1/2"	.24.00
Cigarette Holder, 3" d, ftd	.30.00
Coaster, 5" d	.12.00
Cocktail, 3 oz	.15.00
Comport, 2-1/4"	.17.50
Comport, 4-1/4" d, ftd	.22.00
Comport, 5" d, low, ftd	.22.00
Comport, 5-1/2" d, ftd, low, crimped	.25.00
Comport, 6" d, low, flared	.25.00
Condiment Set, pr cruets, pr salt & pepper shakers, tray	.100.00
Console Bowl, 12" d	.45.00
Cracker Plate, 13" d	.32.00
Creamer	.10.00
Cup	.10.00
Deviled Egg Plate, 12" d	.65.00
Epergne, 9" h	.125.00
Epergne, 12" h, 3-part	.200.00
Finger Bowl, 4" h	.12.00
Finger Bowl Underplate, 6-1/2" d	.8.00
Flower Bowl, 11-1/2" d, crimped	.60.00
Fruit Bowl, 5" d	.10.00
Fruit Bowl, 10" or 11-1/2" d	.65.00
Fruit Bowl, 12", flared	.50.00
Fruit Cup, 6 oz	.12.00

Item	*Crystal*
Fruit Salad Bowl, 6" d	12.00
Gardenia Bowl, 11-1/2" d	48.00
Goblet, 9 oz, 6" h	18.00
Grapefruit Bowl, 5-1/2" d or 6" d	17.50
Hostess Plate, 16" d	100.00
Ice Cream Dish 5 oz	12.00
Ice Cream Plate, rolled edge, 12" d	60.00
Ice Cream Tray, rolled edge, 12" d	45.00
Iced Tea Tumbler, 12 or 13 oz, ftd	20.00
Ivy Bowl, ftd, crimped	35.00
Jelly, 3" d	8.00
Juice Tumbler, 5 oz	12.00
Lazy Susan, 16" d	115.00
Lily Bowl, 10" d	55.00
Mayonnaise Set, 3 pcs	35.00
Mint Tray, 6" l or 7" l, rolled edge, ring handle	18.00
Nappy, 5" or 6" d	15.00
Nut Bowl, 3-1/2" d	10.00
Nut Bowl, 11" d, cupped	55.00
Oil Bottle, orig stopper	35.00
Oil and Vinegar Tray, 8" l	20.00
Oyster Cocktail, 5 oz	18.00
Parfait, 4 oz, ftd	30.00
Pickle Tray, 7" l, oval	15.00
Pitcher, 13 oz, metal lip	75.00
Pitcher, 64 oz, ice lip	125.00

Item	Crystal
Plate, 3" d, jelly	5.00
Plate, 6" d, bread and butter	6.00
Plate, 7" d, dessert	7.50
Plate, 8" d, salad	10.00
Plate, 9-1/2" d, dinner	35.00
Relish, 5" or 6" d, 2-part, ring handle	18.00
Relish, 7" d, 2-part, oval	20.00
Relish, 10" or 10-1/2" d, 3-part, rect	27.50
Relish, 10" d, 4-part	25.00
Relish, 12" l, 3-part	25.00
Salad Bowl, 10" d, deep	75.00
Salad Bowl, 12" d, shallow	42.00
Salt & Pepper Shakers, pr, 2-1/2" h, glass or metal tops	20.00
Salts & Pepper Shakers, set, pr 3-3/4" h, metal tops, 6" tray	35.00
Service Plate, 11-1/2" d, handle	50.00
Service Plate, 13" d	55.00
Sugar Shaker	72.00
Sugar Bowl, 5 oz	10.00
Sugar Bowl, 9 oz, 3-1/4" h, ftd	12.00
Sundae, 5 oz	15.00
Torte Plate, 12" d	48.00
Tray, 8" l	20.00
Urn, cov, 12" h, ftd	150.00
Tumbler, 9 oz, 4-3/4", ftd	15.00
Vase, 3" h	18.00
Vase, 4" h, hat shape	20.00

Item	Crystal
Vase, 4-1/2" h, crimped	25.00
Vase, 5" h, fan	40.00
Vase, 5" h, flared or crimped	25.00
Vase, 10" h, ftd	70.00
Wine, 3 oz	24.00

Sandwich, 8" d crystal plate.

Sharon

Cabbage Rose

Manufactured by Federal Glass Company, Columbus, Ohio, from 1935 to 1939.

Made in amber, crystal, green and pink. Production was limited in crystal.

Reproductions: † Reproductions include the butter dish, cov candy dish, creamer, cov sugar and salt and pepper shakers. Reproduction colors include dark amber, blue, green and pink.

Item	Amber	Green	Pink
Berry Bowl, 5" d 8.50		18.50	15.00
Berry Bowl, 8-1/2" d 10.00		40.00	35.00
Butter Dish, cov † 48.00		85.00	65.00
Cake Plate, 11-1/2" d, ftd 30.00		65.00	50.00
Candy Dish, cov † 45.00		100.00	65.00
Cereal, 6" d 24.00		32.00	30.00
Champagne, 5" d bowl . . . . —		—	12.00
Cheese Dish, cov † 225.00		—	950.00
Cream Soup, 5" d 28.00		60.00	50.00
Creamer, ftd † 15.00		22.00	24.00
Cup and Saucer 15.00		42.00	30.00
Fruit Bowl, 10-1/2" d 24.00		40.00	55.00
Iced Tea Tumbler, ftd 125.00		—	65.00
Jam Dish, 7-1/2" d 40.00		48.00	215.00

Sharon, pink sherbet, two bowls and creamer.

Item	Amber	Green	Pink
Pitcher, 80 oz 145.00		150.00	165.00
Plate, 6" d, bread and butter 16.00		9.00	16.50
Plate, 7-1/2" d, salad 16.50		8.00	30.00
Plate, 9-1/2" d, dinner 17.00		27.50	24.50
Platter, 12-1/2" l, oval 24.00		35.00	40.00
Salt and Pepper Shakers, pr † . . .40.00		80.00	65.00
Sherbet, ftd 14.00		35.00	19.50
Soup, flat, 7-3/4" d, 1-7/8" deep . . .60.00		—	65.00
Sugar, cov † 35.00		55.00	60.00
Tumbler, 9 oz, 4-1/8" h, thick 30.00		65.00	45.00
Tumbler, 9 oz, 4-1/8" h, thin 38.00		65.00	42.00
Tumbler, 12 oz, 5-1/4" h, thick or thin 55.00		95.00	50.00
Tumbler, 15 oz, 6-1/2" h, thick 125.00		—	63.00
Vegetable Bowl, 9-1/2" l, oval 25.00		35.00	42.50

REPRODUCTION! Sharon, pink covered candy dish.

Sharon, amber dinner plate.

Ships

Sailboat, Sportsman Series
White Ship

Manufactured by Hazel Atlas Glass Company, Clarksburg, W.V., and Zanesville, Ohio, late 1930s.

Made in cobalt blue with white, yellow, and red decoration. Pieces with yellow or red decoration are valued slightly higher than the traditional white decoration.

Item	Cobalt Blue with White Decoration
Ashtray	.60.00
Ashtray, metal sailboat	.120.00
Box, cov, three-part	.250.00
Cocktail Mixer, stirrer	.45.00
Cocktail Shaker	.45.00
Cup	.15.00
Ice Bowl	.45.00
Iced Tea Tumbler, 10-1/2 oz, 4-7/8" h	.22.00
Iced Tea Tumbler, 12 oz	.24.00
Juice Tumbler, 5 oz, 3-3/4" h	.12.50
Old Fashioned Tumbler, 8 oz, 3-3/8" h	.22.00
Pitcher, 82 oz, no ice lip	.85.00
Pitcher, 86 oz, ice lip	.75.00
Plate, 5-7/8" d, bread and butter	.24.00
Plate, 8" d, salad	.27.50
Plate, 9" d, dinner	.32.00
Roly Poly, 6 oz	.10.00
Saucer	.18.00
Shot Glass, 2 oz, 2-1/4" h	.250.00
Tumbler, 4 oz, 3-1/4" h, heavy bottom	.27.50
Tumbler, 4 oz, heavy bottom	.12.00
Tumbler, 9 oz, 3-3/4" h	.18.00
Tumbler, 9 oz, 4-5/8" h	.18.00
Whiskey, 3-1/2" h	.45.00

Ships, cobalt blue cocktail shaker.

Ships, cobalt blue luncheon plate.

Ships, cobalt blue dinner plate.

Sierra

Pinwheel

Manufactured by Jeannette Glass Company, Jeannette, Pa., from 1931 to 1933.

Made in green and pink. A few forms are known in Ultramarine.

Item	Green	Pink
Berry, small	.25.00	25.00
Berry Bowl, 8-1/2" d	.40.00	40.00
Butter Dish, cov	.75.00	80.00
Cereal Bowl, 5-1/2" d	.25.00	20.00
Creamer	.25.00	25.00
Cup	.19.50	17.50
Pitcher, 32 oz, 6-1/2" h	.160.00	120.00
Plate, 9" d, dinner	.30.00	32.00
Platter, 11" l, oval	.70.00	65.00
Salt and Pepper Shakers, pr	.50.00	50.00
Saucer	.10.00	10.00
Serving Tray, 10-1/4" l, 2 handles	.25.00	25.00
Sugar, cov	.48.00	48.00
Tumbler, 9 oz, 4-1/2" h, ftd	.90.00	80.00
Vegetable Bowl, 9-1/4" l, oval	.125.00	80.00

Sierra Pinwheel, green butter dish and pink cup and saucer.

Sierra Pinwheel, pink plate.

Spiral

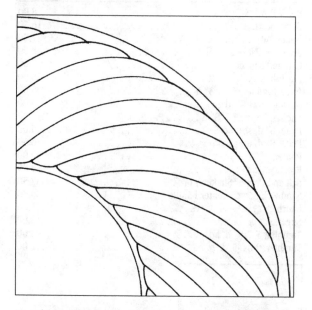

Manufactured by Hocking Glass Company, Lancaster, Ohio, from 1928 to 1930.

Made in crystal, green, and pink. Collector interest is strongest in green.

Item	Green
Berry Bowl, 4-3/4" d	8.00
Berry Bowl, 8" d	16.50
Butter Tub	27.50
Creamer, flat or footed	8.00
Cup and Saucer	9.00
Ice Tub	25.00
Juice Tumbler, 5 oz, 3" h	5.00
Mixing Bowl, 7" d	9.00
Pitcher, 58 oz, 7-5/8" h	35.00
Plate, 6" d, sherbet	5.00
Plate, 8" d, luncheon	6.50
Platter, 12" l	30.00
Preserve, cov	32.00
Salt and Pepper Shakers, pr	37.50
Sandwich Server, center handle	30.00
Sherbet	5.00
Sugar, flat or footed	8.00
Tumbler, 5-7/8" h, ftd	24.00
Tumbler, 9 oz, 5" h	12.00

Spiral, green plate and sherbet.

Star

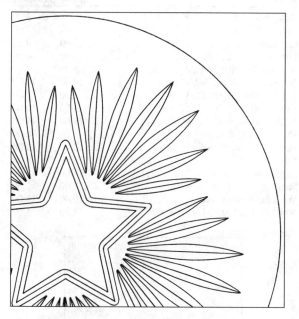

Manufactured by Federal Glass Company, Columbus, Ohio, 1950s.

Made in amber, crystal and crystal with gold trim. Crystal pieces with gold trim would be valued the same as plain crystal.

Item	Amber	Crystal
Bowl, 4-5/8" d	—	5.00
Bowl, 5-5/8" d	—	7.00
Creamer	7.00	9.00
Cup	10.00	10.00
Iced Tea Tumbler, 12 oz, 5-1/8" h	8.00	9.00
Juice Pitcher, 36 oz, 5-3/4" h	10.00	12.00
Juice Tumbler, 4-1/2 oz, 3-3/8" h	4.00	5.00
Pitcher, 60 oz, 7" h	12.00	14.00
Pitcher, 85 oz, 9-1/4" h, ice lip	15.00	15.00
Plate, 6-3/16" d, salad	5.00	6.00
Plate, 9-3/8" d, dinner	12.00	14.00
Saucer	3.00	3.00
Sugar, cov	15.00	15.00
Tumbler, 9 oz, 3-7/8" h, water	7.00	7.50
Vegetable Bowl, 8-3/8" d	10.00	15.00
Whiskey, 1-1/2 oz, 2-1/4" h	4.00	5.00

Star, crystal bowl and two pitchers.

Starlight

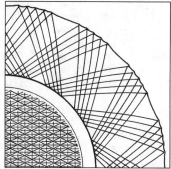

*Starlight, crystal salt
and pepper shakers.*

Manufactured by Hazel Atlas Glass Company, Clarksburg, W.V., and Zanesville, Ohio, from 1938 to 1940.

Made in cobalt blue, crystal, pink and white. Production in cobalt blue was limited to 8-1/2" d bowl, valued at $30.

Item	Crystal	Pink	White
Berry Bowl	9.50	—	—
Bowl, 8-1/2" d, 2 handles	18.00	20.00	18.00
Bowl, 11-1/2" d, deep	25.00	—	25.00
Bowl, 12" d, 2-3/4" deep	25.00	—	25.00
Cereal Bowl, 5-1/2" d, 2 handles	7.00	10.00	7.00
Creamer, oval	10.00	—	5.00
Cup	6.00	—	4.00
Plate, 6" d, sherbet	4.50	—	4.00
Plate, 7-1/2" d, salad	5.00	—	4.50
Plate, 8-1/2" d, luncheon	5.00	—	5.00
Plate, 9" d, dinner	8.50	—	8.50
Relish Dish	15.00	—	15.00
Salad Bowl, 11-1/2" d, deep	27.50	—	27.50
Salt and Pepper Shakers, pr	30.00	—	30.00
Sandwich Plate, 13" d	25.00	20.00	—
Saucer	4.00	—	2.50
Sherbet	15.00	—	12.00
Sugar, oval	10.00	—	10.00

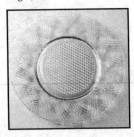

Starlight, crystal plate.

Strawberry

Manufactured by U.S. Glass Company, Pittsburgh, early 1930s.

Made in crystal, green, pink and some iridescent.

Item	Crystal or Iridescent	Green	Pink
Berry Bowl, 4" d	7.50	9.00	10.00
Berry Bowl, 7-1/2" d	16.00	20.00	20.00
Bowl, 6-1/4" d, 2" deep	40.00	60.00	60.00
Butter Dish, cov	125.00	150.00	150.00
Comport, 5-3/4" d	55.00	60.00	60.00
Creamer, large, 4-5/8" h	24.00	35.00	35.00
Creamer, small	12.00	18.50	18.50

Item	Crystal or Iridescent	Green	Pink
Olive Dish, 5" l, one handle	8.50	14.00	14.00
Pickle Dish, 8-1/4" l, oval	8.00	14.00	14.00
Pitcher, 7-3/4" h	150.00	150.00	150.00
Plate, 6" d, sherbet	5.00	13.50	8.00
Plate, 7-1/2" d, salad	10.00	14.00	15.00
Salad Bowl, 6-1/2" d	15.00	20.00	20.00
Sherbet	6.00	13.50	13.50
Sugar, large, cov	60.00	85.00	85.00
Sugar, small, open	12.00	32.00	32.00
Tumbler, 8 oz, 3-5/8" h	20.00	32.00	38.00

Strawberry, pink plate.

Sunburst

Herringbone

Manufactured by Jeannette Glass Company, Jeannette, Pa., late 1930s.

Made in crystal.

Item	*Crystal*
Berry Bowl, 4-3/4" d	6.50
Berry Bowl, 8-1/2" d	15.00
Bowl, 10-1/2" d	22.00
Candlesticks, pr, double	35.00
Creamer, ftd	16.00
Cup and Saucer	9.50
Plate, 5-1/2" d	12.00
Plate, 9-1/4" d, dinner	15.00
Relish, 2 part	14.50
Sandwich Plate, 11-3/4" d	15.00
Sherbet	12.00
Sugar	16.00
Tumbler, 4" h, 9 oz, flat	18.50

Sunburst, clear sandwich plate.

Sunflower

Manufactured by Jeannette Glass Company, Jeannette, Pa., 1930s.

Made in Delphite, green, pink and some opaque colors. Look for a creamer in Delphite, valued at $85.

Item	Green	Pink	Opaque
Ashtray, 5" d	15.00	10.00	—
Cake Plate, 10" d, 3 legs	20.00	16.00	—
Creamer	20.00	20.00	85.00
Cup	14.50	13.50	75.00
Plate, 9" d, dinner	20.00	16.00	—
Saucer	13.50	12.00	85.00
Sugar	23.00	20.00	—
Trivet, 7" d, 3 legs, turned up edge	325.00	315.00	—
Tumbler, 8 oz, 4-3/8" h, ftd	35.00	32.00	—

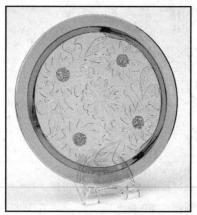

Sunflower, green cake plate.

Swirl (Fire-King)

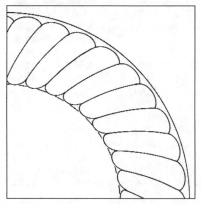

Manufactured by Anchor-Hocking, 1950s.

Made in Azur-ite, ivory, ivory with gold trim, ivory with red trim, Jade-ite (1960s), pink, white and white with gold trim.

Item	Asur-ite	Ivory	Jade-ite
Cereal Bowl, 6-3/8" d	—	—	16.00
Creamer, flat	6.00	4.00	—
Creamer, ftd	—	5.00	6.00
Cup	6.50	3.00	4.00
Fruit or Dessert Bowl, 4-7/8"	4.60	3.00	5.00
Iced Tea Tumbler, 12 oz	7.00	—	—

Item	Asur-ite	Ivory	Jade-ite
Juice Tumbler, 1 oz	5.00	—	—
Mixing Bowl, 6" d	—	8.00	12.00
Mixing Bowl, 7" d	—	15.00	14.00
Mixing Bowl, 9" d	—	18.00	16.00
Plate, 7-1/8" d, salad	8.00	6.50	12.00
Plate, 9-1/8" d, dinner	9.50	6.00	50.00
Platter, 12" x 9"	22.00	7.00	—
Saucer, 5-3/4" d	2.50	3.50	2.00
Serving Plate, 11" d	18.00	—	—
Soup Plate, 7-5/8" d	9.00	12.00	8.50
Sugar lid for flat sugar	6.00	3.00	—
Sugar lid for ftd sugar	—	3.00	20.00
Sugar, flat, tab handles	6.50	4.00	—
Sugar, ftd, open handles	—	3.50	30.00
Tumbler, 9 oz, water	15.00	—	—
Vegetable Bowl, 7-1/4" d	15.00	—	—
Vegetable Bowl, 8-1/4" d	15.00	—	18.00

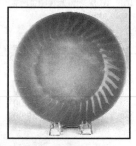

Swirl (Fire-King)
pink plate.

Item	Pink	White	White/Trim
Cereal Bowl, 6-3/8" d	—	—	—
Creamer, flat	9.00	4.50	—
Creamer, ftd	—	5.00	6.00
Cup	7.00	3.00	3.50
Fruit or Dessert Bowl, 4-7/8" .	4.60	4.00	8.00
Iced Tea Tumbler, 12 oz	7.00	—	—
Juice Tumbler, 1 oz	5.00	—	—
Mixing Bowl, 6" d	—	9.00	—
Mixing Bowl, 7" d	—	12.00	—
Mixing Bowl, 9" d	—	16.00	—
Plate, 7-1/8" d, salad	8.00	6.50	10.00
Plate, 9-1/8" d, dinner	21.00	5.00	15.00
Platter, 12" x 9"	18.00	7.00	20.00
Saucer, 5-3/4" d	4.00	2.00	7.50
Serving Plate, 11" d	20.00	—	—
Soup Plate, 7-5/8" d	14.00	5.00	6.50
Sugar lid for flat sugar	6.00	3.00	—
Sugar lid for ftd sugar	—	3.00	—
Sugar, flat, tab handles	6.50	4.00	—
Sugar, ftd, open handles	—	4.00	6.00
Tumbler, 9 oz, water	15.00	—	—
Vegetable Bowl, 7-1/4" d	15.00	—	—
Vegetable Bowl, 8-1/4" d	15.00	7.50	15.00

Swirl

Petal Swirl

Manufactured by Jeannette Glass Company, Jeannette, Pa., from 1937 to 1938.

Made in amber, Delphite, ice blue, pink and Ultramarine. Production was limited in amber and ice blue.

Item	Delphite	Pink	Ultra-marine
Berry Bowl	—	—	18.00
Bowl, 10" d, ftd, closed handles	—	25.00	30.00
Butter Dish, cov	—	175.00	245.00
Candleholders, pr, double branch	—	40.00	45.00
Candleholders, pr, single branch	115.00	—	—
Candy Dish, cov	—	130.00	150.00
Candy Dish, open, 3 legs	—	20.00	29.50
Cereal Bowl, 5-1/4" d	14.00	10.00	15.00
Coaster, 1" x 3-1/4"	—	15.00	14.00
Console Bowl, 10-1/2" d, ftd	—	20.00	35.00
Creamer	12.00	9.50	18.00
Cup and Saucer	17.50	14.00	22.50
Plate, 6-1/2" d, sherbet	6.50	5.00	8.00
Plate, 7-1/4" d, luncheon	—	6.50	12.00
Plate, 8" d, salad	9.00	8.50	12.00

Swirl, Ultramarine sugar and creamer.

Item	*Delphite*	*Pink*	*Ultra-marine*
Plate, 9-1/4" d, dinner	12.00	13.00	22.50
Plate, 10-1/2" d, dinner	18.00	—	30.00
Platter, 12" l, oval	35.00	—	—
Salad Bowl, 9" d	30.00	18.00	35.00
Salad Bowl, 9" d, rimmed	—	20.00	30.00

*Swirl, ultramarine
8-1/2" footed vase.*

*Swirl, ultramarine
covered candy dish.*

Item	Delphite	Pink	Ultra-marine
Salt and Pepper Shakers, pr .... —		—	50.00
Sandwich Plate, 12-1/2" d ..... —		20.00	27.50
Sherbet, low, ftd .... —		13.00	23.00
Soup, tab handles, lug .... —		25.00	35.00
Sugar, ftd .... —		12.00	18.00
Tray, 10-1/2" l, two handles ...25.00		—	—
Tumbler, 9 oz .... —		18.00	42.00
Tumbler, 13 oz, 5-1/8" h ...... —		45.00	90.00
Vase, 6-1/2" h, ftd, ruffled ..... —		22.00	—
Vase, 8-1/2" h, ftd .... —		—	36.00

Swirl, 9" salad bowl.

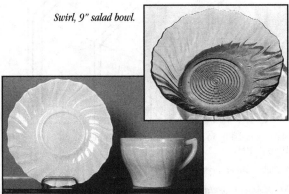

Swirl, delphite cup and saucer.

Tea Room

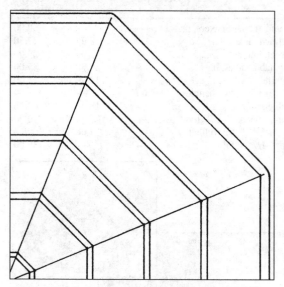

Manufactured by Indiana Glass Company, Dunkirk, Ind., from 1926 to 1931.

Made in amber, crystal, green and pink.

Note: *Amber production limited to creamer and sugar ($80 each), pitcher ($425), 8 oz tumbler ($75).*

Item	Crystal	Green	Pink
Banana Split Bowl, 7-1/2" l 75.00		100.00	145.00
Candlesticks, pr, low . . . . —		48.00	85.00
Celery Bowl, 8-1/2"d . . . . —		35.00	27.50
Creamer, 3-1/4" h . . . . —		30.00	28.00
Creamer, 4-1/2" h, ftd . . . . —		20.00	18.00
Creamer and Sugar on Tray . . . . —		180.00	75.00
Cup . . . . —		65.00	60.00
Finger Bowl 79.00		50.00	40.00
Goblet, 9 oz . . . . —		75.00	65.00
Ice Bucket . . . . —		85.00	80.00
Lamp, electric 140.00		175.00	145.00
Mustard, cov . . . . —		160.00	140.00

Tea Room, pink sugar and creamer.

Item	Crystal	Green	Pink
Parfait	—	72.00	65.00
Pitcher, 64 oz	400.00	150.00	135.00
Plate, 6-1/2" d, sherbet	—	35.00	32.00
Plate, 8-1/4" d, luncheon	—	37.50	35.00
Plates, 10-1/2" d, two handles	—	50.00	45.00
Relish, divided	—	30.00	25.00
Salad Bowl, 8-3/4" d, deep	—	150.00	135.00
Salt and Pepper Shakers, pr, ftd	—	60.00	55.00
Saucer	—	30.00	25.00

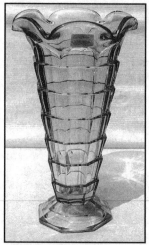

Tea Room, 11" pink vase.

Item	Crystal	Green	Pink
Sherbet	—	39.50	35.00
Sugar, 3" h, cov	—	115.00	100.00
Sugar, 4-1/2" h, ftd	—	20.00	18.00
Sugar, cov, flat	—	200.00	170.00
Sundae, ftd, ruffled	—	85.00	70.00
Tumbler, 6 oz, ftd	—	35.00	32.00
Tumbler, 8 oz, 5-1/4" h, ftd	—	35.00	32.00
Tumbler, 11 oz, ftd	—	45.00	40.00
Tumbler, 12 oz, ftd	—	60.00	55.00
Vase, 6-1/2" h, ruffled edge	—	145.00	125.00
Vase, 9-1/2" h, ruffled	50.00	175.00	100.00
Vase, 9-1/2" h, straight	175.00	95.00	225.00
Vase, 11" h, ruffled edge	—	350.00	395.00
Vase, 11" h, straight	—	200.00	395.00
Vegetable Bowl, 9-1/2" l, oval	—	75.00	65.00

Tea Room, 11 oz footed tumbler.

Thistle

Manufactured by MacBeth-Evans, Charleroi, Pa., about 1929 to 1930.

Made in crystal, green, pink and yellow. Production was limited in crystal and yellow.

Reproductions: † Recent reproductions have been found in pink, a darker emerald green and wisteria. Several of the reproductions have a scalloped edge. Reproductions include the cake plate, fruit bowl, pitcher, salt and pepper shakers, and a small tumbler.

Item	Green	Pink
Cake Plate, 13" d, heavy †	150.00	125.00
Cereal Bowl, 5-1/2" d	29.50	29.50
Cup, thin	32.00	24.00
Fruit Bowl, 10-1/4" d †	295.00	195.00
Plate, 8" d, luncheon	24.00	20.00
Plate, 10-1/4" d, grill	32.00	28.00
Saucer	12.00	12.00

Thistle, green plate.

Thumbprint

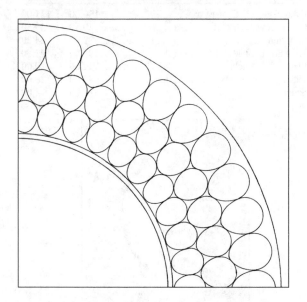

Manufactured by Federal Glass Company, Columbus, Ohio, from 1927 to 1930.

Made in green.

Item	Green
Berry Bowl, 4-3/4" d	10.00
Berry Bowl, 8" d	25.00
Cereal Bowl, 5" d	10.00
Creamer, ftd	12.00
Cup	8.00
Fruit Bowl, 5" d	10.00
Juice Tumbler, 4" h	6.00
Plate, 6" d, sherbet	4.50
Plate, 8" d, luncheon	7.00
Plate, 9-1/4" d, dinner	24.00
Salt and Pepper Shakers, pr.	65.00
Saucer	4.00
Sherbet	9.00
Sugar, ftd	12.00
Tumbler, 5" h	8.00
Tumbler, 5-1/2" h	10.00
Whiskey, 2-1/4" h	6.50

Thumbprint, green plate.

Tulip

Manufactured by Dell Glass Company, Millville, N. J., early 1930s.

Made in amber, amethyst, blue, crystal and green.

Item	Amber or Crystal	Amethyst or Blue	Green
Bowl, 6" d	20.00	18.00	20.00
Bowl, 13-1/4" l, oblong oval	40.00	50.00	40.00
Candleholders, pr, 3-3/4" h	24.50	30.00	27.50
Candy, cov	32.00	45.00	32.00
Creamer	15.00	20.00	25.00
Cup	12.00	18.00	16.00
Decanter, orig stopper	42.00	50.00	42.00
Ice Tub, 4-7/8" wide, 3" deep	24.00	35.00	24.00
Juice Tumbler	15.00	17.50	15.00
Plate, 6" d	10.00	12.00	10.00
Plate, 7-1/4" d	12.00	24.00	24.00
Plate, 10-1/4" d	35.00	40.00	35.00
Saucer	10.00	8.50	12.00
Sherbet, 3-3/4" h, flat	8.50	12.00	20.00
Sugar	15.00	20.00	15.00
Whiskey	19.50	20.00	20.00

Tulip, green creamer.

Turquoise Blue (Fire-King)

Turquoise Blue (Fire-King), snack plate with indent for cup.

Turquoise Blue (Fire-King), snack set in original box.

Manufactured by Anchor-Hocking from 1957 to 1958.

Made in turquoise blue. Some forms have a gold edge.

Item	Turquoise Blue
Ashtray, 3-1/2" d	7.50
Ashtray, 4-5/8" d	8.50
Ashtray, 5-3/4" d	12.00
Batter Bowl, spout	200.00
Berry Bowl, 4-1/2" d	10.00
Cereal Bowl, 5" d	15.00
Creamer	8.50
Cup	5.00
Egg Plate, 9-3/4" d	18.00
Mixing Bowl, 1 pt, tear	15.00
Mixing Bowl, 1 qt, round	18.00
Mixing Bowl, 1 qt, tear	20.00
Mixing Bowl, 2 qt, round	24.00
Mixing Bowl, 2 qt, tear	28.00
Mixing Bowl, 3 qt, round	30.00
Mixing Bowl, 3 qt, tear	30.00
Mixing Bowl, 4 qt, round	35.00
Mug, 8 oz	15.00
Plate, 6-1/8" d	12.50
Plate, 7" d	12.00
Plate, 9" d	8.00
Plate, 9" d, cup indent	7.50
Plate, 10" d, dinner	30.00
Relish, 11-1/8" l, 3 part	15.00
Saucer	2.00
Soup/Salad Bowl, 6-5/8"	24.00
Sugar	10.00
Vegetable Bowl, 8" d	18.00

Twisted Optic

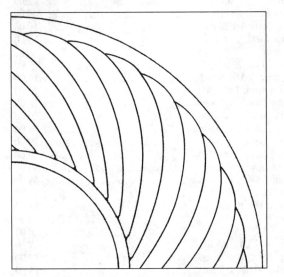

Manufactured by Imperial Glass Company, Bellaire, Ohio, from 1927 to 1930.

Made in amber, blue, canary, green and pink.

Item	Amber	Blue or Canary	Green or Pink
Basket, 10" h	42.00	75.00	45.00
Bowl, 7" d, ruffled	—	—	—
Bowl, 9" d	18.50	28.50	18.50
Bowl, 11-1/2" d, 4-1/4" h	24.00	48.00	24.00
Candlesticks, pr, 3" h	22.00	40.00	22.00
Candlesticks, pr, 8" h	30.00	50.00	30.00
Candy Jar, cov, flat	25.00	50.00	25.00
Candy Jar, cov, flat or ftd, flange edge	35.00	60.00	33.00
Candy Jar, cov, ftd, short or tall	40.00	70.00	40.00
Cereal Bowl, 5" d	6.50	10.00	6.50
Cologne Bottle, stopper	45.00	65.00	45.00
Console Bowl, 10-1/2" d	25.00	35.00	25.00
Cream Soup, 4-3/4" d	12.00	18.00	12.00
Creamer	8.00	14.00	8.00
Cup	7.50	10.00	5.00
Mayonnaise	20.00	35.00	20.00
Pitcher, 64 oz.	32.00	—	30.00
Plate, 6" d, sherbet	2.50	4.50	2.50
Plate, 7" d, salad	3.50	6.50	3.50
Plate, 7-1/2 x 9" l, oval	6.00	10.00	6.00
Plate, 8" d, luncheon	6.00	9.00	6.00
Powder Jar, cov	38.00	65.00	38.00
Preserve Jar	30.00	—	30.00
Salad Bowl, 7" d	12.00	15.00	12.00
Sandwich Plate, 10" d	10.00	17.50	10.00

Item	Amber	Blue or Canary	Green or Pink
Sandwich Server, center handle	22.00	35.00	22.00
Sandwich Server, two-handles, flat	15.00	20.00	15.00
Saucer	2.50	4.50	2.50
Sherbet	7.50	12.00	7.00
Sugar	8.00	14.00	8.00
Tumbler, 4-1/2" h, 9 oz	6.50	—	6.50
Tumbler, 5-1/4" h, 12 oz	9.50	—	9.50
Vase, 7-1/4" h, 2 handles, rolled edge	20.00	50.00	—
Vase, 8" h, 2 handles, fan	32.00	65.00	30.00
Vase, 8" h, 2 handles, straight edge	30.00	65.00	30.00

U.S. Swirl

Manufactured by U.S. Glass Company, late 1920s.

Made in crystal, green, iridescent and pink. Production in crystal and iridescent was limited.

Item	Green	Pink
Berry Bowl, 4-3/8" d	8.00	10.00
Berry Bowl, 7-7/8" d	15.00	17.00
Bowl, 5-1/2" d, handle	10.00	12.00
Bowl, 8-1/4" l, 2-3/4" h, oval	40.00	40.00
Bowl, 8-3/8" l, 1-3/4" h, oval	50.00	50.00
Butter Dish, cov	115.00	115.00
Candy, cov, 2 handles	30.00	32.00
Creamer	15.00	17.50
Pitcher, 48 oz, 8" h	55.00	50.00
Plate, 6-1/8" d, sherbet	3.00	2.50
Plate, 7-7/8" d, salad	6.00	6.50
Salt and Pepper Shakers, pr	48.00	45.00
Sherbet, 3-1/4" h	5.00	6.00
Sugar, cov	35.00	32.00
Tumbler, 8 oz, 3-5/8" h	12.00	12.00
Tumbler, 12 oz, 4-3/4" h	15.00	17.50
Vase, 6-1/2" h	25.00	25.00

U.S. Swirl, green pitcher.

Vernon

No. 616

Manufactured by Indiana Glass Company, Dunkirk, Ind., from 1930 to 1932.

Made in crystal, green and yellow.

Item	Crystal	Green	Yellow
Creamer, ftd 12.00		25.00	25.00
Cup 10.00		15.00	18.00
Plate, 8" d, luncheon 7.00		10.00	12.00
Sandwich Plate, 11-1/2" d 14.00		25.00	25.00
Saucer 4.00		6.00	6.00
Sugar, ftd .12.00		25.00	25.00
Tumbler, 5" h, ftd 15.00		35.00	35.00

Vernon, yellow tumbler.

Victory

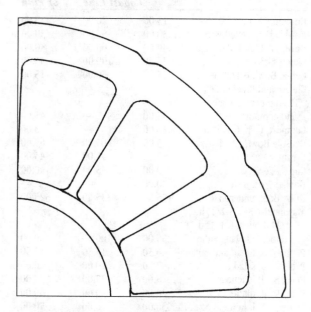

Manufactured by Diamond Glass-Ware Company, Indiana, Pa.,
from 1929 to 1932.

Made in amber, black, cobalt blue, green and pink.

Item	Amber	Black or Cobalt Blue	Green or Pink
Bonbon, 7" d	15.00	20.00	15.00
Bowl, 11" d, rolled edge	30.00	50.00	30.00
Bowl, 12-1/2" d, flat edge	30.00	60.00	30.00
Candlesticks, pr, 3" h	35.00	100.00	35.00
Cereal Bowl, 6-1/2" d	15.00	30.00	15.00
Cheese and Cracker Set, 12" d indented plate and comport	45.00	—	45.00
Comport, 6" h, 6-1/4" d	18.00	—	18.00
Console Bowl, 12" d	35.00	65.00	65.00
Creamer	17.50	45.00	45.00
Cup	10.00	35.00	40.00
Goblet, 7 oz, 5" h	20.00	—	—
Gravy Boat, underplate	185.00	325.00	325.00
Mayonnaise Set, 3-1/2" h, 5-1/2" d bowl, 8-1/2" d indented plate, ladle	55.00	100.00	100.00
Plate, 6" d, bread and butter	6.50	17.50	17.50
Plate, 7" d, salad	7.50	20.00	20.00
Plate, 8" d, luncheon	8.00	27.00	27.00
Plate, 9" d, dinner	20.00	40.00	40.00
Platter, 12" l, oval	30.00	70.00	70.00
Sandwich Server, center handle	30.00	65.00	65.00
Saucer	5.00	12.50	12.50
Sherbet, ftd	15.00	27.50	27.50

Item	Amber	Black or Cobalt Blue	Green or Pink
Soup Bowl, 8-1/2" d, flat	.20.00	45.00	45.00
Sugar	.15.00	45.00	45.00
Vegetable Bowl, 9" l, oval	.35.00	85.00	85.00

Victory, pink creamer and sugar.

Vitrock

Flower Rim

Manufactured by Hocking Glass Company, Lancaster, Ohio, from 1934 to 1937.

Made in white and white with fired-on colors.

Item	Fire-On Colors	White
Berry Bowl, 4" d	9.50	7.50
Cereal Bowl, 7-1/2" d	12.00	8.50
Cream Soup, 5-1/2" d	16.00	14.00
Creamer, oval	10.00	7.50
Cup	8.50	6.00
Fruit Bowl, 6" d	10.00	8.00
Plate, 7-1/4" d, salad	7.50	4.50
Plate, 8-3/4" d, luncheon	12.00	6.50
Plate, 10" d, dinner	15.00	10.00
Platter, 11-1/2" l	50.00	35.00
Saucer	7.50	4.50
Soup Bowl, flat	48.00	35.00
Sugar	12.00	7.50
Vegetable Bowl, 9-1/2" d	24.00	18.00

Vitrock, white bowl and plate.

Waterford

Waffle

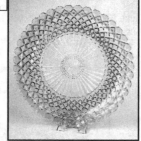

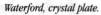
Waterford, crystal plate.

Manufactured by Hocking Glass Company, Lancaster, Ohio, from 1938 to 1944.

Made in crystal, Forest Green (1950s), pink, white and yellow. Forest Green production was limited; currently an ashtray is valued at $5. Yellow was also limited. Collector interest is low in white.

Item	Crystal	Pink
Ashtray, 4" d	7.50	—
Berry Bowl, 4-3/4" d	8.50	18.00
Berry Bowl, 8-1/4" d	12.00	30.00
Butter Dish, cov	30.00	250.00
Cake Plate, 10-1/4" d, handles	15.00	20.00
Cereal Bowl, 5-1/2" d	18.50	32.00
Coaster, 4" d	7.50	—
Creamer, oval	6.00	15.00
Cup	7.50	18.00
Goblet, 5-1/4" h	15.00	—
Goblet, 5-5/8" h	20.00	—
Juice Pitcher, 42 oz, tilted	30.00	—
Lamp, 4" spherical base	45.00	—
Pitcher, 80 oz, tilted, ice lip	32.00	150.00
Plate, 6" d, sherbet	4.50	9.50
Plate, 7-1/8" d, salad	9.00	18.00
Plate, 9-5/8" d, dinner	12.50	24.00
Platter, 14" l	14.00	—
Relish, 13-3/4" d, 5 part	16.00	—
Salt and Pepper Shakers, pr	12.00	—
Sandwich Plate, 13-3/4" d	15.00	32.00
Saucer	3.00	5.00
Sherbet, ftd	4.50	15.00
Sherbet, ftd, scalloped base	8.00	—
Sugar	7.50	15.00
Sugar Lid, oval	5.00	25.00
Tray	7.50	—
Tumbler, 10 oz, 4-7/8" h, ftd	18.00	27.50

Windsor

Windsor Diamond

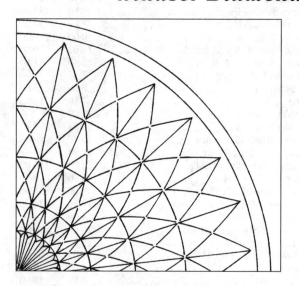

Manufactured by Jeannette Glass Company, Jeannette, Pa., from 1936 to 1946.

Made in crystal, green and pink with limited production in amberina red, Delphite and ice blue.

Item	Crystal	Green	Pink
Ashtray, 5-3/4" d 15.00		45.00	45.00
Berry Bowl, 4-3/4" d 5.00		12.00	10.00
Berry Bowl, 8-1/2" d 7.50		18.50	22.00
Bowl, 5" l, pointed edge 10.00		—	25.00
Bowl, 7" x 11-3/4", boat shape 18.00		35.00	32.00
Bowl, 7-1/2" d, 3 legs 8.00		—	24.00
Bowl, 8" d, 2 handles 9.00		24.00	20.00
Bowl, 8" l, pointed edge 10.00		—	48.00
Bowl, 10-1/2" l, pointed edge 25.00		—	32.00
Butter Dish, cov 27.50		95.00	60.00
Cake Plate, 10-3/4" d, ftd 12.00		22.00	20.00
Candlesticks, pr, 3" h 22.00		—	85.00
Candy Jar, cov 18.00		—	—
Cereal Bowl, 5-3/8" d 10.00		32.50	25.00
Chop Plate, 13-5/8" d 24.00		42.00	50.00
Coaster, 3-1/4" d 8.50		18.00	25.00
Comport 9.00		—	—
Cream Soup, 5" d 6.00		30.00	25.00
Creamer 5.00		15.00	20.00
Cup and Saucer 10.00		27.00	15.00
Fruit Console, 12-1/2" d 45.00		—	115.00
Pitcher, 16 oz, 4-1/2" h 25.00		—	115.00
Pitcher, 52 oz, 6-3/4" h 20.00		55.00	35.00
Plate, 6" d, sherbet 3.75		8.00	5.00
Plate, 7" d, salad 4.50		20.00	18.00
Plate, 9" d, dinner 9.00		25.00	25.00
Platter, 11-1/2" l, oval 7.00		25.00	25.00

Item	Crystal	Green	Pink
Powder Jar	15.00	—	55.00
Relish Platter, 11-1/2" l, divided	10.00	—	200.00
Salad Bowl, 10-1/2" d	12.00	—	—
Salt and Pepper Shakers, pr	20.00	48.00	42.00
Sandwich Plate, 10" d, closed handles	10.00	—	24.00
Sandwich Plate, 10" d, open handles .	12.50	18.00	20.00
Sherbet, ftd	3.50	15.00	13.00
Sugar, cov	10.00	40.00	30.00
Tray, 4" sq or 4-1/8" x 9"	5.00	12.00	10.00
Tray, 4-1/8" x 9", handles	9.00	—	50.00

Windsor, crystal plate and pink pitcher.

Item	Crystal	Green	Pink
Tray, 8-1/2" x 9-3/4"	.7.00	35.00	25.00
Tray, 8-1/2" x 9-3/4", handles	.14.00	45.00	85.00
Tumbler, 4" h, ftd	.7.00	—	—
Tumbler, 5 oz, 3-1/4" h	.9.00	42.00	25.00
Tumbler, 9 oz, 4" h	.7.50	38.00	22.00
Tumbler, 11 oz, 4-5/8" h	.8.00	—	—
Tumbler, 12 oz, 5" h	.11.00	55.00	30.00
Tumbler, 11 oz, 5" h, ftd	.12.00	—	—
Vegetable Bowl, 9-1/2" l, oval	.7.50	29.00	25.00

Windsor, pink butter dish, covered.

Glossary

AOP: All-over pattern, often found in descriptions to indicate a design that covers the entire piece rather than in just one location.

Berry Bowl: Used to describe both individual serving dishes and master bowl used as a set to serve berries (strawberries, etc.). Often accompanied by creamer or milk pitcher and sugar bowl.

Bouillon: Generally, cup-shaped bowl for serving broth or clear soups, usually has handles.

Cheese and Cracker Set: Serving piece often consists of a comport to hold cheese and large plate for crackers; forms differ. Sometimes, a sherbet is used as comport.

Cheese Dish: Serving dish, often with domed top, to cover cheese wedge.

Children's Wares: Dish and tea sets designed to be used by children for play.

Chop Plate: Large round plate used to serve individual portions of meat and fowl.

Cider Set: Consists of covered cookie jar (used to hold cider), tray and roly-poly cups and ladle.

Closed Handle: Solid glass handle.

Comport: Container used as serving dish, open with handles, sometimes covered.

Compote: Another name for comport.

Console Set: Decorative large bowl with matching candlesticks.

Cream Soup: Bowl used to serve cream-type or chilled soups, usually has handles.

Cup and Saucer: Used to refer to place-setting cup and saucer; some patterns include larger coffee cup or more diminutive tea cup.

Demitasse Cup and Saucer: Term used to describe smaller cup and saucer used for after-dinner beverage.

Domino Tray: Tray used to hold sugar blocks shaped like dominoes.

Egg Cup: Stemware with short stem used to hold egg, usually used with underplate.

Goblet: Stemware used to hold water.

Grill Plate: Dinner-sized plate with lines that divide plate into compartments.

Ice Lip: Small piece of glass inside of top of pitcher to hold ice in pitcher. May also mean a pinched lip that prevents ice from falling from pitcher.

Icer: Vessel with compartment to hold crushed ice to keep main vessel cold, i.e., mayonnaise, cream soup, shrimp, etc.

Individual Sized Pieces: Smaller sized pieces, often designed for bed tray use. Not to be confused with children's wares.

Liner: Underplate or under bowl used to accompany another piece, i.e., finger bowl or sherbet.

Light (Lite): Branch found on candlestick used to hold additional candles, i.e., 2 light, 3 light.

Nappy: Shallow bowl used as serving dish or in place-setting; often has small handle.

Oil/Vinegar: Term used to describe cruet or bottle with stopper to hold oil and/or vinegar for salads.

Platter: Small, medium or large oval plate used to serve roasts and fowl.

Ring Handle: Figural round handle, ring-shaped.

Salver: Large round plate used as serving piece.

Sandwich Server: Round plate, often with center handle (made of glass or metal) used to serve tea-type sandwiches.

Sherbet: Part of a place-setting used to hold sherbet, often served with matching underplate about the same size as a saucer.

Snack Set: Plate or small tray with indent to hold punch or coffee-type cup.

Spooner: Small, often squatty, open vase-type vessel used to hold spoons upright. Typically, part of table set.

Spoon Tray: Small bowl-shaped vessel used to hold spoons horizontally, often oval. Often used on buffets, etc., to hold extra place-setting spoons.

Stand: Base or additional piece used to hold punch bowl, etc.

Table Set: Name given to set of matching covered butter dish, creamer, covered (or open) sugar and spooner. An extended table service may include syrup, toothpick holder and salt and pepper shakers.

Tab Handle: Small solid glass handle useful to grab bowl, etc.

Toddy Set: Set consists of covered cookie jar (used to hold toddy), tray and roly-poly cups and ladle.

Tumbler: Any footed or flat vessel used to hold water or other liquids. Specialized tumblers include ginger ale, juice, iced tea, lemonade, old fashioned and whiskey.

Wine: Term used to describe stemware used to hold wine. Depression-era wines have a small capacity, by today's standards.

References

General Depression Glass References

Tom and Neila Bredehoft, *Fifty Years of Collectible Glass, 1920-1970*, Antique Trader Books, Volume 1, 1997, Volume 2, 2000.

Monica Lynn Clements and Patricia Rosser Clements, *Cobalt Blue Glass*, Schiffer Publishing, 1998.

—*Price Guide to Pink Glass*, Schiffer Publishing, 1999.

Randy and Debbie Coe, *Elegant Glass--Early, Depression and Beyond*, Schiffer Publishing, 2001.

Gene Florence, *Collectible Glassware from the 40s, 50s, & 60s, 5th Edition*, Collector Books, 2000.

—*Collector's Encyclopedia of Depression Glass, 14th Edition*, Collector Books, 2000.

—*Elegant Glassware of the Depression Era, 9th Edition*, Collector Books, 2000.

—*Kitchen Glassware of the Depression Era, 5th Edition*, Collector Books, 1995, revised 1999.

—*Pocket Guide to Depression Glass & More, 12th Edition*, Collector Books, 2001.

—*Stemware Identification*, Collector Books, 1996.

—*Very Rare Glassware of the Depression Years*, 1st Series (1988, 1990 value update), 2nd Series (1990), 3rd Series (1993, 1995 value update), 4th Series (1995), 5th Series (1996), 6th Series (1999), Collector Books.

Jay L. Glickman, *Yellow-Green Vaseline! A Guide to the Magic Glass*, Antique Publications, 1991.

Phillip Hopper, *Forest Green Glass with Price Guide*, Schiffer Publishing, 2000.

—*Royal Ruby*, Schiffer Publishing, 1998.

—*More Royal Ruby*, Schiffer Publishing, 1999.

Ralph and Terry Kovel, *Kovel's Depression Glass & Americana Dinnerware Price List, 7th Edition*, Three Rivers Press, 2001.

Carl F. Luckey with Debbie Coe, *Special Consultant, Identification and Value Guide to Depression Era Glassware, 4th Edition*, Krause Publications, 2001.

Barbara and Jim Mauzy, *Mauzy's Comprehensive Handbook of Depression Glass Prices*, Schiffer Publishing, 1999.

—*Mauzy's Depression Glass, A Photographic Reference with Prices*, 2nd edition, Schiffer Publishing, 2001.

James Measell and Barry Wiggins, *Great American Glass of the Roaring 20s and Depression Era*, Antique Publications, 1998.

C. L. Miller, Depression Era Dime Store Glass, Schiffer Publishing, 1999.

Naomi L. Over, *Ruby Glass of the 20th Century*, Antique Publications, 1990, 1993-94 value update.

—*Ruby Glass of the 20th Century, Book 2*, Antique Publications, 1999.

Sherry Riggs and Paula Pendergrass, *Candleholders of the Depression Era and Beyond*, Schiffer Publishing, 2001.

Ellen T. Schroy, *Warman's Depression Glass*, 2nd edition, Krause Publications, 2000.

The Daze, *The Daze Past*, Volumes 1, 2, and 3, The Daze.

Marlene Toohey, *A Collector's Guide to Black Glass*, Antique Publications, 1988.
—*A Collector's Guide to Black Glass, Book 2*, Antique Publications, 1999.
Kent G. Washburn, *Price Survey, 4th Edition*, published by author, 1994.
Hazel Marie Weatherman, *Colored Glassware of the Depression Era, Book 2*, published by author, 1974, available in reprint
—*1984 Supplement & Price Trends for Colored Glassware of the Depression Era, Book 1*, published by author, 1984.

Specific Company References

Duncan: Gail Krause, *The Encyclopedia of Duncan Glass*, published by author, 1984; *A Pictorial History of Duncan & Miller Glass,* published by author, 1986; *The Years of Duncan*, published by author, 1980; Leslie Piña, *Depression Era Glass* by Duncan, Schiffer Publishing, 1992.

Fenton: Robert E. Eaton, Jr., *Fenton Glass: The First 25 Years Comprehensive Price Guide*, The Glass Press, 1995, 1997 value update, distributed by Antique Publications; *Fenton Glass: The 1980s Decade Comprehensive Price Guide*, The Glass Press,

1996, 1997 value update, distributed by Antique Publications; William Heacock, *Fenton Glass: The First Twenty-Five Years* (1978), *The Second Twenty-Five Years* (1980), *The Third Twenty-Five Years* (1989), available from Antique Publications; Alan Linn, *Fenton Story of Glass Making*, Antique Publications, 1996; James Measell, *Fenton Glass, The 80s Decade*, Antique Publications, 1966, Members of the Fenton Art Glass Collectors of America, Fenton Glass: *The Third 25 Years Comprehensive Price Guide to Fenton Glass*, Antique Publications, 1995, distributed by Antique Publications; Ferill J. Rice (ed.), *Caught in the Butterfly Net*, Fenton Art Glass Collectors of America, The Glass Press, 1995; Margaret and Kenn Whitmyer, *Fenton Art Glass 1907-1939*, Collector Books, 1996.

Fire-King: Monica Clements and Patricia Rosser Clements, *Guide to Fire King Glassware*, Schiffer Publishing, 1999; Gene Florence, *Anchor Hocking's Fire-King & More*, Collector Books, 1997; Joe Keller and David Ross, *Jadite - An Identification and Price Guide*, Schiffer Publishing, 1999; Garry and Dale Kilgo, Jerry and Gail Wilkins, *Collectors Guide to Anchor Hocking's Fire-King Glassware*, K & W Collectibles Publisher, 1991; *Fire-King Glassware, A Collector's Guide to Anchor Hocking*, 2nd Edition, K & W Collectibles Publisher, 1998.

Fostoria: Frances Bones, *Fostoria Glassware 1887-1982*, Collector Books, 1999; Ann Kerr, *Fostoria: An Identification and Value Guide, Volume I, Pressed, Blown & Hand Molded Shapes*, Collector Books, 1994, 1997 values; *Fostoria: An Identification and Value Guide, Volume II, Etched and Carved & Cut Designs*,

Collector Books, 1996; Milbra Long and Emily Seate, *Fostoria Stemware, The Crystal for America*, Collector Books, 1997; *Fostoria Tableware, 1924-1943*, Collector Books, 1999; *Fostoria Tableware, 1944-1986*, Collector Books, 1999; Leslie Piña, *Fostoria American Line 2056*, Schiffer Publishing, 1999; *Fostoria Designer George Sakier*, Schiffer Publishing, 1996; *Fostoria*, Schiffer Publishing, 1995; Joann Schleismann, *Price Guide to Fostoria, 3rd Edition*, Park Avenue Publications; Sidney P. Seligson, *Fostoria American, A Complete Guide, 2nd Edition*, published by author.

Imperial: Margaret and Douglas Archer, *Imperial Glass*, Collector Books, 1978, 1993 value update; Myrna and Bob Garrison, *Imperial Cape Cod Tradition to Treasure, 2nd Edition*, published by authors, 1991; National Imperial Glass Collectors Society, *Imperial Glass Encyclopedia, Volume I: A-Cane*, Antique Publications, 1995; *Imperial Glass Encyclopedia, Volume II: Cape Cod to L*, Antique Publications, 1998; *Imperial Glass Encyclopedia, Volume III, M-Z*, Antique Publications, 1999; National Imperial Glass Collectors Society, *Imperial Glass 1966 Catalog*, reprint, 1991 price guide, Antique Publications.

Morgantown: Jerry Gallagher, *A Handbook of Old Morgantown Glass, Volume I: A Guide to Identification and Shape*, published by author, 1995; Jeffrey B. Snyder, *Morgantown Glass: Depression through 1960s*, Schiffer Publishing, 1998.

New Martinsville: James Measell, *New Martinsville Glass*, Antique Publications, 1994.

Tiffin: Fred Bickenhauser, *Tiffin Glassmasters, Book I (1979), Book II (1981), Book III (1985)*, Glassmasters Publications; Ed Goshe, Ruth Hemminger and Leslie Piña, *Tiffin Depression-Era Stems and Tablewares*, Schiffer Publishing, 1998; *40s, 50s, & 60s Stemware by Tiffin*, Schiffer Publihsing, 1999; Kelly O'Kane, *Tiffin Glassmasters, The Modern Years*, published by author, 1998; Bob Page and Dale Fredericksen, *Tiffin Is Forever*, Page-Fredericksen, 1994; Leslie Piña and Jerry Gallagher, *Tiffin Glass*, Schiffer Publishing, 1996.

Westmoreland: Lorraine Kovar, *Westmoreland Glass, Volumes I and II* (1991), *Volume III* (1998), Antique Publications, 1991; *Westmoreland Glass 1950-1984 Volume I Comprehensive Price Guide*, published by author, 1998; *Price Guide to Westmoreland's Paneled Grape Pattern*, published by author, 1997; Charles West Wilson, *Westmoreland Glass*, Collector Books, 1996.

Resources

Collectors' Clubs

International Associations

Canadian Depression Glass Association
119 Wexford Road
Brampton, Ontario L6Z 2T5
Canada

Fenton Art Glass Collectors of America, Inc.
PO Box 384
Williamstown, WV 26187

Fire-King Collectors Club
1167 Teal Rd, SW
Dellroy, OH 44620

Fostoria Glass Collectors, Inc.
PO Box 1625
Orange, CA 92856

Fostoria Glass Society of America, Inc.
PO Box 826
Moundsville, WV 26041
Internet: www.fostoriagladd.org

H. C. Fry Glass Society
PO Box 41
Beaver, PA 15009

Heisey Collectors of America, Inc.
169 N. Church Street
Newark, OH 43055

National Cambridge Collectors Inc.
PO Box 416
Cambridge, OH 43725

National Candlewick Collectors Club
275 Milledge Terrace
Athens, GA 30606

National Depression Glass Association
PO Box 8264
Wichita, KS 67208-0264

National Duncan Glass Society
PO Box 965
Washington, PA 15301

National Fenton Glass Society
PO Box 4008
Marietta, OH 45750

National Imperial Glass Collectors Society
PO Box 534
Bellaire, OH 43906

National Westmoreland Glass Collectors Club
PO Box 372
Westmoreland City, PA 15692

Old Morgantown Glass

Collectors Guild Inc.
PO Box 894
Morgantown, WV 26507-0894

Three Rivers Depression Era Glass Society
Donna Hennen
3275 Sylvan Road
Bethel Park, PA 15102
412-835-1903

Tiffin Glass Collectors' Club
PO Box 554
Tiffin, OH 44883

Westmoreland Glass Society, Inc.
2712 Glenwood
Independence, MO 64052.

Regional

There are many regional clubs where people gather to discuss Depression-era glassware. Check with the National Depression Glass Association for a club in your region if none are listed below:

Big "D" Pression Glass Club
10 Windling Creek Trail
Garland, TX 75043

Black Hills Depression Glass Club
1310 Milwaukee
Rapid City, SD 57701

Buckeye Dee Geer's
2501 Campbell Street
Sandusky, OH 44870

Carolina Depression Glass Club
PO Box 128
Easley, SC 29640

**Central Florida Depression
Era Glass Club**
PO Box 948042
Maitland, FL 32794-8042

**Central Jersey Depression
Glass Club**
181 Riviera Drive
Brick Town, NJ 08723

**Charter Oak Depression
Glass Club**
PO Box 604
Chester, CT 06412

**Cigar City Depression
Glass Club**
PO Box 17322
Tampa, FL 33612

**Clearwater Depression
Glass Club**
10038 62nd Terrace North
St. Petersburg, FL 33708

CSRA D. G. Club
1129 Magnolia Avenue
Augusta, GA 30904

**Crescent City Depression
Glass Club**
PO Box 55981
Metairie, LA 70055

**Depression Era Glass
Society of Wisconsin**
1534 S. Wisconsin Ave.
Racine, WI 53403

**Depression Glass Club of
Greater Rochester**
PO Box 10362
Rochester, NY 14610

**Depression Glass Club of
North East Florida**
2604 Jolly Rd
Jacksonville, FL 33207

**Evergreen Depression Era
Collectors**
312 Golden Gate
Fircrest, WA 98466

**Garden State Depression
Glass Club**
93 Idlewild Lane
Matawan, NJ 07747

**Greater San Diego
Depression Glass Club**
PO Box 3573
San Diego, CA 92103-3573

**Greater Tulsa Depression
Era Glass Club**
PO Box 470763
Tulsa, OK 74147-0763

Hazelnut Depression Glass Club
129 Southcliff Drive
Findlay, OH 45840

Heart of America Glass Collectors
14404 E. 36th Terrace
Independence, MO, 64055

Houston Glass Club
PO Box 1254
Rosenberg, TX 77471-1254

Hudson Valley Depression Club
129 Southcliff Drive
Findlay, OH 45840

Kansas City Depression Glass Club
12950 East 51st Terrace
Independence, MO 64055

Illinois Valley Depression Glass Club
RR 1, Box 52
Rushville, IL 62681

Iowa Depression Glass Association
5871 Vista Drive, Apt 725
West Des Moines, IA 50266

Land of Sunshine Depression Glass Club
PO Box 560275
Orlando, FL 32856-0275

Lincoln Land Depression Glass Club
1625 Dial Court
Springfield, IL 62704

Long Island Depression Glass Society
PO Box 147
West Sayville NY 11796

Low Country Depression Glass Club
209 Trestle Wood Drive
Summersville, SC 29483

Montclair Depression Glass Club
1254 Karesh Avenue
Pomona, CA 91767

Mountain Laurel Depression Glass Club
942 Main Street
Hartford, CT 06103

North Jersey Dee Geer's
82 High Street
Butler, NJ 07405

Northeast Florida Depression Glass Club
PO Box 338
Whitehouse, FL 32220

Nutmeg Depression Glass Club
230 Hillside Avenue
Naugatuck, CT 06770

Old Dominion Depression Glass Club
8415 W. Rugby Road
Manassas, VA 22111

Peach State Depression Glass Club
4174 Reef Road
Marietta, GA 30066

Permian Basin Depression Glass Club
708 N Adams Street
Odessa,TX 79762

Pikes Peak Depression Glass Club
2029 Devon
Colorado Springs, CO 80909

Pocono Mountains Depression Glass Club
c/o Gwen Hawn
Pocono Lake, PA 18610

Portland's Rain of Glass, Inc.
PO Box 819
Portland, OR 97207-0819

Sandlapper Depression Glass Club
503 Leyswood Drive
Greenville, SC 29615

South Bay Depression Glass Society
PO Box 7400
Torrance, CA 90504-7400

South Florida Depression Glass Club
PO Box 845
Boca Raton, FL 33429

Southern Illinois Diamond H Seekers
1203 N. Yale
O'Fallon, IL 62269

Spokane Falls Depression Glass Etc.
PO Box 113
Veradale, WA 99037

Three Rivers Depression Era Glass Society
3275 Sylvan Road
Bethel Park, PA 15102

Top of Texas Depression Era Glass Club
42149 1st Street
Lubbock, TX 79424

Tri-State Depression Era Glass Club
RD #6, Box 560D
Washington, PA 15301

20-30-40 Society, Inc.
PO Box 856
LaGrange, IL 60525

Western North Carolina
PO Box 116
Mars Hill, NC 28743

Western Reserve Depression Glass Club
8669 Courtland Drive
Strongsville, OH 44136.

Internet Sites

The following Internet Web sites offer information about Depression-era glassware in the form of online articles, references, chats, etc.

There are hundreds of Web sites to purchase Depression-era glassware as well as numerous e-auctions.

DG Shopper Online
The Depression Glass Super Site
http://www.dgshopper.com
PO Box 3411
Albany, OR 97321-0716

Dictionary of Glass Marks
http://www.heartland-discoveries.com

Facets Antiques & Collectibles Mall
http://www.Facets.net

Just Glass
http://www.justglass.com
PO Box 20146
Cincinnati, OH 45220.

Mega Show
http://www.glassshow.com

Publications

**Antique & Collector's
Reproduction News**
PO Box 12130
Des Moines, IA 50312

**Kitchen Antiques &
Collectible News**
4645 Laurel Ridge Drive
Harrisburg, PA 17110

The Candlewick Collector
6534 South Avenue
Holland, OH 45328

The DAZE, Inc.
PO Box 57
Otisville, MI 48463
http://www.thedaze.com

The Fire-King News
K & W Collectibles, Inc.
PO Box 473
Addison, AL 35540

**Westmoreland Glass
Collectors Newsletter**
PO Box 143
North Liberty, IA 52317

Video Tapes

**Fenton: Glass Artistry in the
Making**
Fenton Art Glass, Michael
Dickensen, 1992

**Popular Patterns of the
Depression Era**
Living Glass Videotape Series
RoCliff Communications
8422 N Park Court
Kansas City, MO 64155

Index by Manufacturer

H

Index by Pattern

R

S

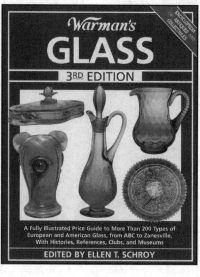